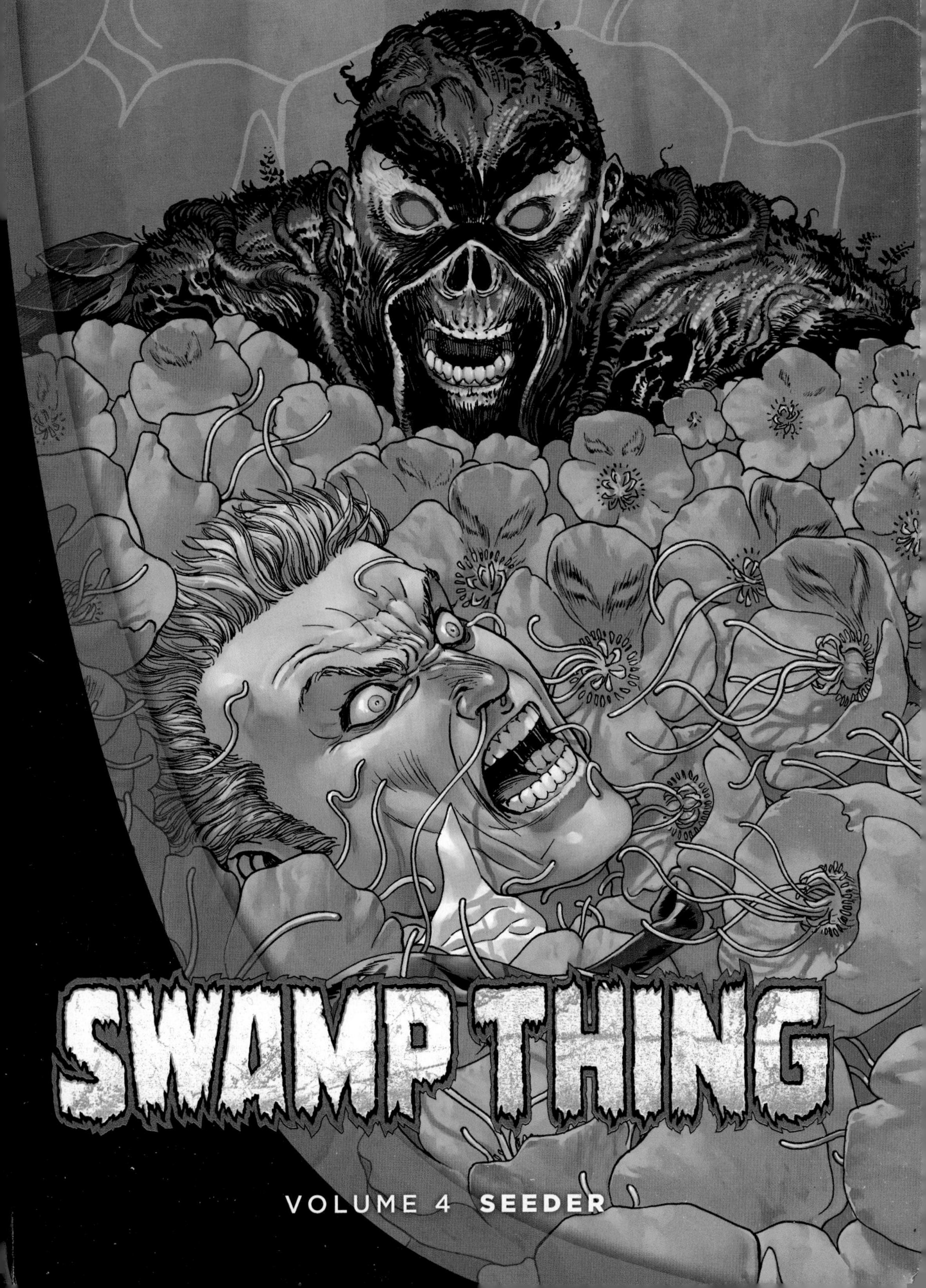

# SWAMP THING

VOLUME 4 **SEEDER**

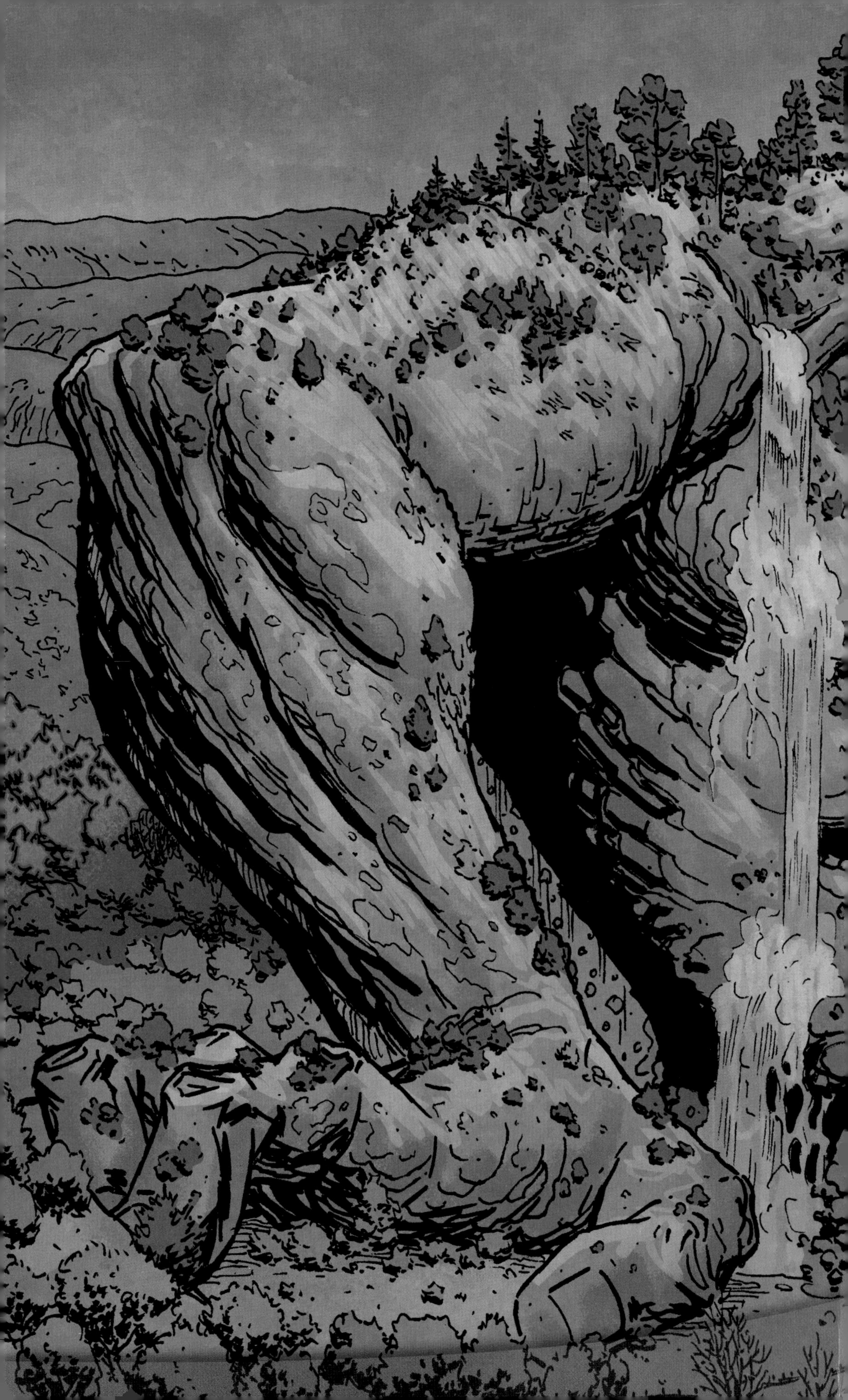

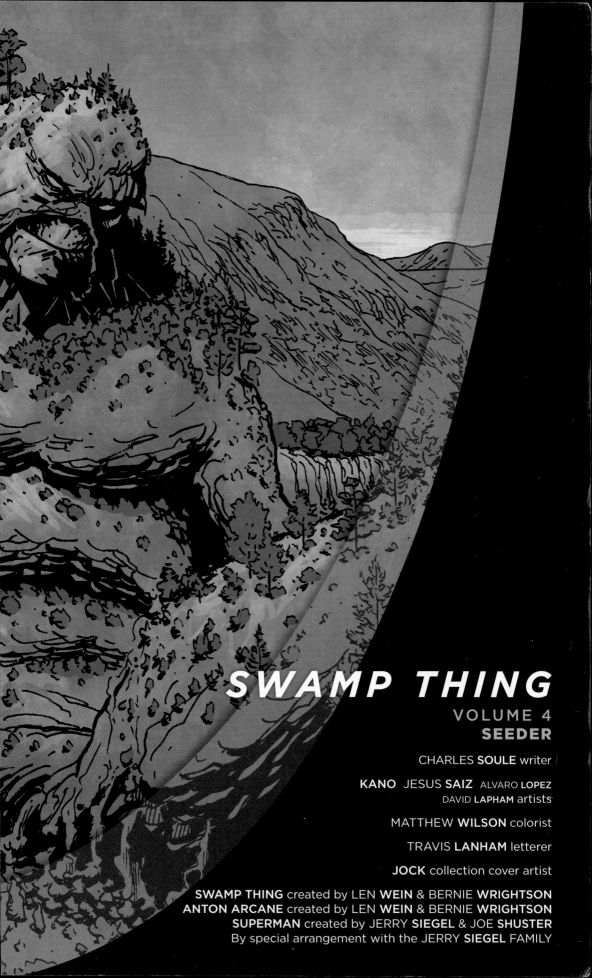

# SWAMP THING

## VOLUME 4
### SEEDER

CHARLES **SOULE** writer

**KANO**   JESUS **SAIZ**   ALVARO **LOPEZ**
DAVID **LAPHAM** artists

MATTHEW **WILSON** colorist

TRAVIS **LANHAM** letterer

**JOCK** collection cover artist

SWAMP THING created by LEN **WEIN** & BERNIE **WRIGHTSON**
ANTON ARCANE created by LEN **WEIN** & BERNIE **WRIGHTSON**
SUPERMAN created by JERRY **SIEGEL** & JOE **SHUSTER**
By special arrangement with the JERRY **SIEGEL** FAMILY

MATT IDELSON Editor – Original Series  CHRIS CONROY Associate Editor – Original Series
ROWENA YOW Editor  ROBBIN BROSTERMAN Design Director – Books  ROBBIE BIEDERMAN Publication Design

BOB HARRAS Senior VP – Editor-in-Chief, DC Comics

DIANE NELSON President  DAN DIDIO and JIM LEE Co-Publishers  GEOFF JOHNS Chief Creative Officer
JOHN ROOD Executive VP – Sales, Marketing and Business Development  AMY GENKINS Senior VP – Business and Legal Affairs
NAIRI GARDINER Senior VP – Finance  JEFF BOISON VP – Publishing Planning
MARK CHIARELLO VP – Art Direction and Design  JOHN CUNNINGHAM VP – Marketing
TERRI CUNNINGHAM VP – Editorial Administration  ALISON GILL Senior VP – Manufacturing and Operations
HANK KANALZ Senior VP – Vertigo and Integrated Publishing  JAY KOGAN VP – Business and Legal Affairs, Publishing
JACK MAHAN VP – Business Affairs, Talent  NICK NAPOLITANO VP – Manufacturing Administration
SUE POHJA VP – Book Sales  COURTNEY SIMMONS Senior VP – Publicity  BOB WAYNE Senior VP – Sales

SWAMP THING VOLUME 4: SEEDER

DC Comics, 1700 Broadway, New York, NY 10019
A Warner Bros. Entertainment Company.
Printed by RR Donnelley, Salem, VA, USA. 5/2/14. First Printing.

ISBN: 978-1-4012-4639-6

Library of Congress Cataloging-in-Publication Data is Available.

SUSTAINABLE
FORESTRY
INITIATIVE

Certified Chain of Custody
20% Certified Forest Content,
80% Certified Sourcing
www.sfiprogram.org
SFI-01042
APPLIES TO TEXT STOCK ONLY

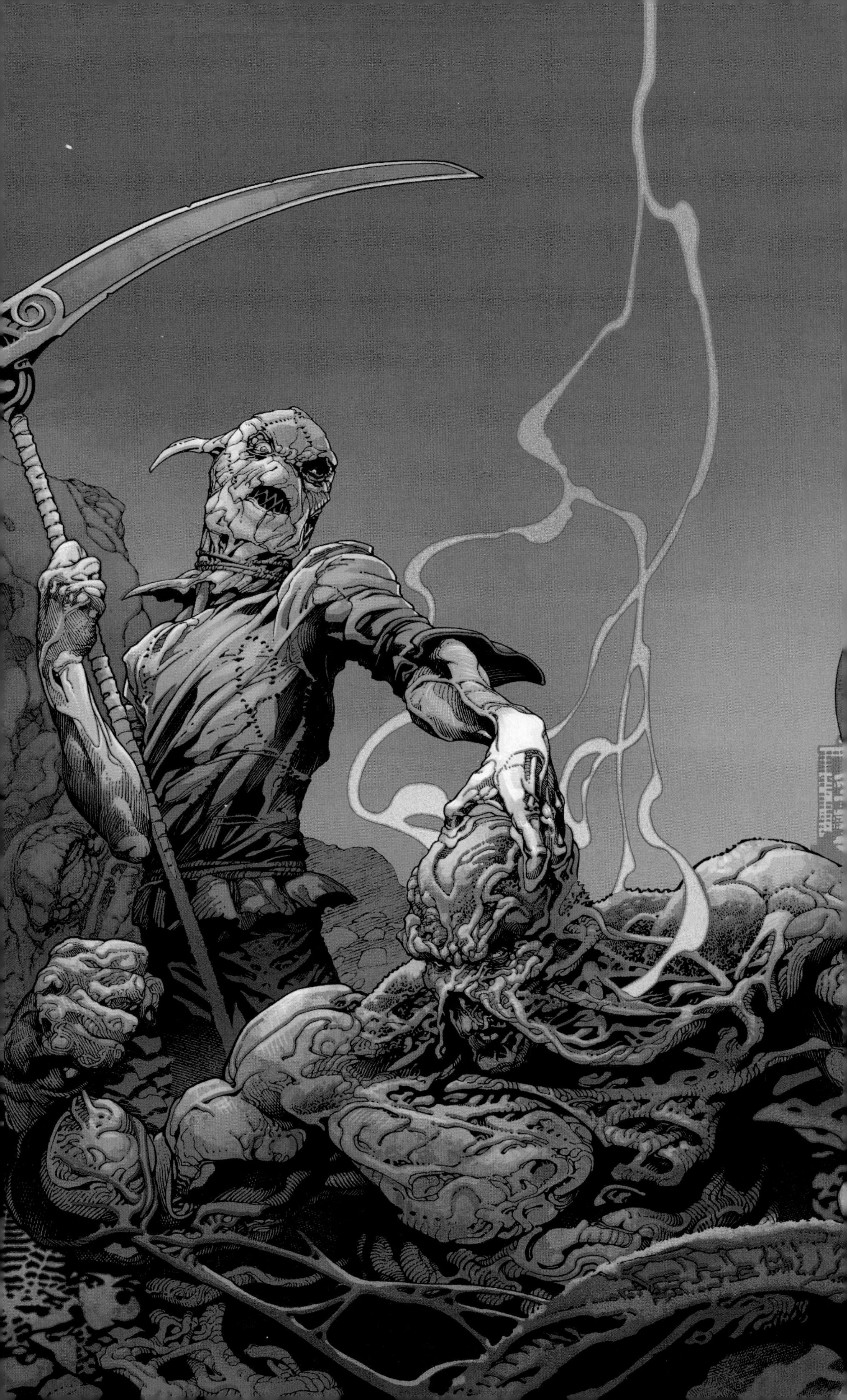

## URBAN JUNGLE

**CHARLES SOULE** writer **KANO** artist cover art by **ANDY BRASE & MATTHEW WILSON**

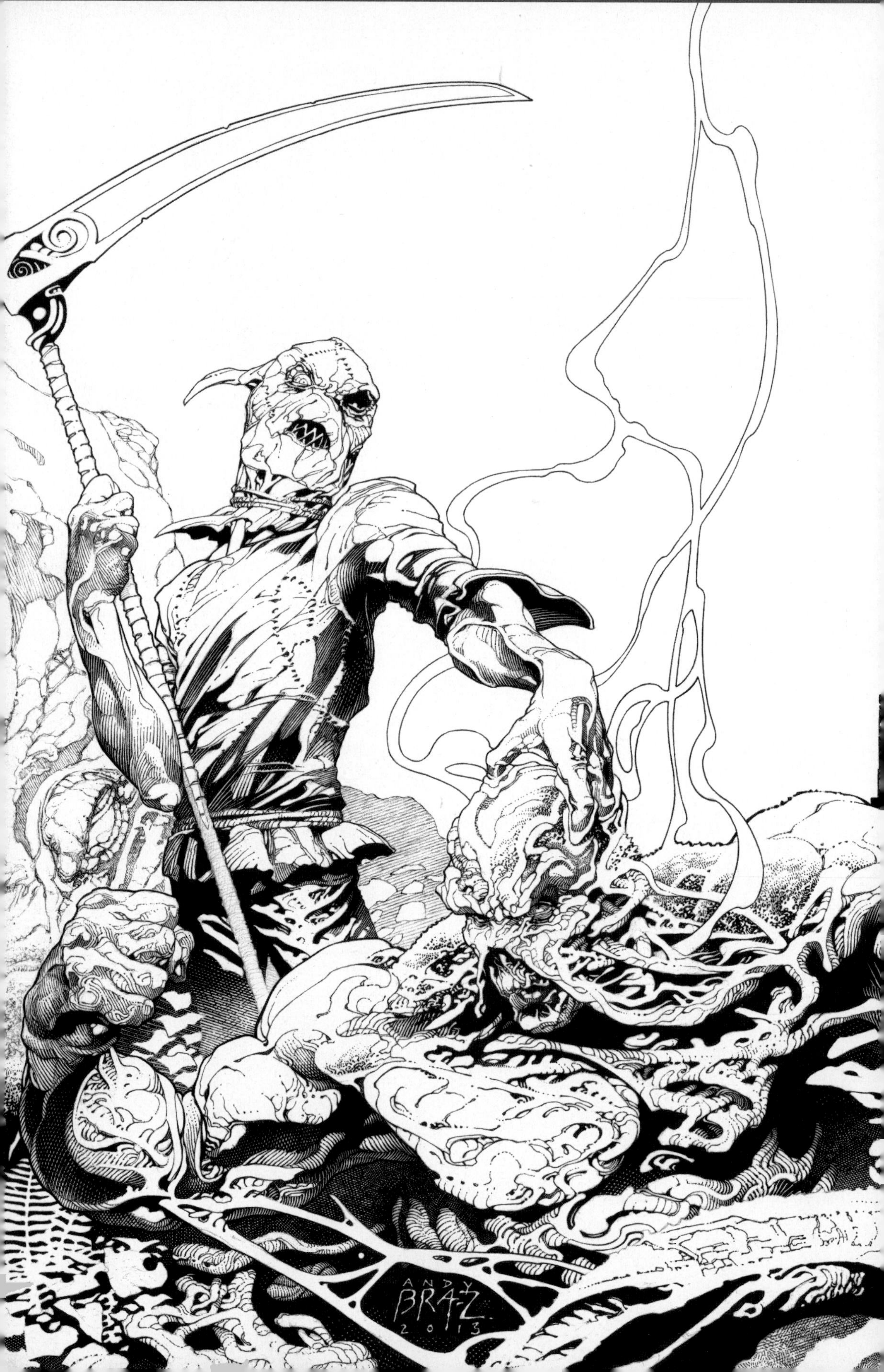

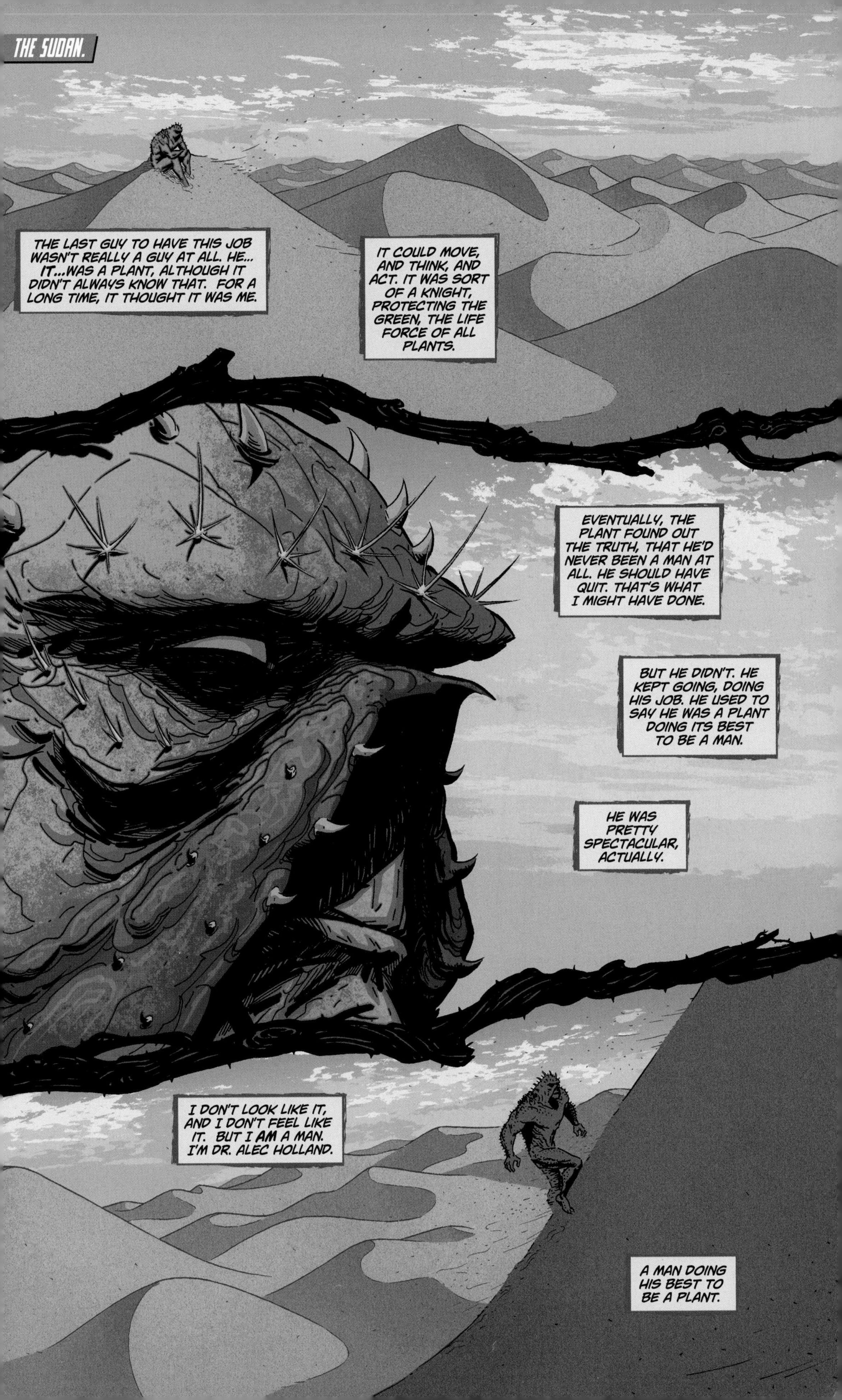
THE SUDAN.
THE LAST GUY TO HAVE THIS JOB WASN'T REALLY A GUY AT ALL. HE... IT...WAS A PLANT, ALTHOUGH IT DIDN'T ALWAYS KNOW THAT. FOR A LONG TIME, IT THOUGHT IT WAS ME.
IT COULD MOVE, AND THINK, AND ACT. IT WAS SORT OF A KNIGHT, PROTECTING THE GREEN, THE LIFE FORCE OF ALL PLANTS.
EVENTUALLY, THE PLANT FOUND OUT THE TRUTH, THAT HE'D NEVER BEEN A MAN AT ALL. HE SHOULD HAVE QUIT. THAT'S WHAT I MIGHT HAVE DONE.
BUT HE DIDN'T. HE KEPT GOING, DOING HIS JOB. HE USED TO SAY HE WAS A PLANT DOING ITS BEST TO BE A MAN.
HE WAS PRETTY SPECTACULAR, ACTUALLY.
I DON'T LOOK LIKE IT, AND I DON'T FEEL LIKE IT. BUT I AM A MAN. I'M DR. ALEC HOLLAND.
A MAN DOING HIS BEST TO BE A PLANT.

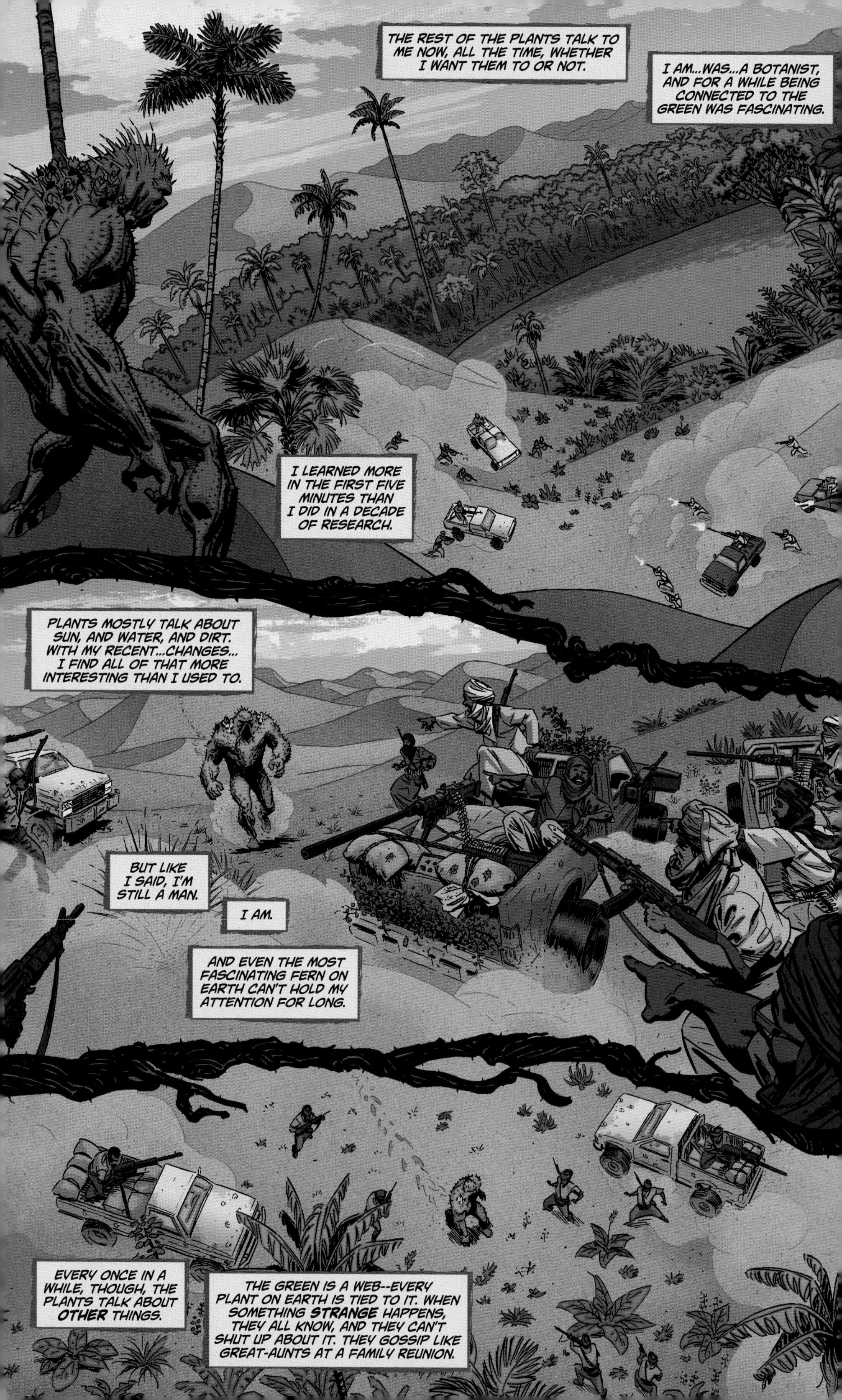
THE REST OF THE PLANTS TALK TO ME NOW, ALL THE TIME, WHETHER I WANT THEM TO OR NOT.
I AM...WAS...A BOTANIST, AND FOR A WHILE BEING CONNECTED TO THE GREEN WAS FASCINATING.
I LEARNED MORE IN THE FIRST FIVE MINUTES THAN I DID IN A DECADE OF RESEARCH.
PLANTS MOSTLY TALK ABOUT SUN, AND WATER, AND DIRT. WITH MY RECENT...CHANGES... I FIND ALL OF THAT MORE INTERESTING THAN I USED TO.
BUT LIKE I SAID, I'M STILL A MAN.
I AM.
AND EVEN THE MOST FASCINATING FERN ON EARTH CAN'T HOLD MY ATTENTION FOR LONG.
EVERY ONCE IN A WHILE, THOUGH, THE PLANTS TALK ABOUT OTHER THINGS.
THE GREEN IS A WEB--EVERY PLANT ON EARTH IS TIED TO IT. WHEN SOMETHING STRANGE HAPPENS, THEY ALL KNOW, AND THEY CAN'T SHUT UP ABOUT IT. THEY GOSSIP LIKE GREAT-AUNTS AT A FAMILY REUNION.

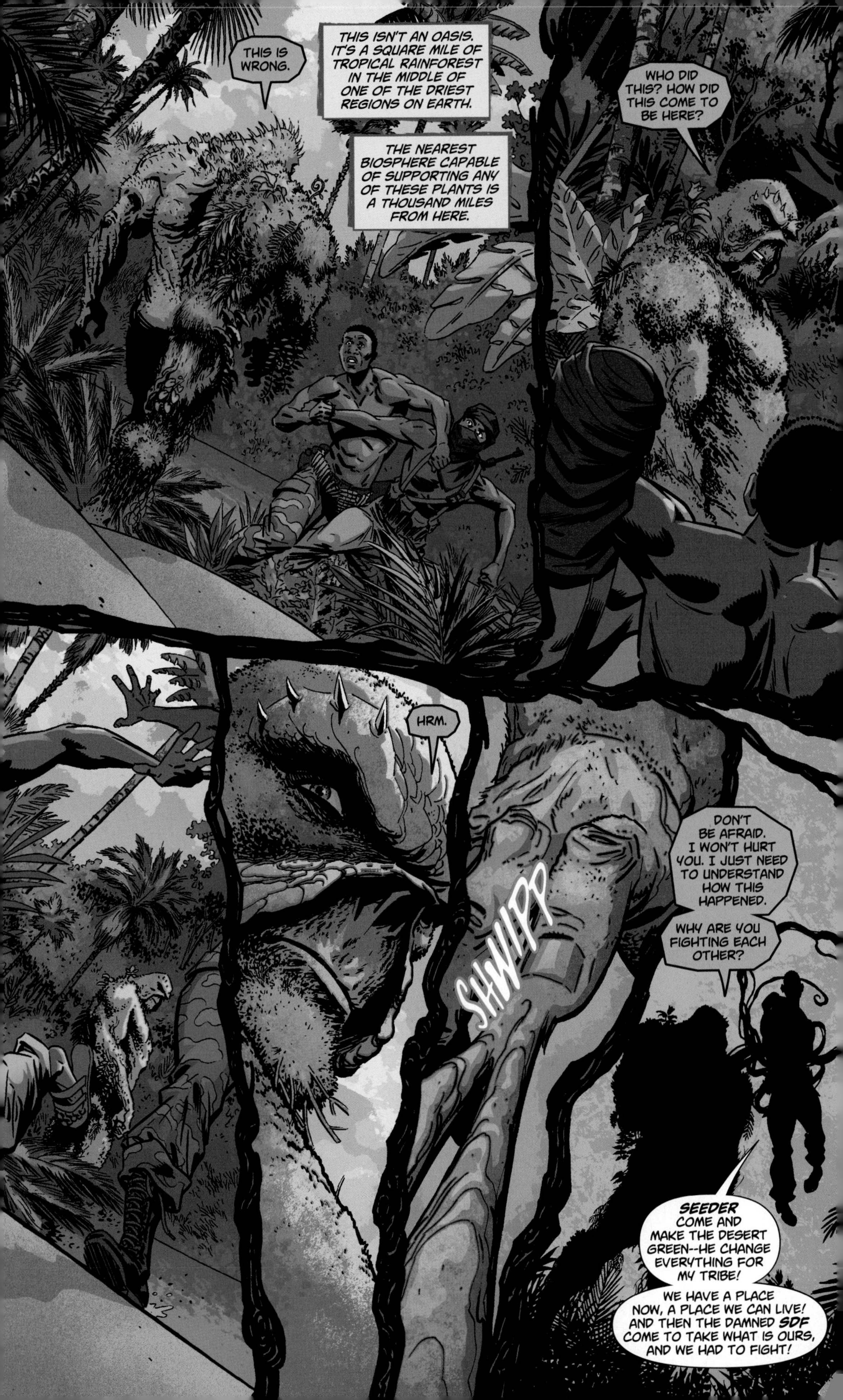

THIS IS WRONG.
THIS ISN'T AN OASIS. IT'S A SQUARE MILE OF TROPICAL RAINFOREST IN THE MIDDLE OF ONE OF THE DRIEST REGIONS ON EARTH.
THE NEAREST BIOSPHERE CAPABLE OF SUPPORTING ANY OF THESE PLANTS IS A THOUSAND MILES FROM HERE.
WHO DID THIS? HOW DID THIS COME TO BE HERE?
HRM.
DON'T BE AFRAID. I WON'T HURT YOU. I JUST NEED TO UNDERSTAND HOW THIS HAPPENED.
WHY ARE YOU FIGHTING EACH OTHER?
SHWIPP
SEEDER COME AND MAKE THE DESERT GREEN--HE CHANGE EVERYTHING FOR MY TRIBE!
WE HAVE A PLACE NOW, A PLACE WE CAN LIVE! AND THEN THE DAMNED SDF COME TO TAKE WHAT IS OURS, AND WE HAD TO FIGHT!

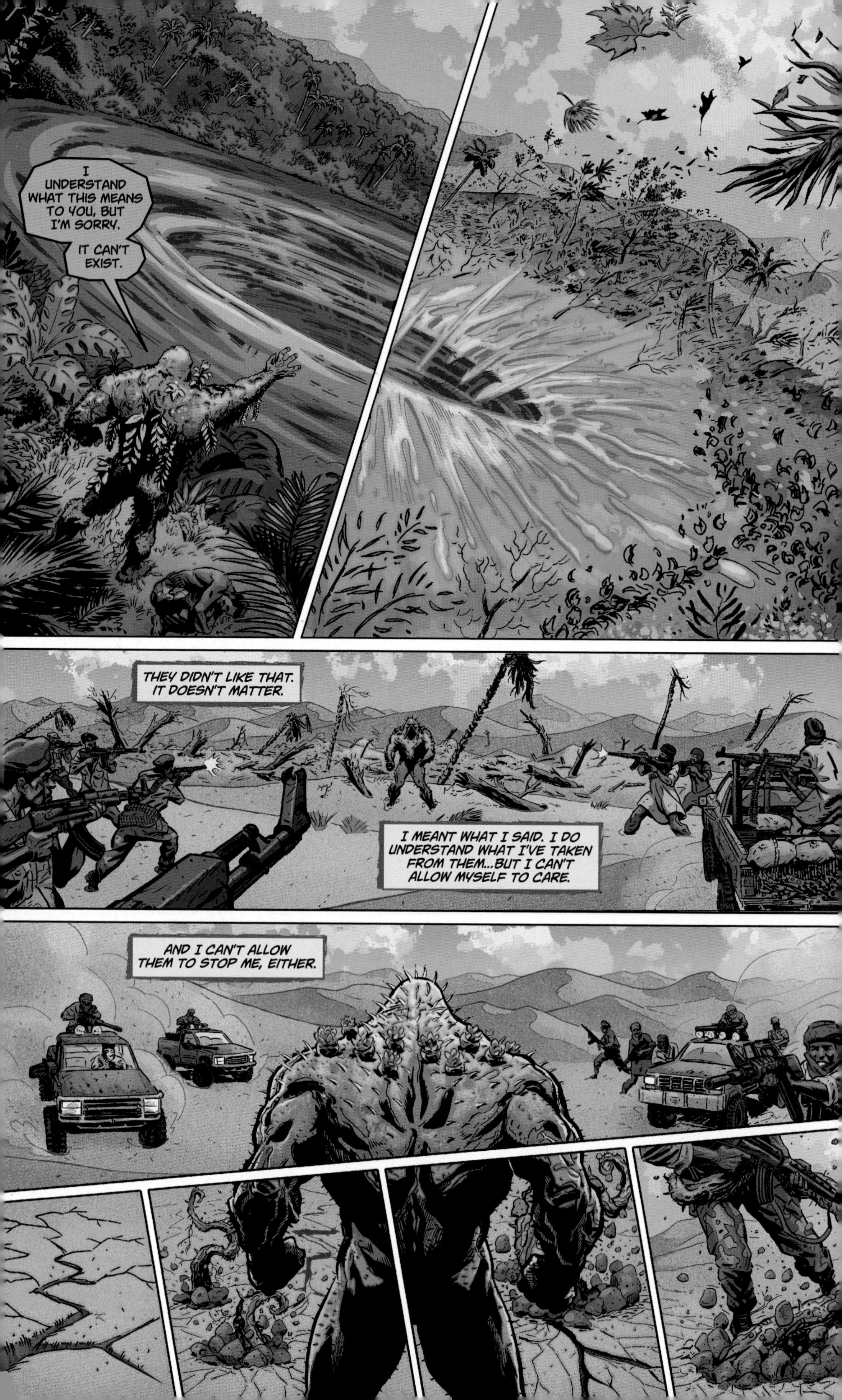
I UNDERSTAND WHAT THIS MEANS TO YOU, BUT I'M SORRY.
IT CAN'T EXIST.
THEY DIDN'T LIKE THAT. IT DOESN'T MATTER.
I MEANT WHAT I SAID. I DO UNDERSTAND WHAT I'VE TAKEN FROM THEM...BUT I CAN'T ALLOW MYSELF TO CARE.
AND I CAN'T ALLOW THEM TO STOP ME, EITHER.

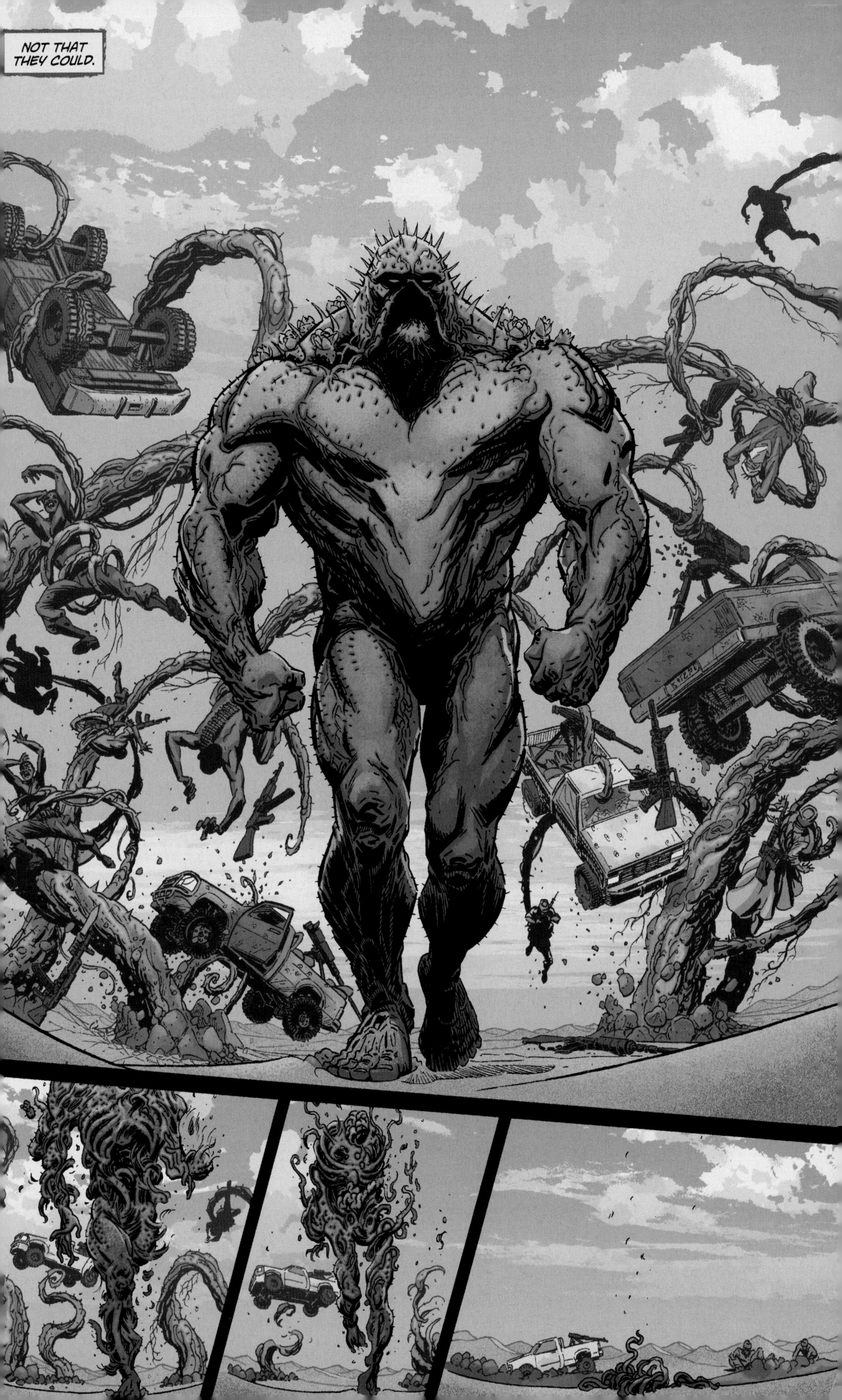
NOT THAT
THEY COULD.

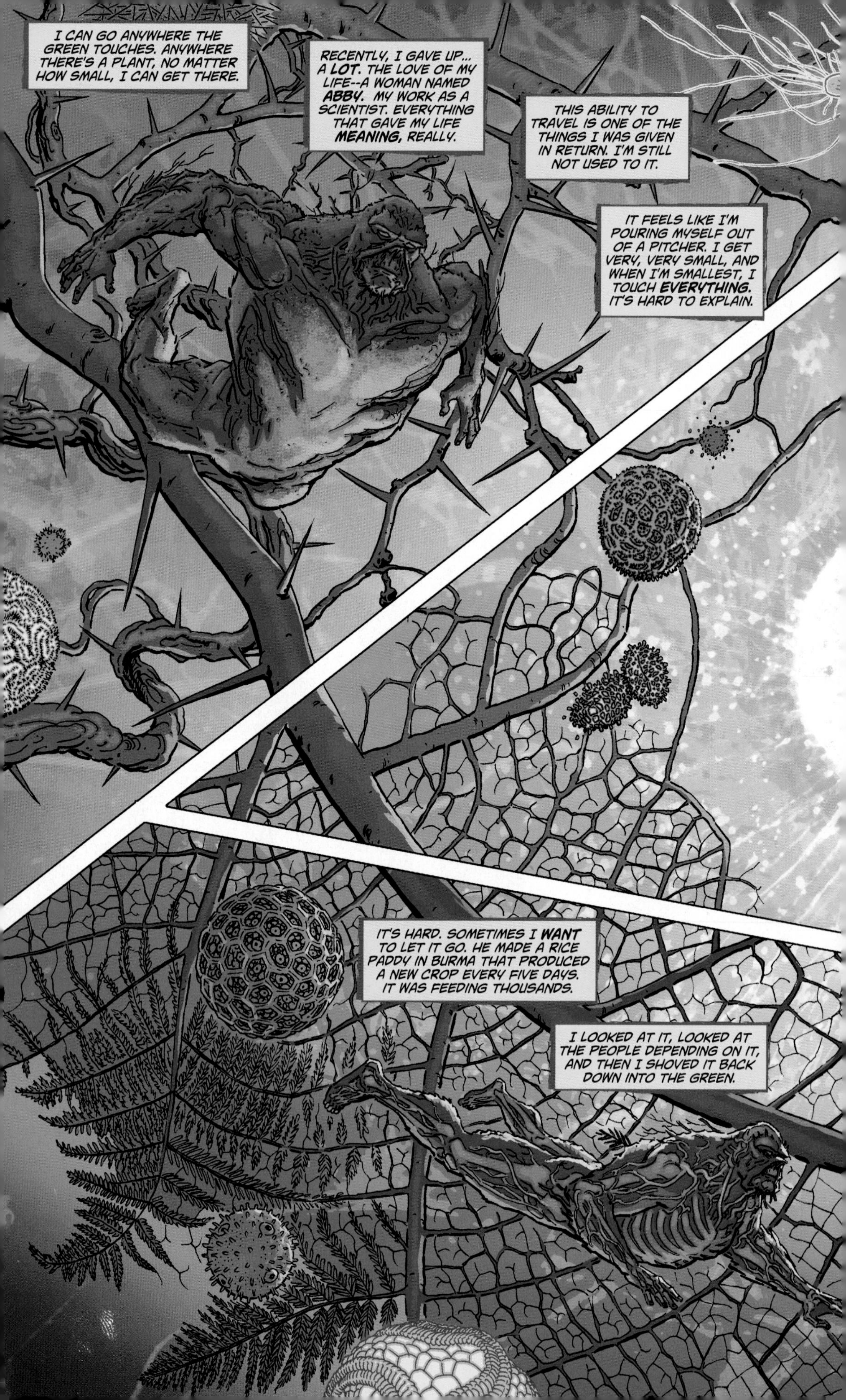
I CAN GO ANYWHERE THE GREEN TOUCHES. ANYWHERE THERE'S A PLANT, NO MATTER HOW SMALL, I CAN GET THERE.
RECENTLY, I GAVE UP... A **LOT**. THE LOVE OF MY LIFE--A WOMAN NAMED **ABBY**. MY WORK AS A SCIENTIST. EVERYTHING THAT GAVE MY LIFE **MEANING**, REALLY.
THIS ABILITY TO TRAVEL IS ONE OF THE THINGS I WAS GIVEN IN RETURN. I'M STILL NOT USED TO IT.
IT FEELS LIKE I'M POURING MYSELF OUT OF A PITCHER. I GET VERY, VERY SMALL, AND WHEN I'M SMALLEST, I TOUCH **EVERYTHING**. IT'S HARD TO EXPLAIN.
IT'S HARD. SOMETIMES I **WANT** TO LET IT GO. HE MADE A RICE PADDY IN BURMA THAT PRODUCED A NEW CROP EVERY FIVE DAYS. IT WAS FEEDING THOUSANDS.
I LOOKED AT IT, LOOKED AT THE PEOPLE DEPENDING ON IT, AND THEN I SHOVED IT BACK DOWN INTO THE GREEN.

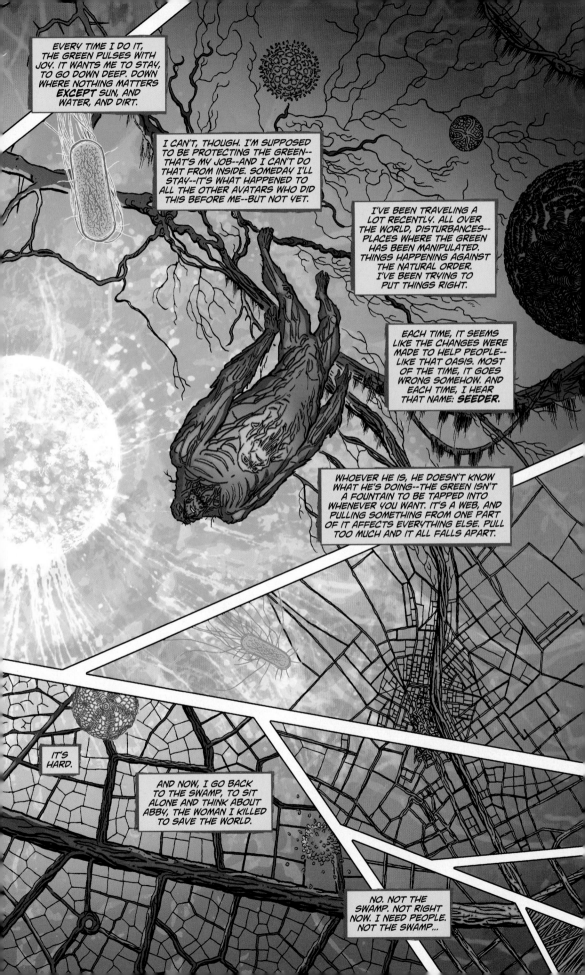

EVERY TIME I DO IT, THE GREEN PULSES WITH JOY. IT WANTS ME TO STAY, TO GO DOWN DEEP. DOWN WHERE NOTHING MATTERS *EXCEPT* SUN, AND WATER, AND DIRT.

I CAN'T, THOUGH. I'M SUPPOSED TO BE PROTECTING THE GREEN-- THAT'S MY JOB--AND I CAN'T DO THAT FROM INSIDE. SOMEDAY I'LL STAY--IT'S WHAT HAPPENED TO ALL THE OTHER AVATARS WHO DID THIS BEFORE ME--BUT NOT YET.

I'VE BEEN TRAVELING A LOT RECENTLY. ALL OVER THE WORLD, DISTURBANCES-- PLACES WHERE THE GREEN HAS BEEN MANIPULATED. THINGS HAPPENING AGAINST THE NATURAL ORDER. I'VE BEEN TRYING TO PUT THINGS RIGHT.

EACH TIME, IT SEEMS LIKE THE CHANGES WERE MADE TO HELP PEOPLE-- LIKE THAT OASIS. MOST OF THE TIME, IT GOES WRONG SOMEHOW. AND EACH TIME, I HEAR THAT NAME: *SEEDER.*

WHOEVER HE IS, HE DOESN'T KNOW WHAT HE'S DOING--THE GREEN ISN'T A FOUNTAIN TO BE TAPPED INTO WHENEVER YOU WANT. IT'S A WEB, AND PULLING SOMETHING FROM ONE PART OF IT AFFECTS EVERYTHING ELSE. PULL TOO MUCH AND IT ALL FALLS APART.

IT'S HARD.

AND NOW, I GO BACK TO THE SWAMP, TO SIT ALONE AND THINK ABOUT ABBY, THE WOMAN I KILLED TO SAVE THE WORLD.

NO. NOT THE SWAMP. NOT RIGHT NOW. I NEED PEOPLE. NOT THE SWAMP...

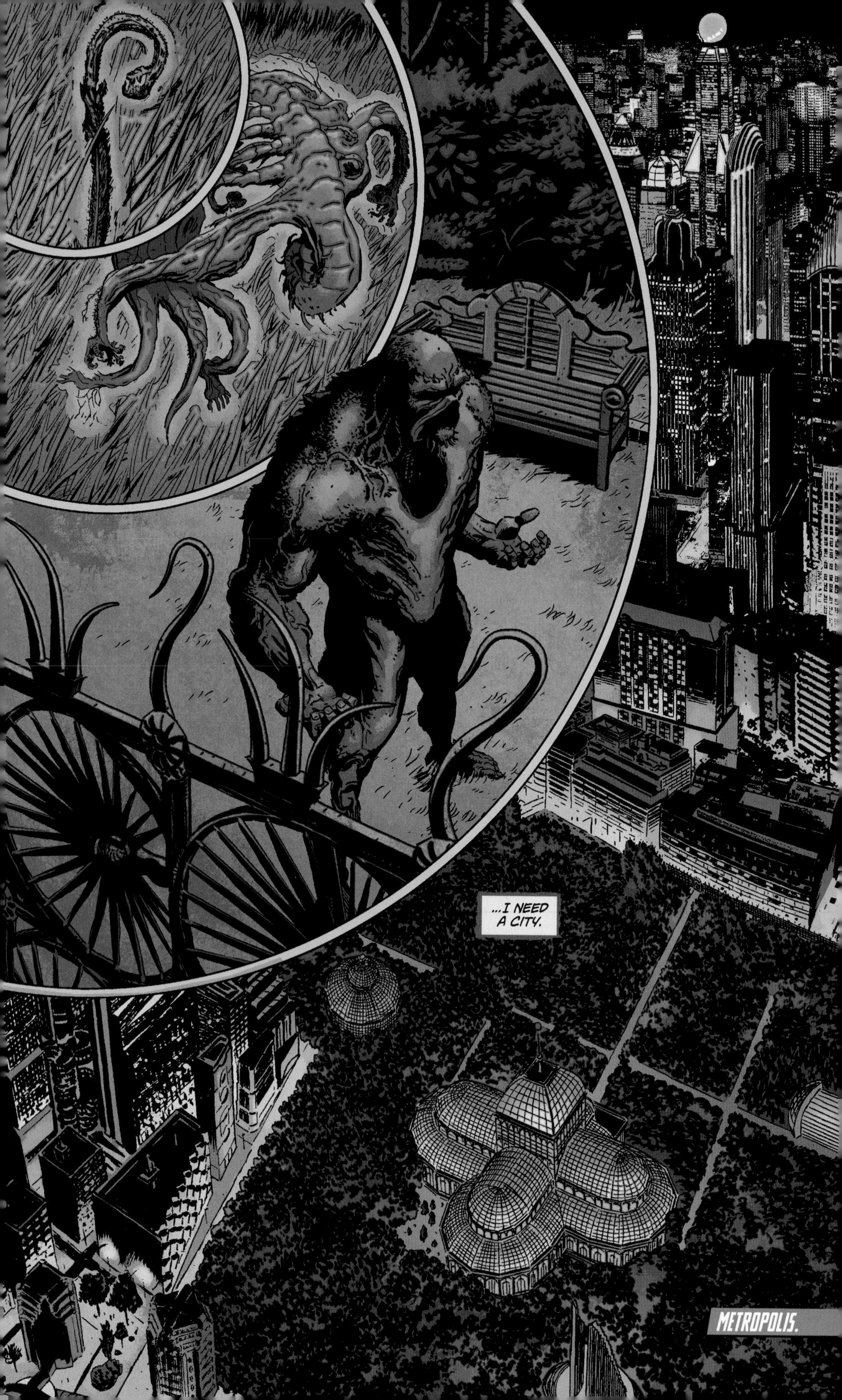

...I NEED
A CITY.
METROPOLIS.

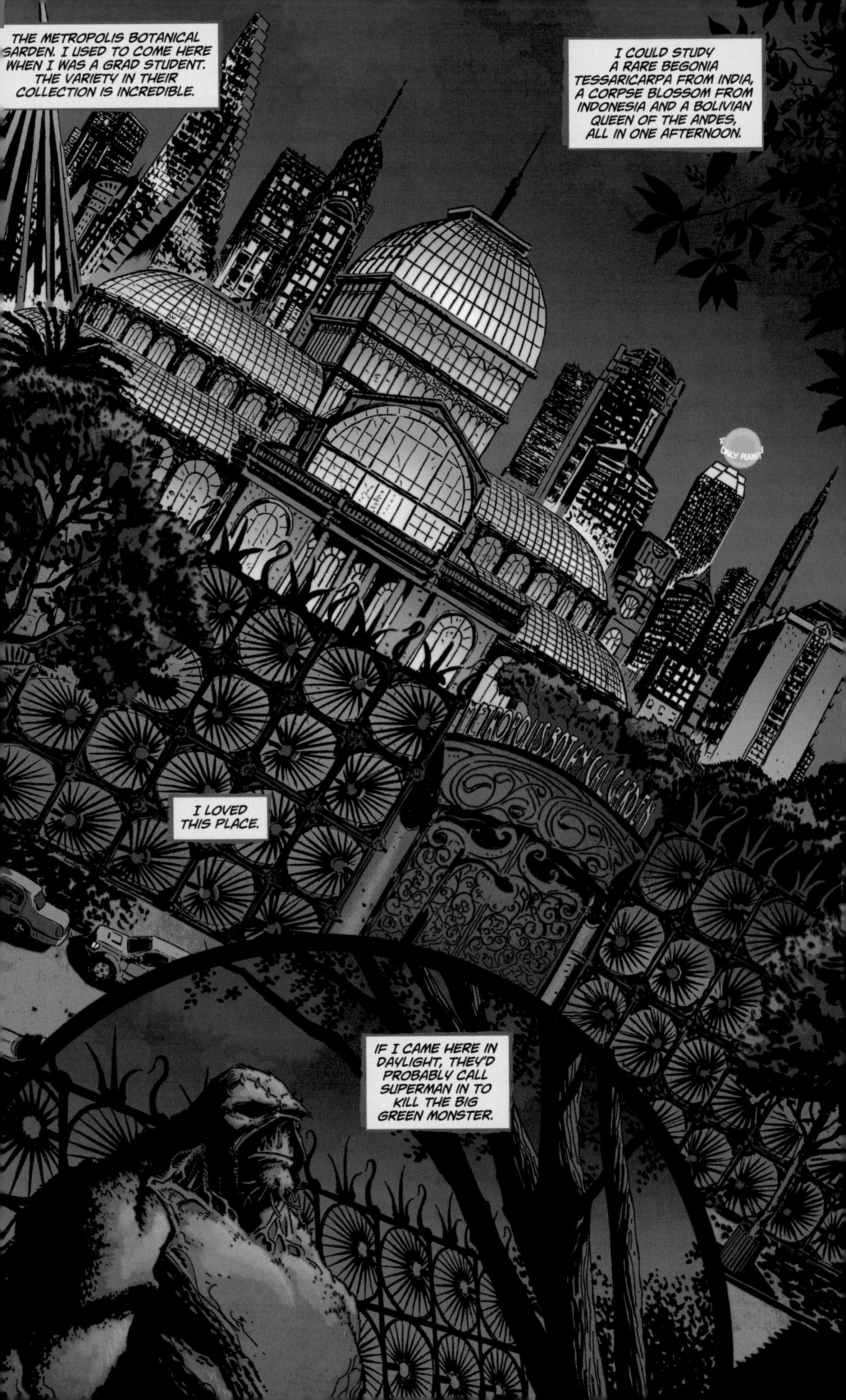
THE METROPOLIS BOTANICAL GARDEN. I USED TO COME HERE WHEN I WAS A GRAD STUDENT. THE VARIETY IN THEIR COLLECTION IS INCREDIBLE.
I COULD STUDY A RARE BEGONIA TESSARICARPA FROM INDIA, A CORPSE BLOSSOM FROM INDONESIA AND A BOLIVIAN QUEEN OF THE ANDES, ALL IN ONE AFTERNOON.
DAILY PLANET
METROPOLIS BOTANICAL GARDENS
I LOVED THIS PLACE.
IF I CAME HERE IN DAYLIGHT, THEY'D PROBABLY CALL SUPERMAN IN TO KILL THE BIG GREEN MONSTER.

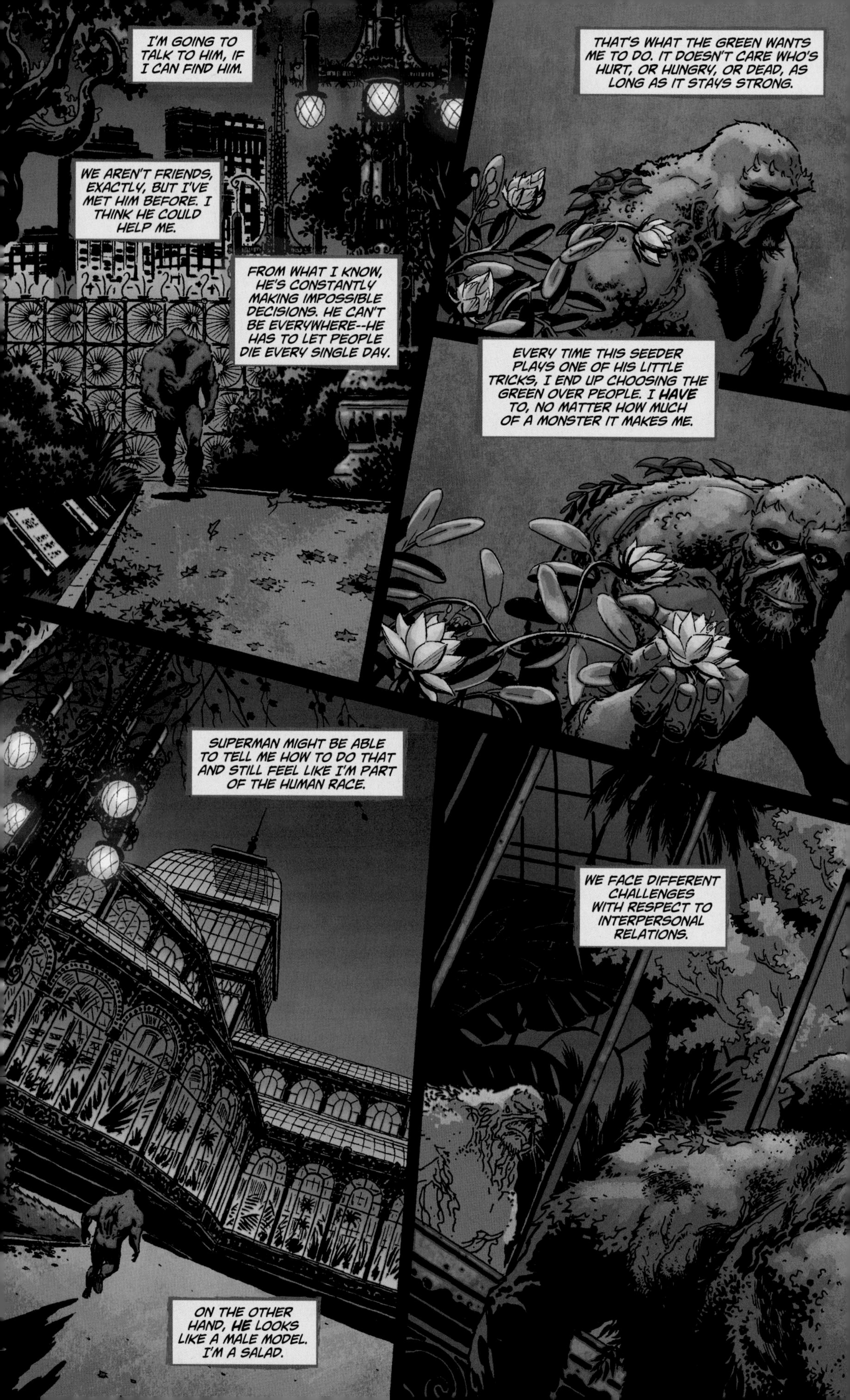
I'M GOING TO TALK TO HIM, IF I CAN FIND HIM.
WE AREN'T FRIENDS, EXACTLY, BUT I'VE MET HIM BEFORE. I THINK HE COULD HELP ME.
FROM WHAT I KNOW, HE'S CONSTANTLY MAKING IMPOSSIBLE DECISIONS. HE CAN'T BE EVERYWHERE--HE HAS TO LET PEOPLE DIE EVERY SINGLE DAY.
THAT'S WHAT THE GREEN WANTS ME TO DO. IT DOESN'T CARE WHO'S HURT, OR HUNGRY, OR DEAD, AS LONG AS IT STAYS STRONG.
EVERY TIME THIS SEEDER PLAYS ONE OF HIS LITTLE TRICKS, I END UP CHOOSING THE GREEN OVER PEOPLE. I HAVE TO, NO MATTER HOW MUCH OF A MONSTER IT MAKES ME.
SUPERMAN MIGHT BE ABLE TO TELL ME HOW TO DO THAT AND STILL FEEL LIKE I'M PART OF THE HUMAN RACE.
ON THE OTHER HAND, HE LOOKS LIKE A MALE MODEL. I'M A SALAD.
WE FACE DIFFERENT CHALLENGES WITH RESPECT TO INTERPERSONAL RELATIONS.

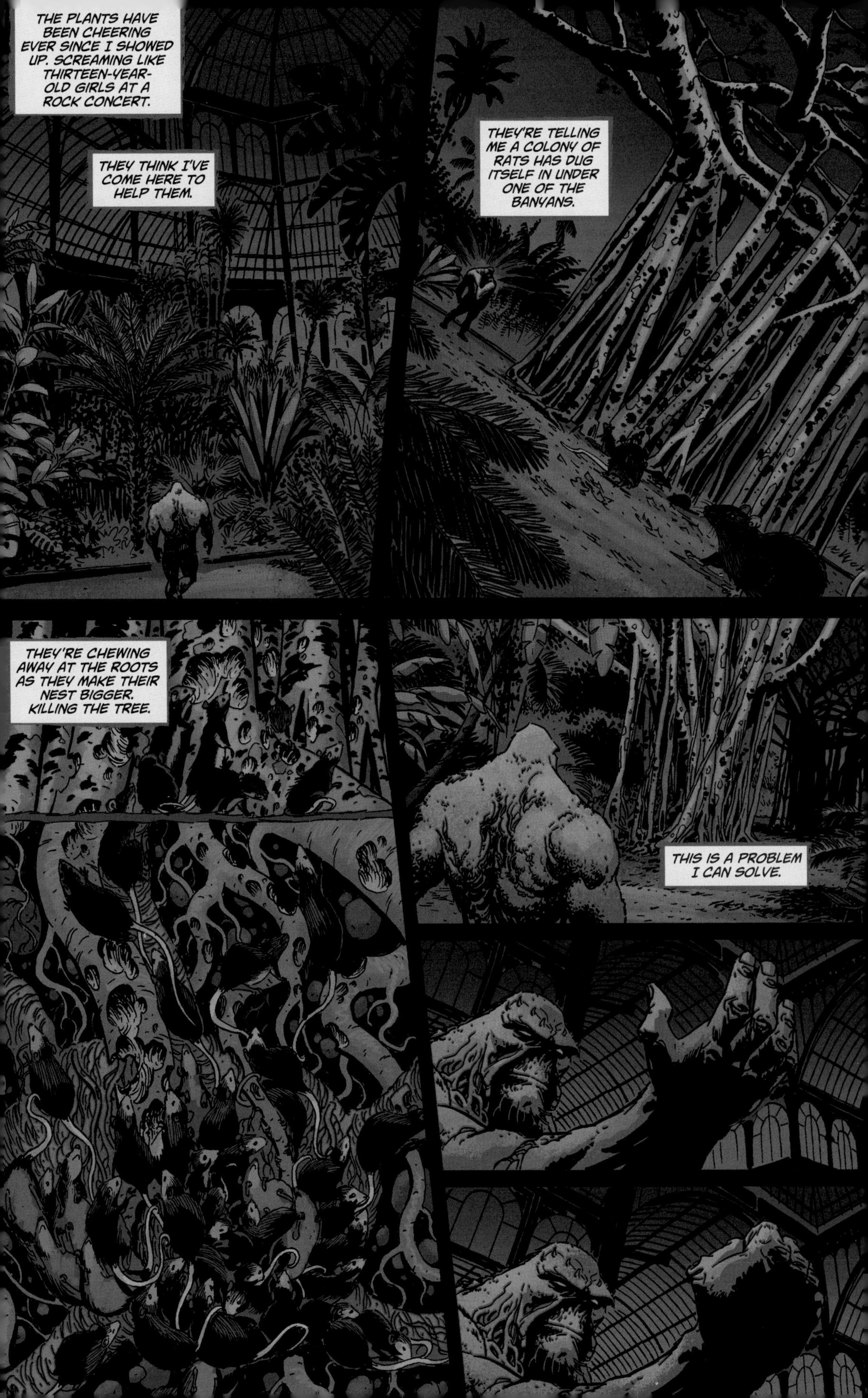
THE PLANTS HAVE BEEN CHEERING EVER SINCE I SHOWED UP. SCREAMING LIKE THIRTEEN-YEAR-OLD GIRLS AT A ROCK CONCERT.
THEY THINK I'VE COME HERE TO HELP THEM.
THEY'RE TELLING ME A COLONY OF RATS HAS DUG ITSELF IN UNDER ONE OF THE BANYANS.
THEY'RE CHEWING AWAY AT THE ROOTS AS THEY MAKE THEIR NEST BIGGER. KILLING THE TREE.
THIS IS A PROBLEM I CAN SOLVE.

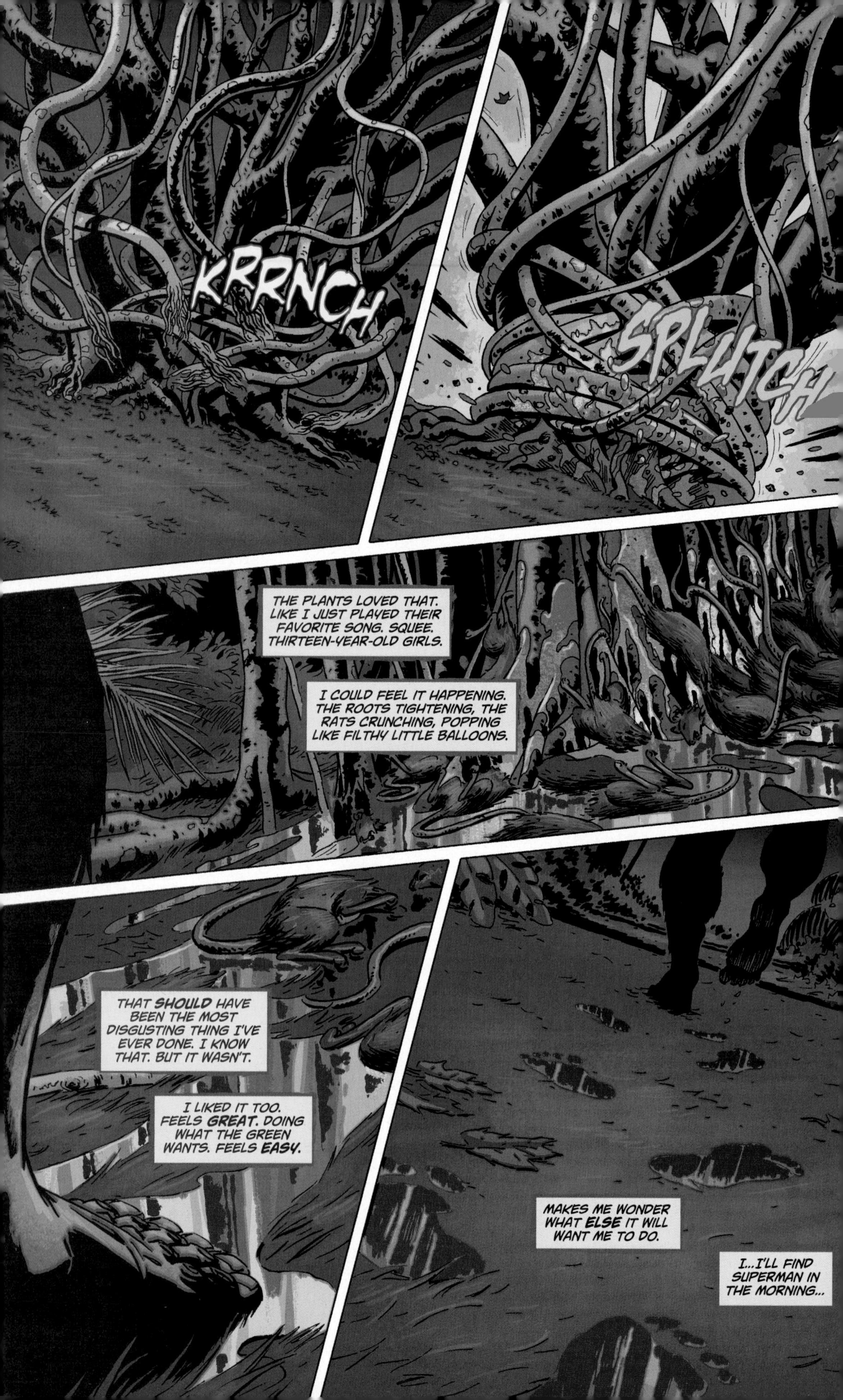
KRRNCH
SPLUTCH
THE PLANTS LOVED THAT. LIKE I JUST PLAYED THEIR FAVORITE SONG. SQUEE. THIRTEEN-YEAR-OLD GIRLS.
I COULD FEEL IT HAPPENING. THE ROOTS TIGHTENING, THE RATS CRUNCHING, POPPING LIKE FILTHY LITTLE BALLOONS.
THAT **SHOULD** HAVE BEEN THE MOST DISGUSTING THING I'VE EVER DONE. I KNOW THAT. BUT IT WASN'T.
I LIKED IT TOO. FEELS **GREAT**. DOING WHAT THE GREEN WANTS. FEELS **EASY**.
MAKES ME WONDER WHAT **ELSE** IT WILL WANT ME TO DO.
I...I'LL FIND SUPERMAN IN THE MORNING...

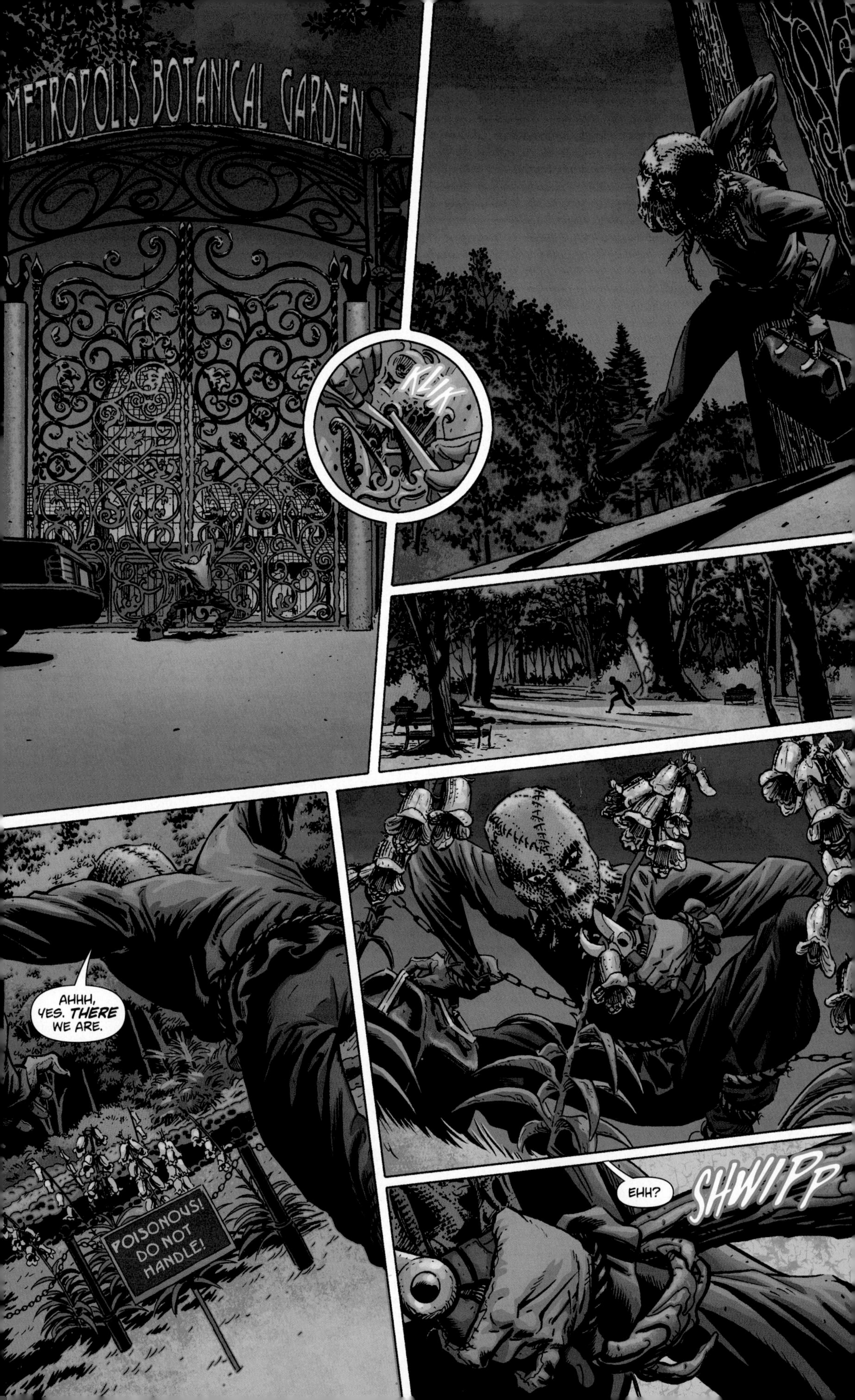
METROPOLIS BOTANICAL GARDEN
KLIK
AHHH, YES. THERE WE ARE.
POISONOUS! DO NOT HANDLE!
EHH?
SHWIPP

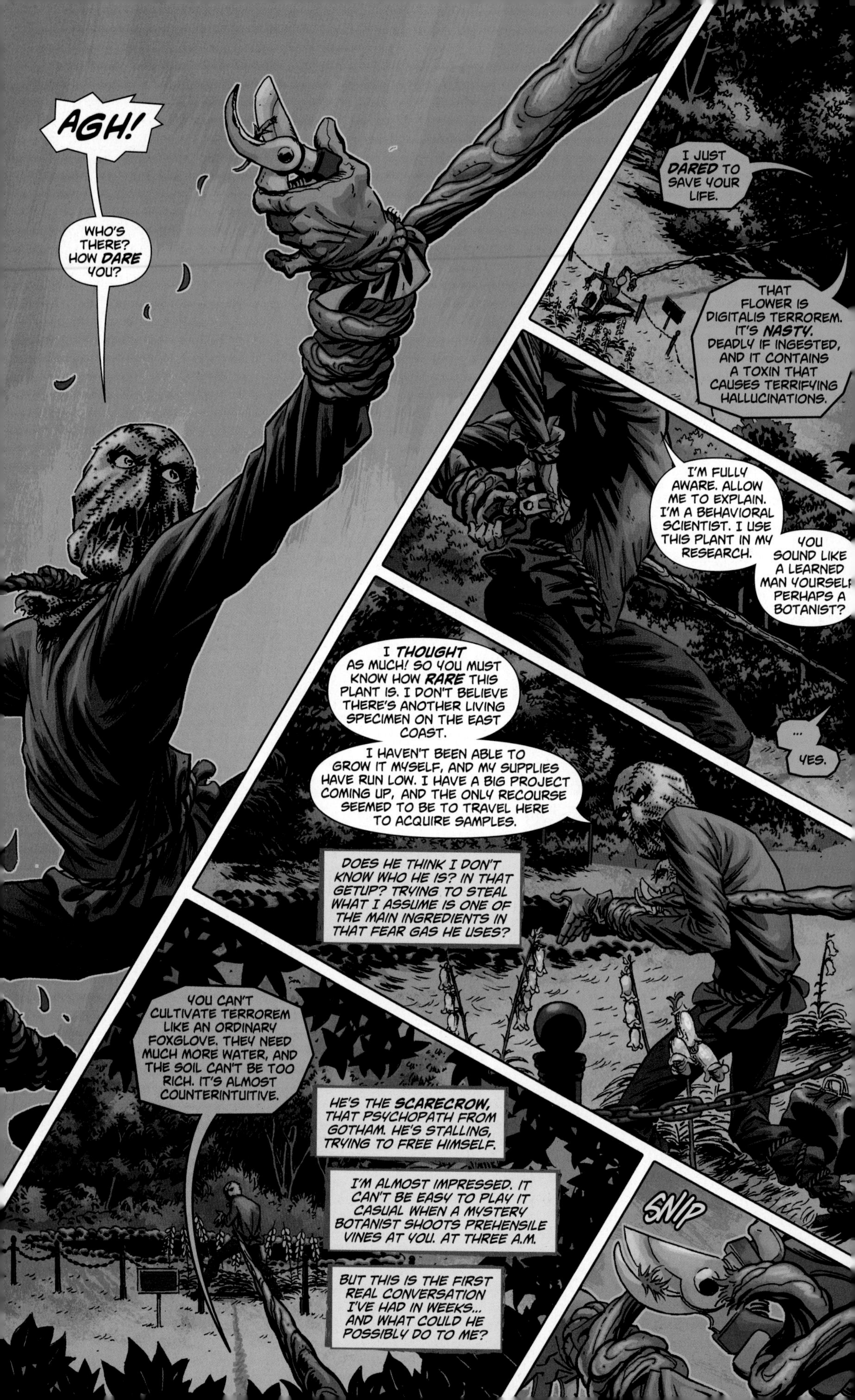
AGH!
WHO'S THERE? HOW DARE YOU?
I JUST DARED TO SAVE YOUR LIFE.
THAT FLOWER IS DIGITALIS TERROREM. IT'S NASTY. DEADLY IF INGESTED, AND IT CONTAINS A TOXIN THAT CAUSES TERRIFYING HALLUCINATIONS.
I'M FULLY AWARE. ALLOW ME TO EXPLAIN. I'M A BEHAVIORAL SCIENTIST. I USE THIS PLANT IN MY RESEARCH.
YOU SOUND LIKE A LEARNED MAN YOURSELF. PERHAPS A BOTANIST?
...
YES.
I THOUGHT AS MUCH! SO YOU MUST KNOW HOW RARE THIS PLANT IS. I DON'T BELIEVE THERE'S ANOTHER LIVING SPECIMEN ON THE EAST COAST.
I HAVEN'T BEEN ABLE TO GROW IT MYSELF, AND MY SUPPLIES HAVE RUN LOW. I HAVE A BIG PROJECT COMING UP, AND THE ONLY RECOURSE SEEMED TO BE TO TRAVEL HERE TO ACQUIRE SAMPLES.
DOES HE THINK I DON'T KNOW WHO HE IS? IN THAT GETUP? TRYING TO STEAL WHAT I ASSUME IS ONE OF THE MAIN INGREDIENTS IN THAT FEAR GAS HE USES?
YOU CAN'T CULTIVATE TERROREM LIKE AN ORDINARY FOXGLOVE. THEY NEED MUCH MORE WATER, AND THE SOIL CAN'T BE TOO RICH. IT'S ALMOST COUNTERINTUITIVE.
HE'S THE SCARECROW, THAT PSYCHOPATH FROM GOTHAM. HE'S STALLING, TRYING TO FREE HIMSELF.
I'M ALMOST IMPRESSED. IT CAN'T BE EASY TO PLAY IT CASUAL WHEN A MYSTERY BOTANIST SHOOTS PREHENSILE VINES AT YOU. AT THREE A.M.
BUT THIS IS THE FIRST REAL CONVERSATION I'VE HAD IN WEEKS... AND WHAT COULD HE POSSIBLY DO TO ME?
SNIP

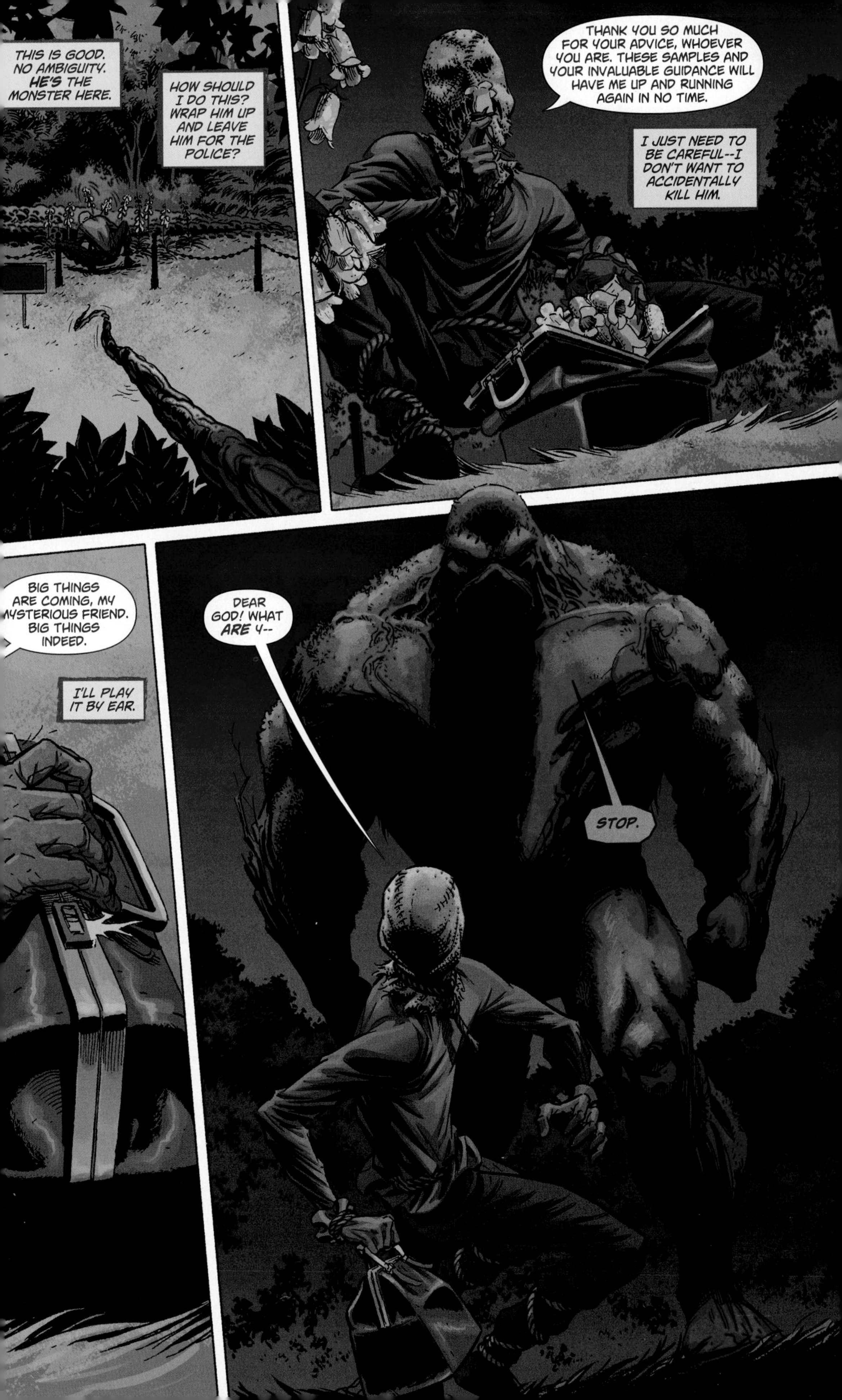

THIS IS GOOD. NO AMBIGUITY. HE'S THE MONSTER HERE.
HOW SHOULD I DO THIS? WRAP HIM UP AND LEAVE HIM FOR THE POLICE?
THANK YOU SO MUCH FOR YOUR ADVICE, WHOEVER YOU ARE. THESE SAMPLES AND YOUR INVALUABLE GUIDANCE WILL HAVE ME UP AND RUNNING AGAIN IN NO TIME.
I JUST NEED TO BE CAREFUL--I DON'T WANT TO ACCIDENTALLY KILL HIM.
BIG THINGS ARE COMING, MY MYSTERIOUS FRIEND. BIG THINGS INDEED.
I'LL PLAY IT BY EAR.
DEAR GOD! WHAT ARE Y--
STOP.

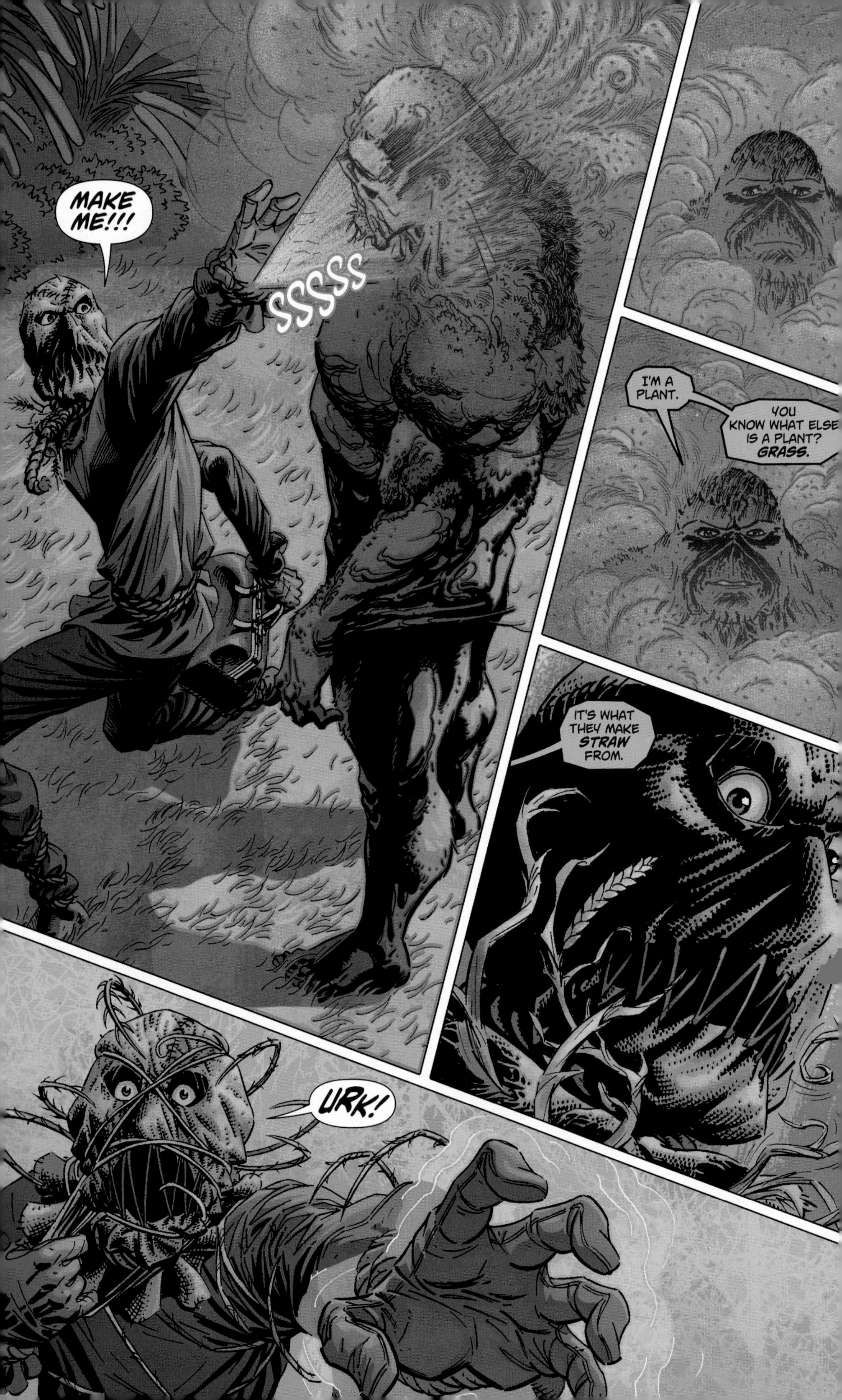
MAKE ME!!!
SSSSS
I'M A PLANT.
YOU KNOW WHAT ELSE IS A PLANT? GRASS.
IT'S WHAT THEY MAKE STRAW FROM.
URK!

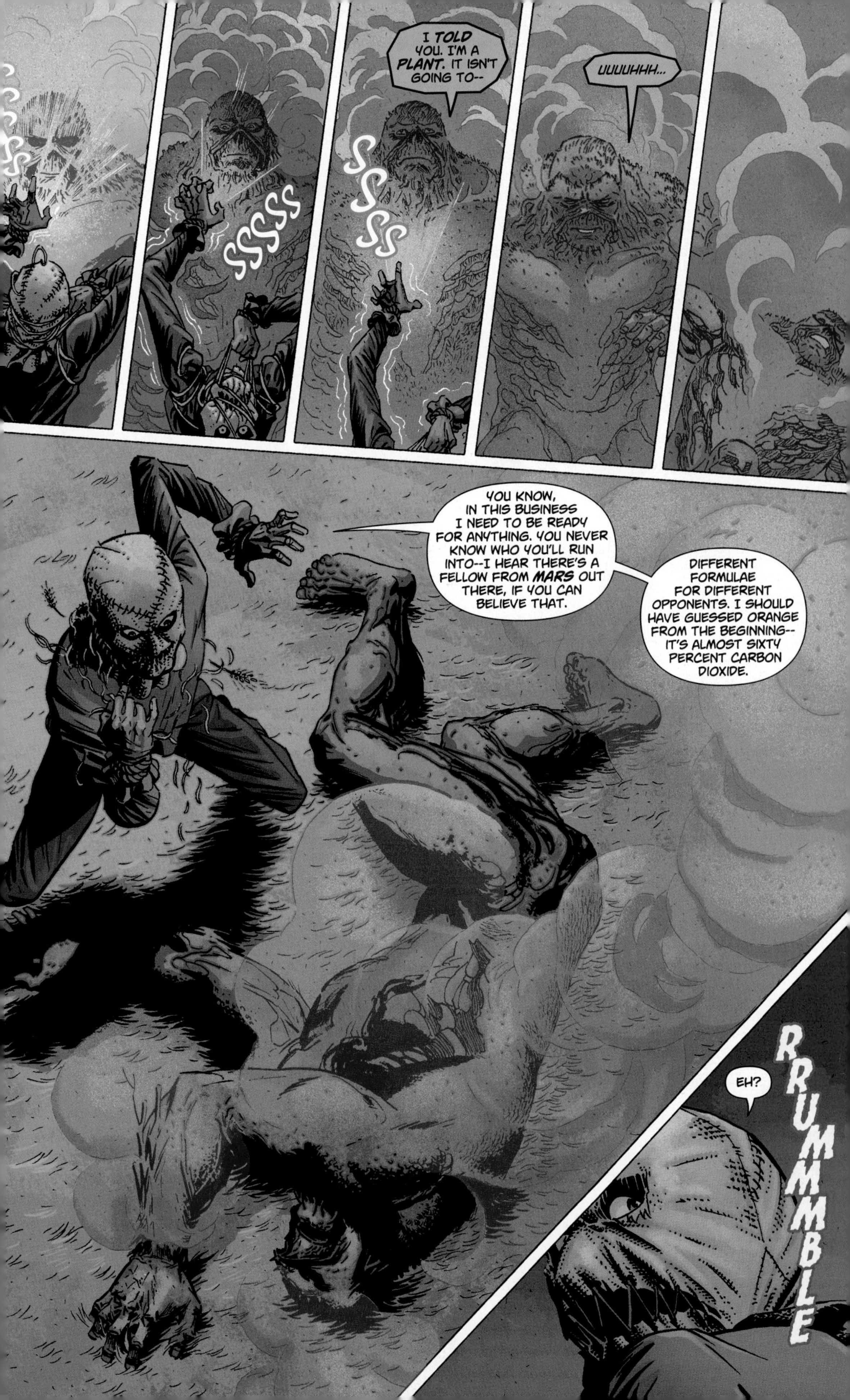
SSSSS
SSSSS
I TOLD YOU. I'M A PLANT. IT ISN'T GOING TO--
SSSSS
UUUUHHH...
YOU KNOW, IN THIS BUSINESS I NEED TO BE READY FOR ANYTHING. YOU NEVER KNOW WHO YOU'LL RUN INTO--I HEAR THERE'S A FELLOW FROM MARS OUT THERE, IF YOU CAN BELIEVE THAT.
DIFFERENT FORMULAE FOR DIFFERENT OPPONENTS. I SHOULD HAVE GUESSED ORANGE FROM THE BEGINNING-- IT'S ALMOST SIXTY PERCENT CARBON DIOXIDE.
RRUMMBLE
EH?

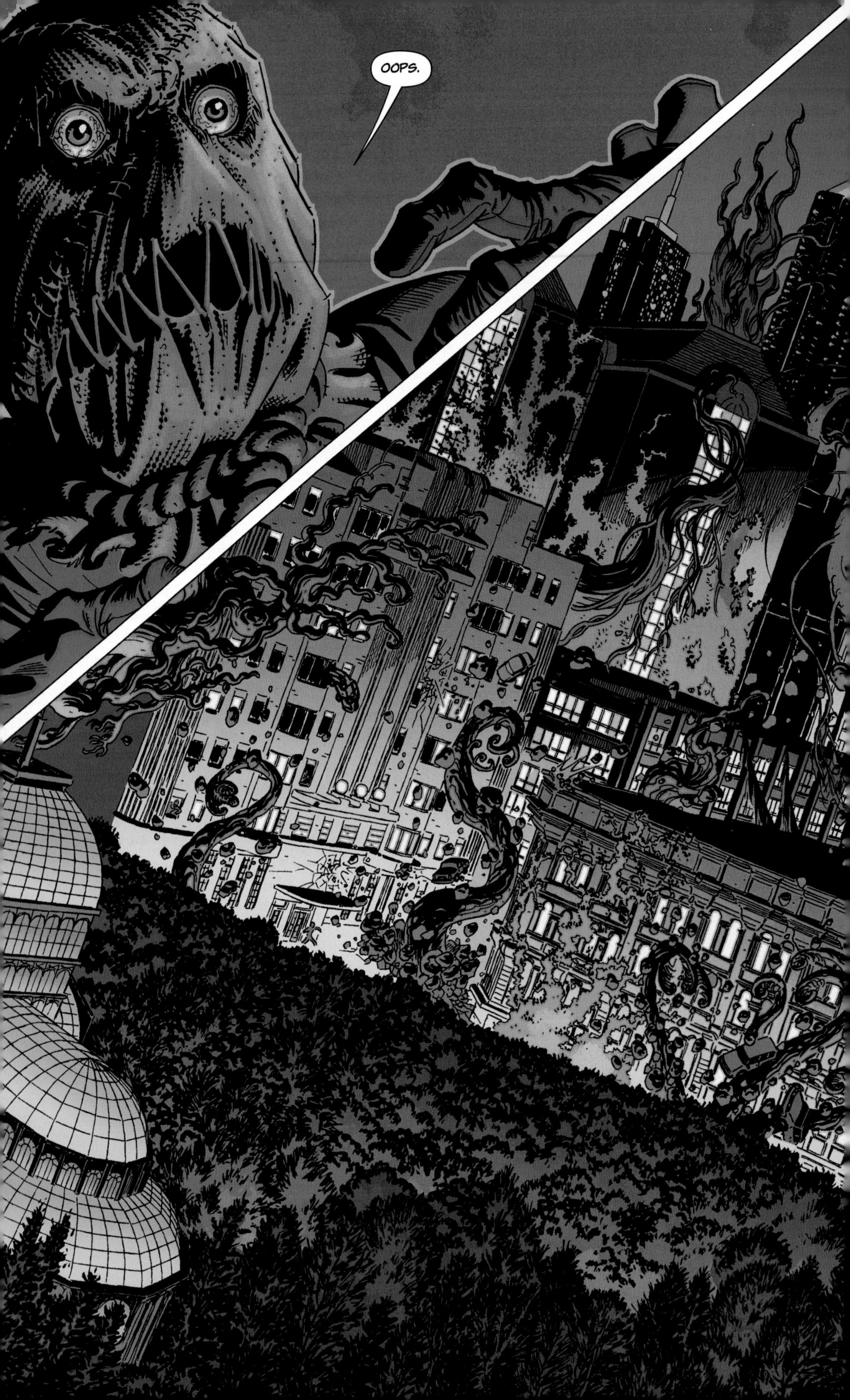
OOPS.

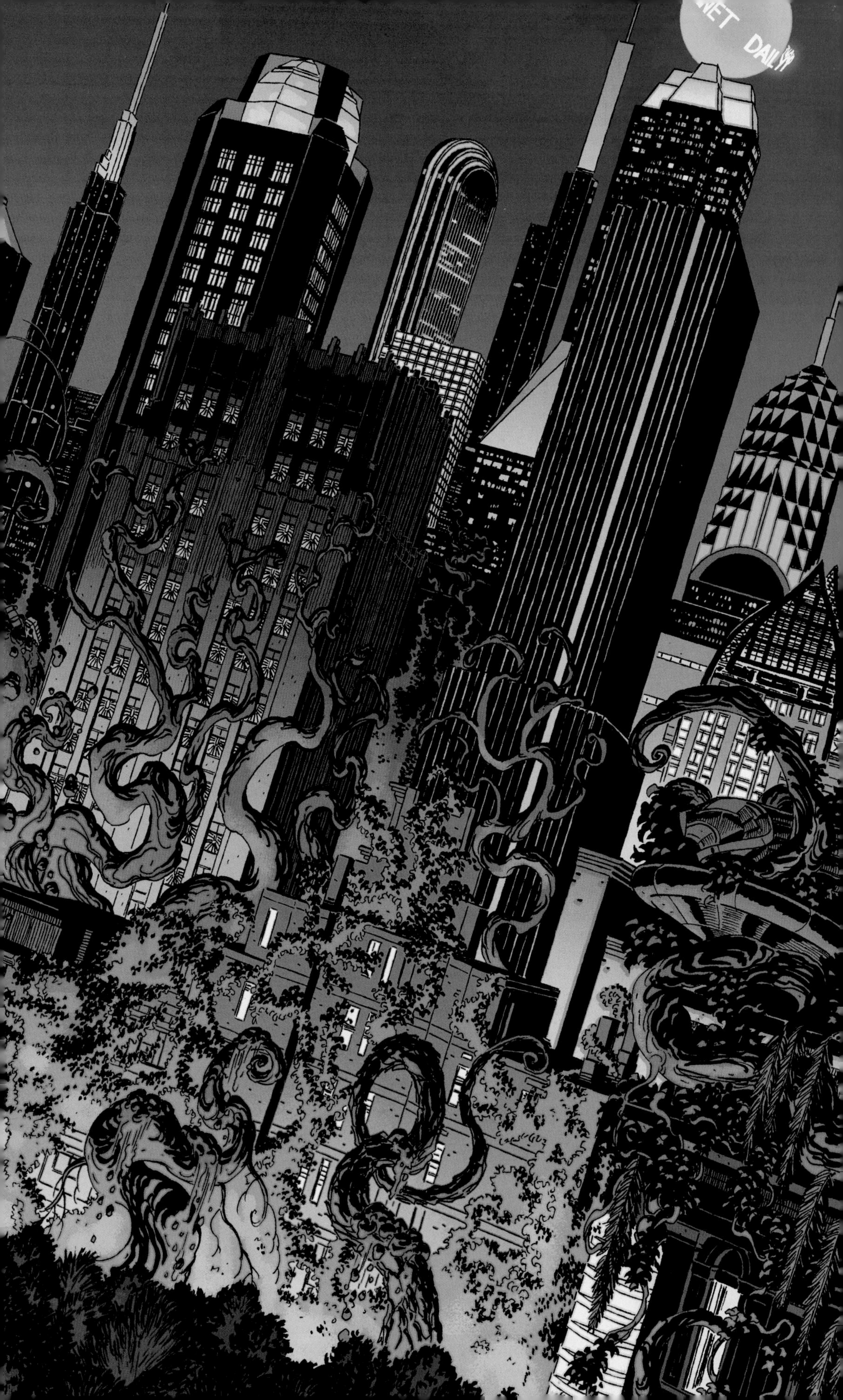
NET DAILY

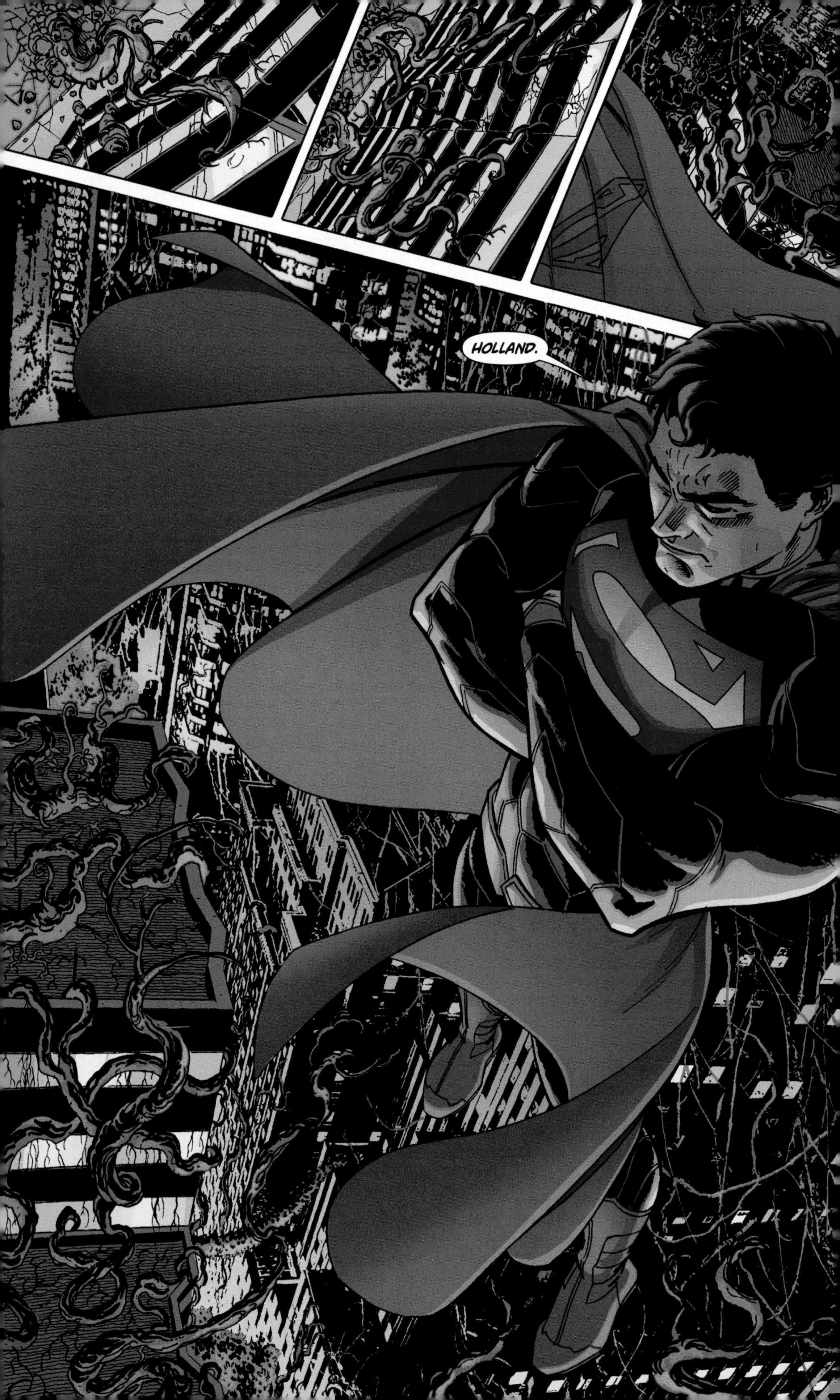
HOLLAND.

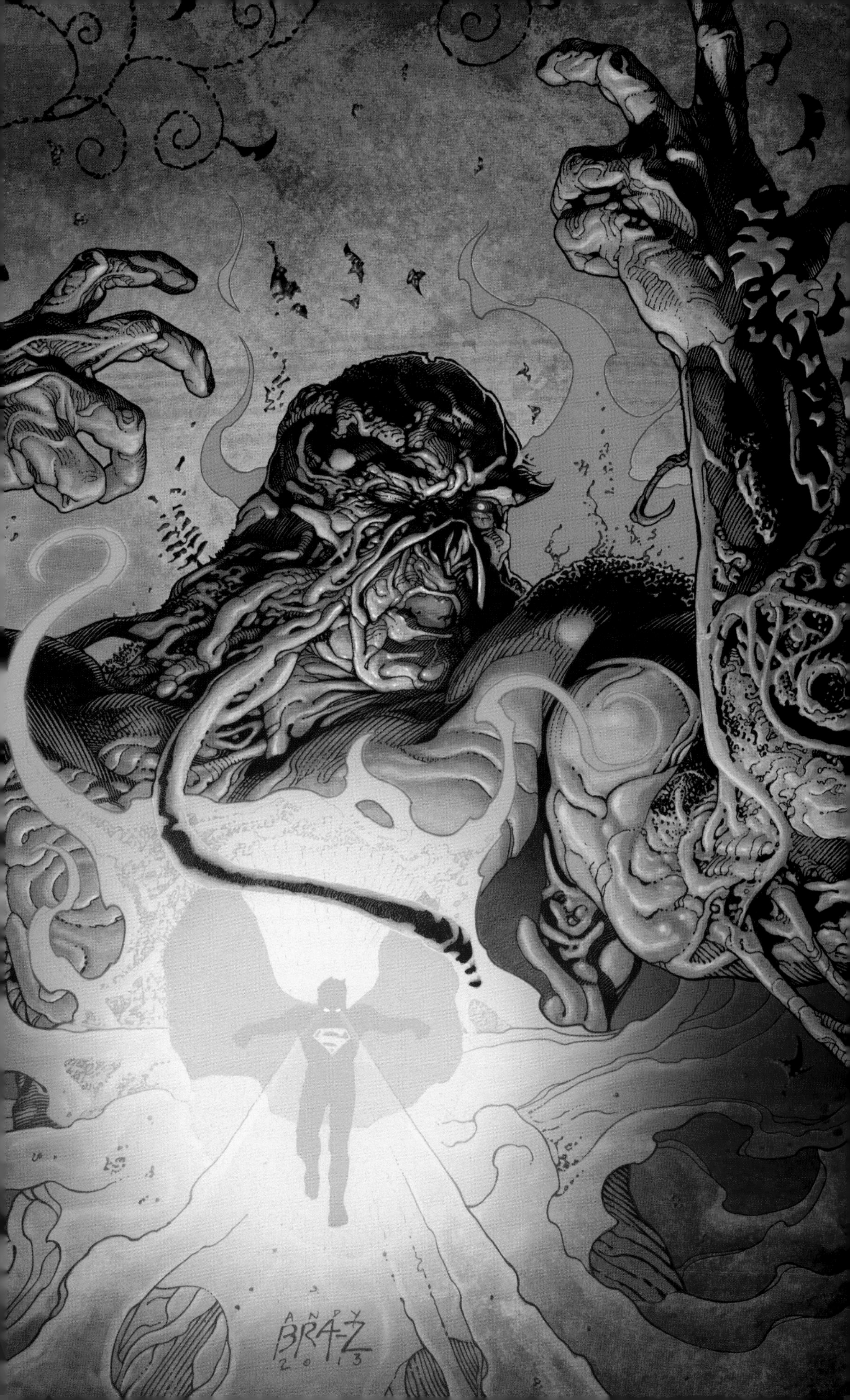
ANDY
BRA-Z
2013

# THIS GREEN HELL

**CHARLES SOULE** writer   **KANO** penciller   **ALVARO LOPEZ** inker   cover art by **ANDY BRASE**

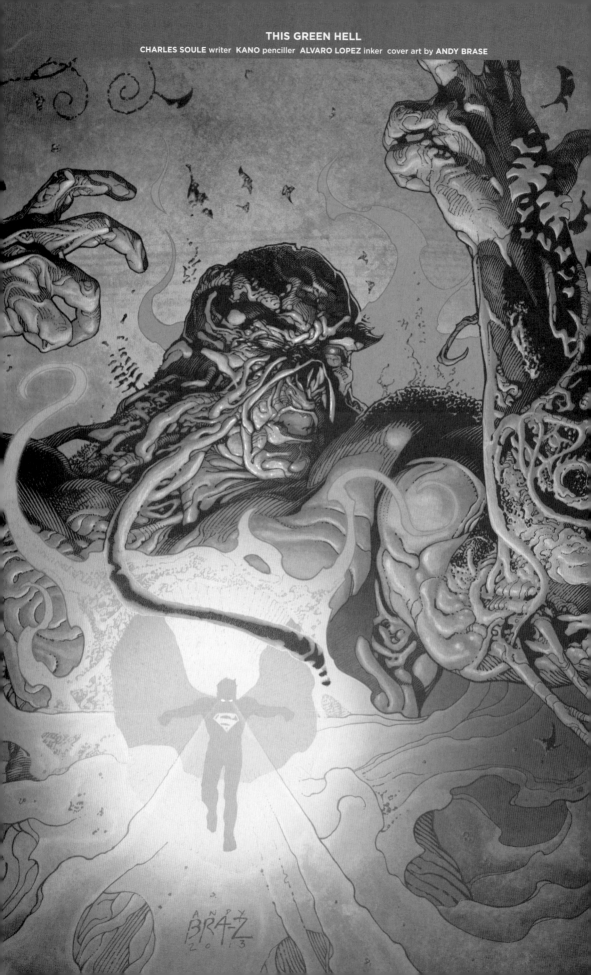

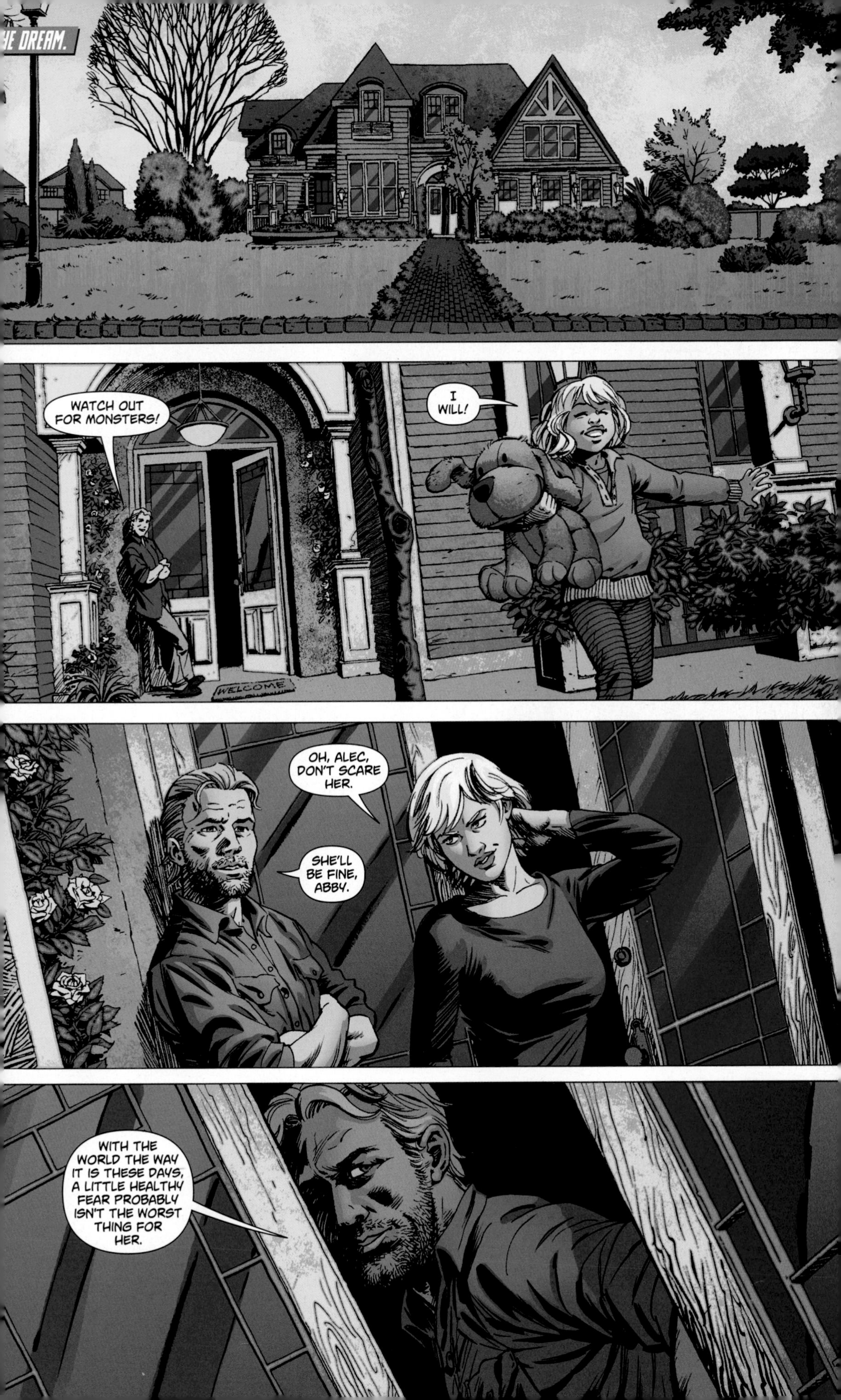

HE DREAM.
WATCH OUT FOR MONSTERS!
I WILL!
WELCOME
OH, ALEC, DON'T SCARE HER.
SHE'LL BE FINE, ABBY.
WITH THE WORLD THE WAY IT IS THESE DAYS, A LITTLE HEALTHY FEAR PROBABLY ISN'T THE WORST THING FOR HER.

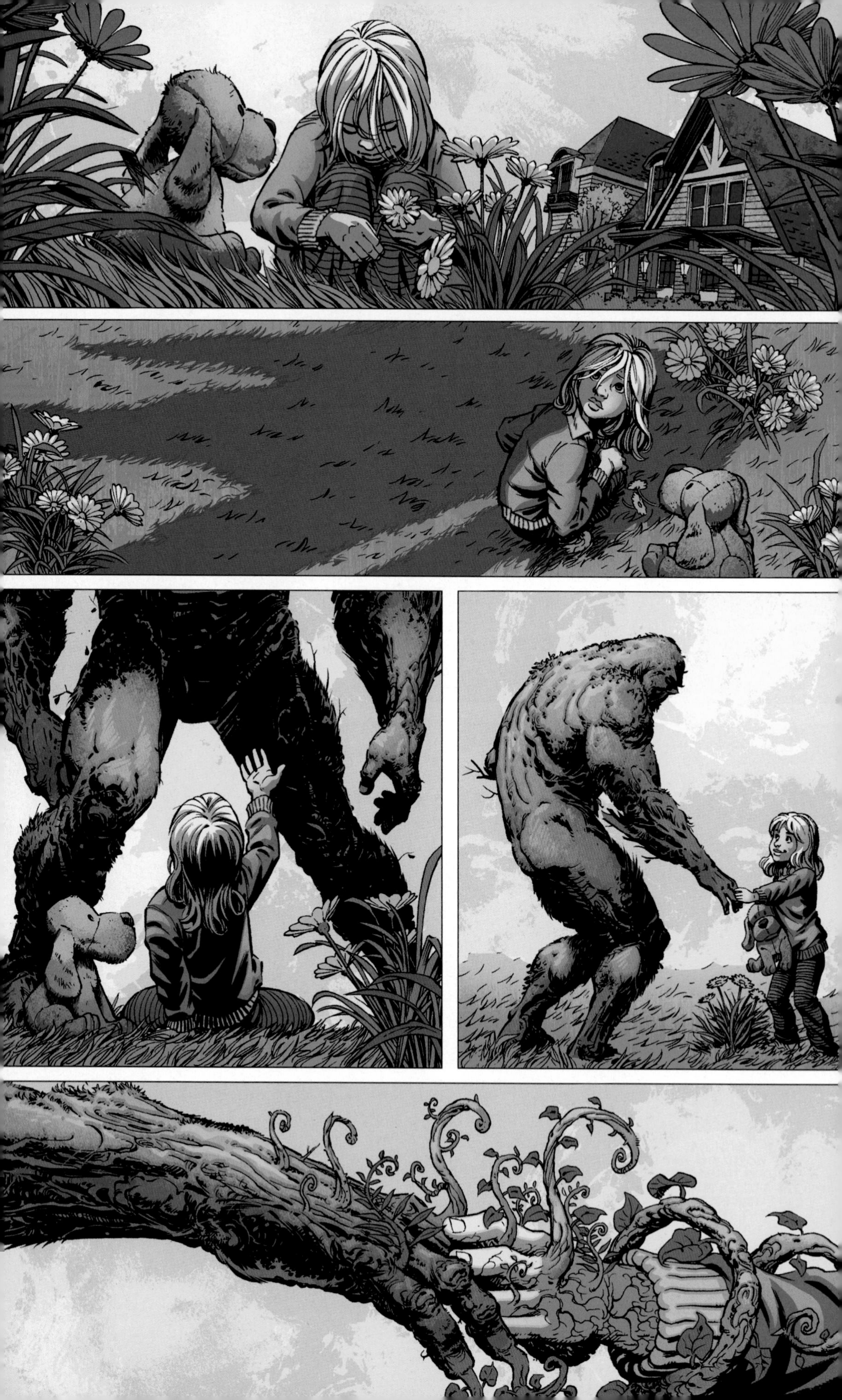

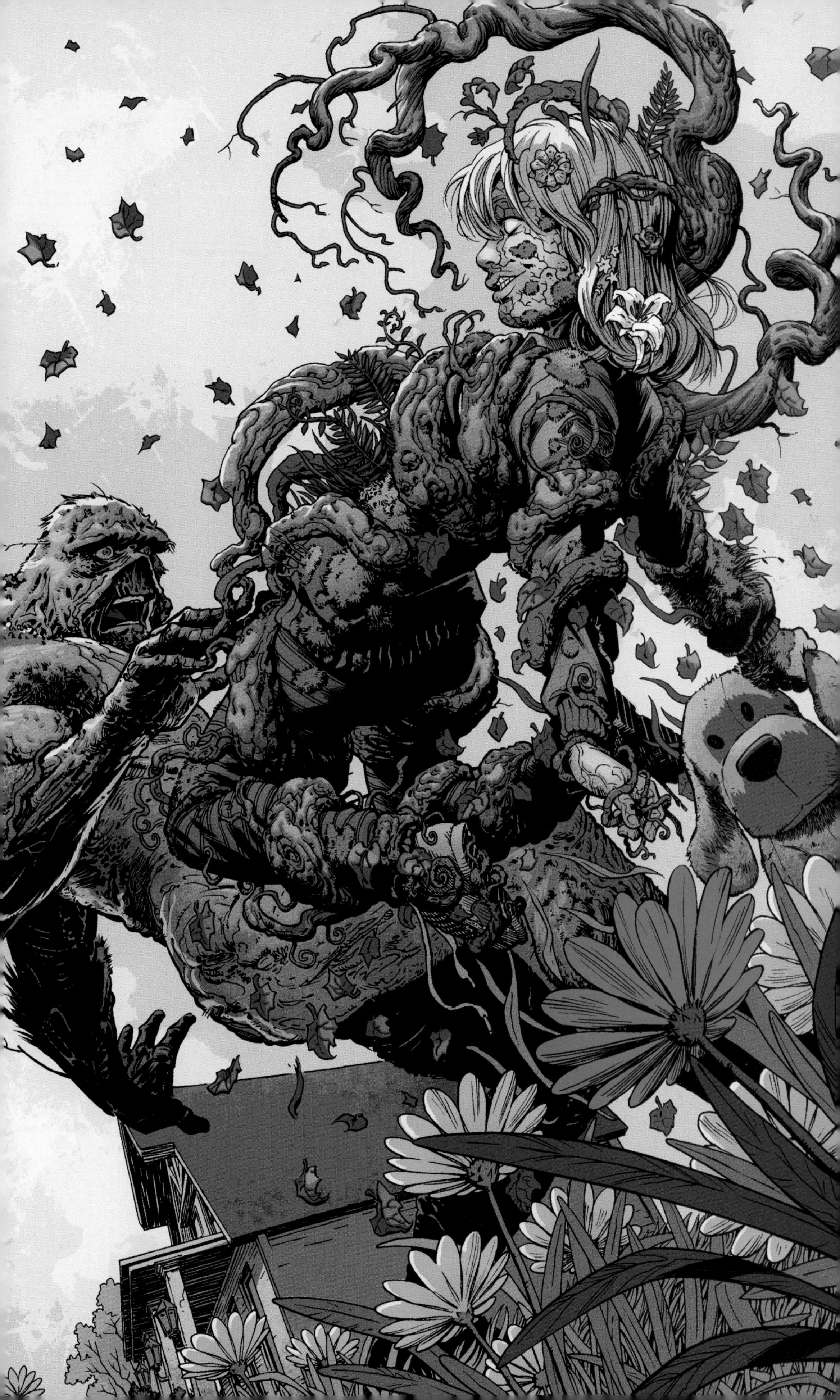

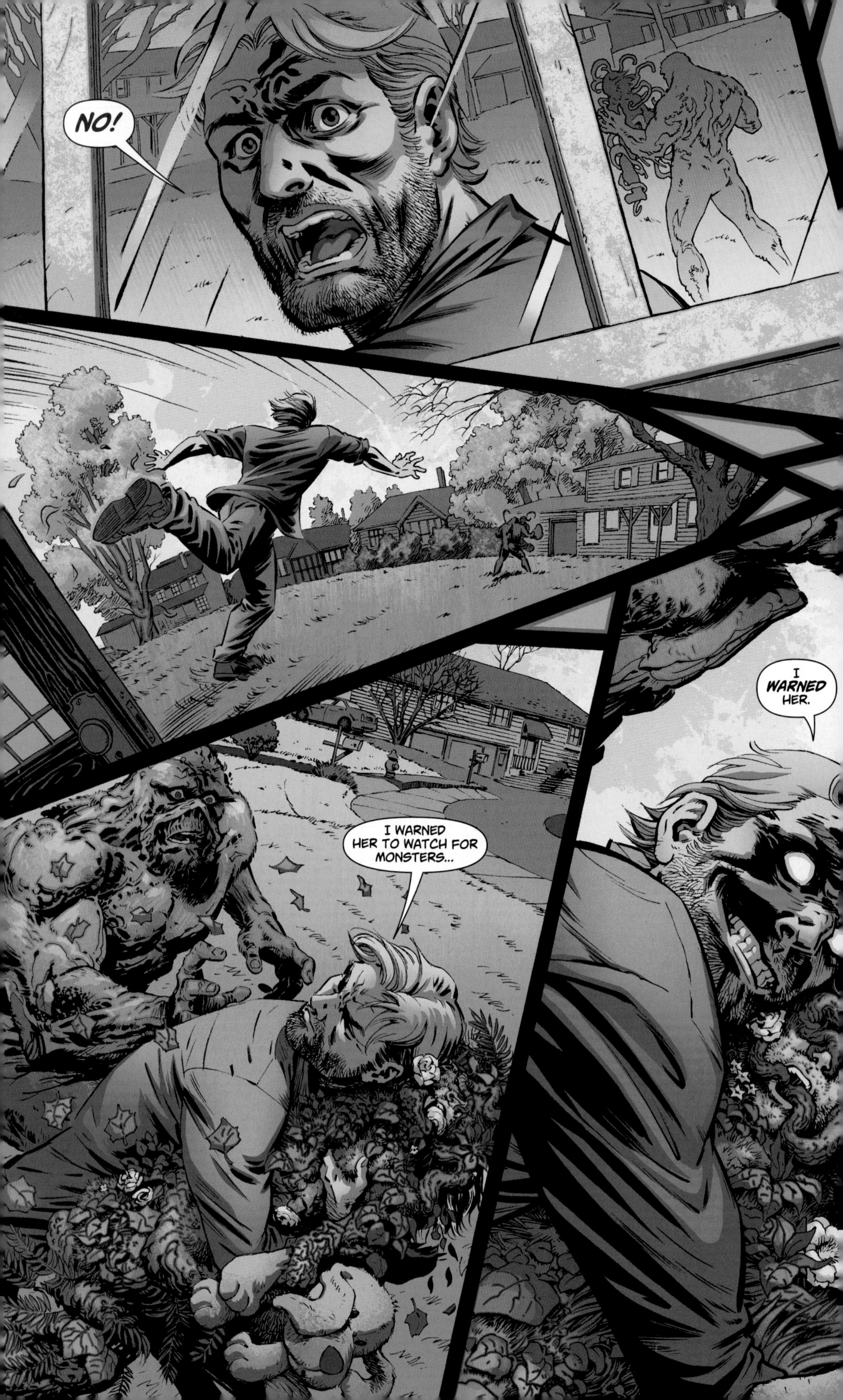
NO!
I WARNED HER TO WATCH FOR MONSTERS...
I WARNED HER.

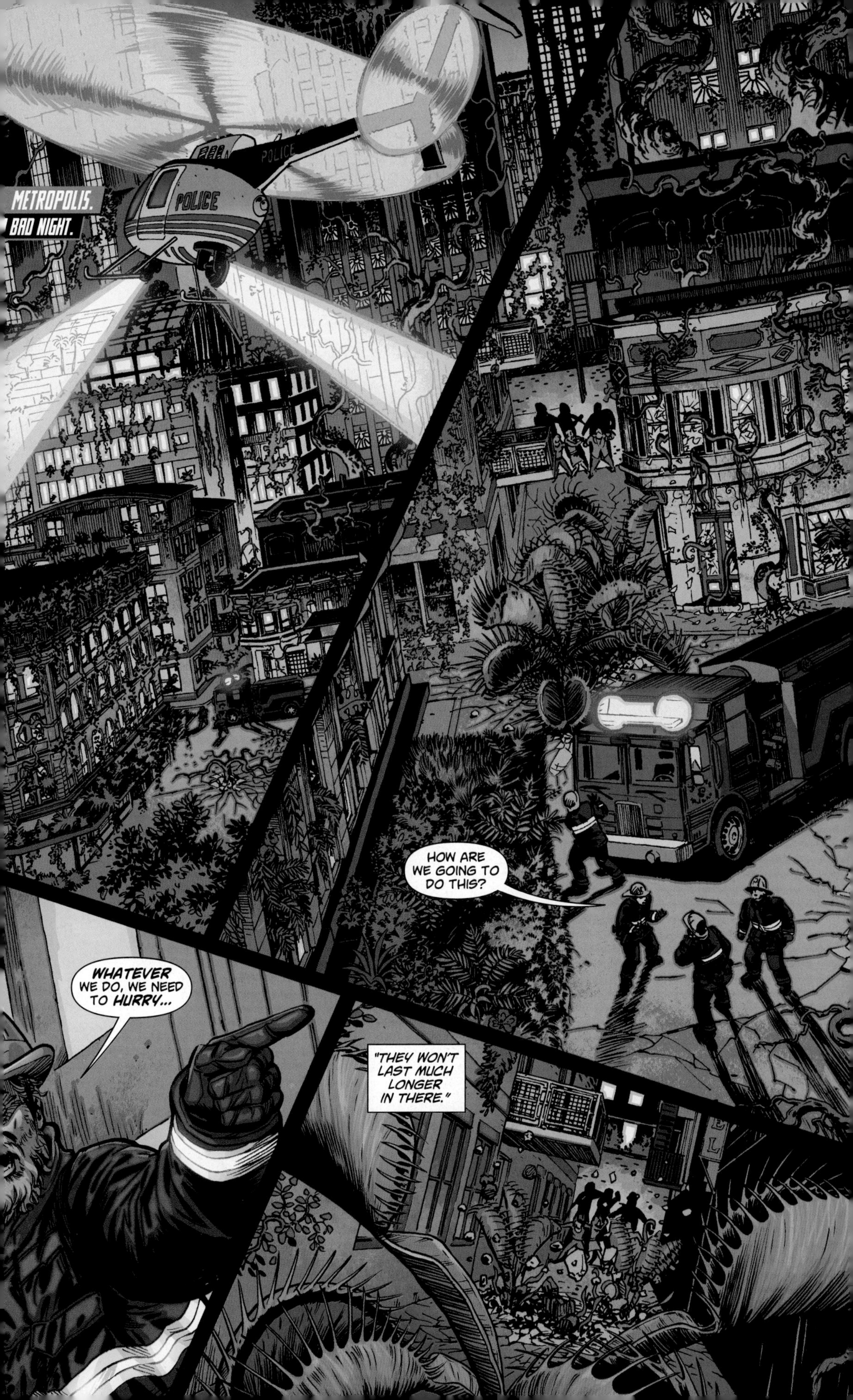
METROPOLIS.
BAD NIGHT.
POLICE
POLICE
HOW ARE WE GOING TO DO THIS?
WHATEVER WE DO, WE NEED TO HURRY...
"THEY WON'T LAST MUCH LONGER IN THERE."

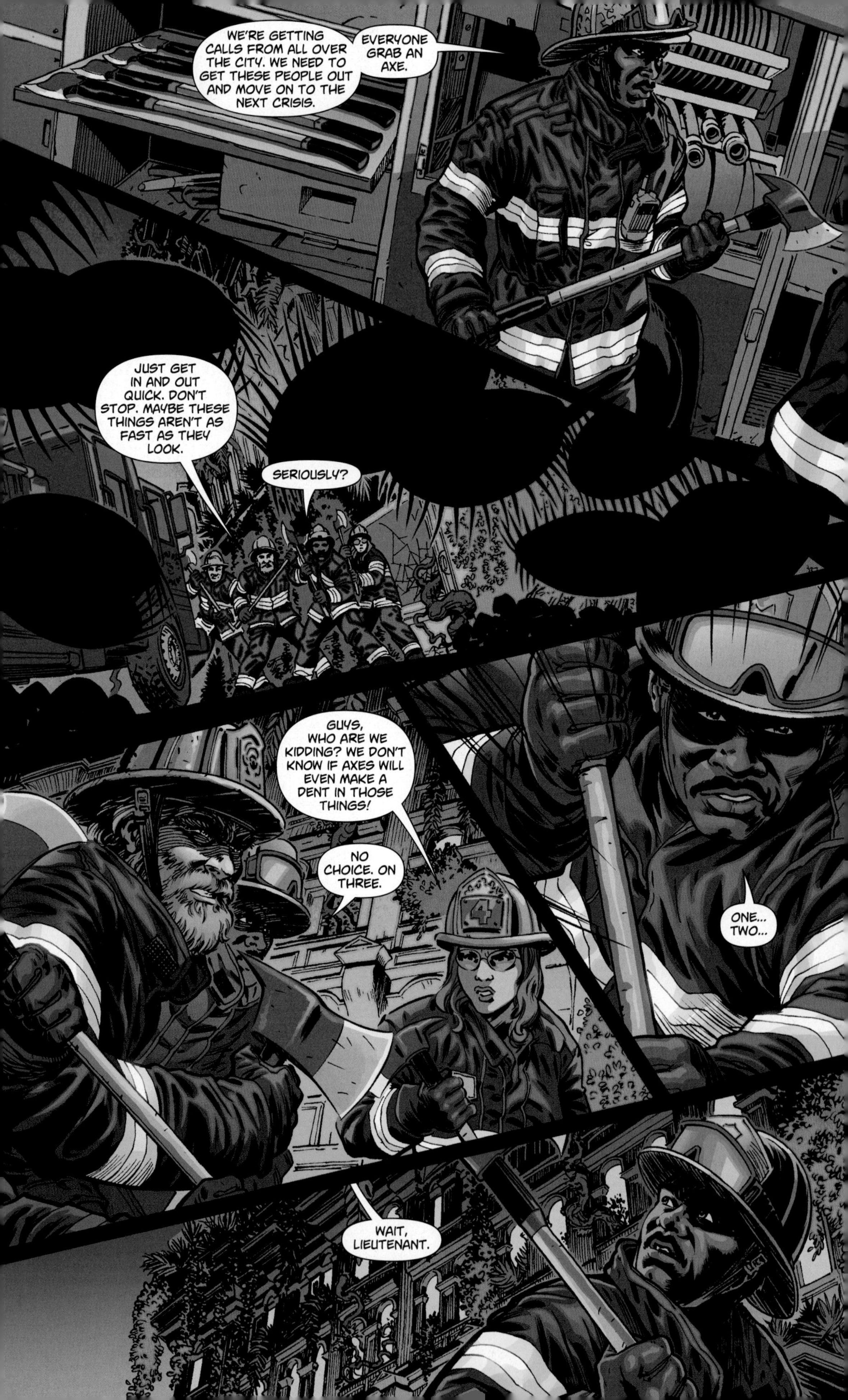
WE'RE GETTING CALLS FROM ALL OVER THE CITY. WE NEED TO GET THESE PEOPLE OUT AND MOVE ON TO THE NEXT CRISIS.
EVERYONE GRAB AN AXE.
JUST GET IN AND OUT QUICK. DON'T STOP. MAYBE THESE THINGS AREN'T AS FAST AS THEY LOOK.
SERIOUSLY?
GUYS, WHO ARE WE KIDDING? WE DON'T KNOW IF AXES WILL EVEN MAKE A DENT IN THOSE THINGS!
NO CHOICE. ON THREE.
ONE... TWO...
WAIT, LIEUTENANT.

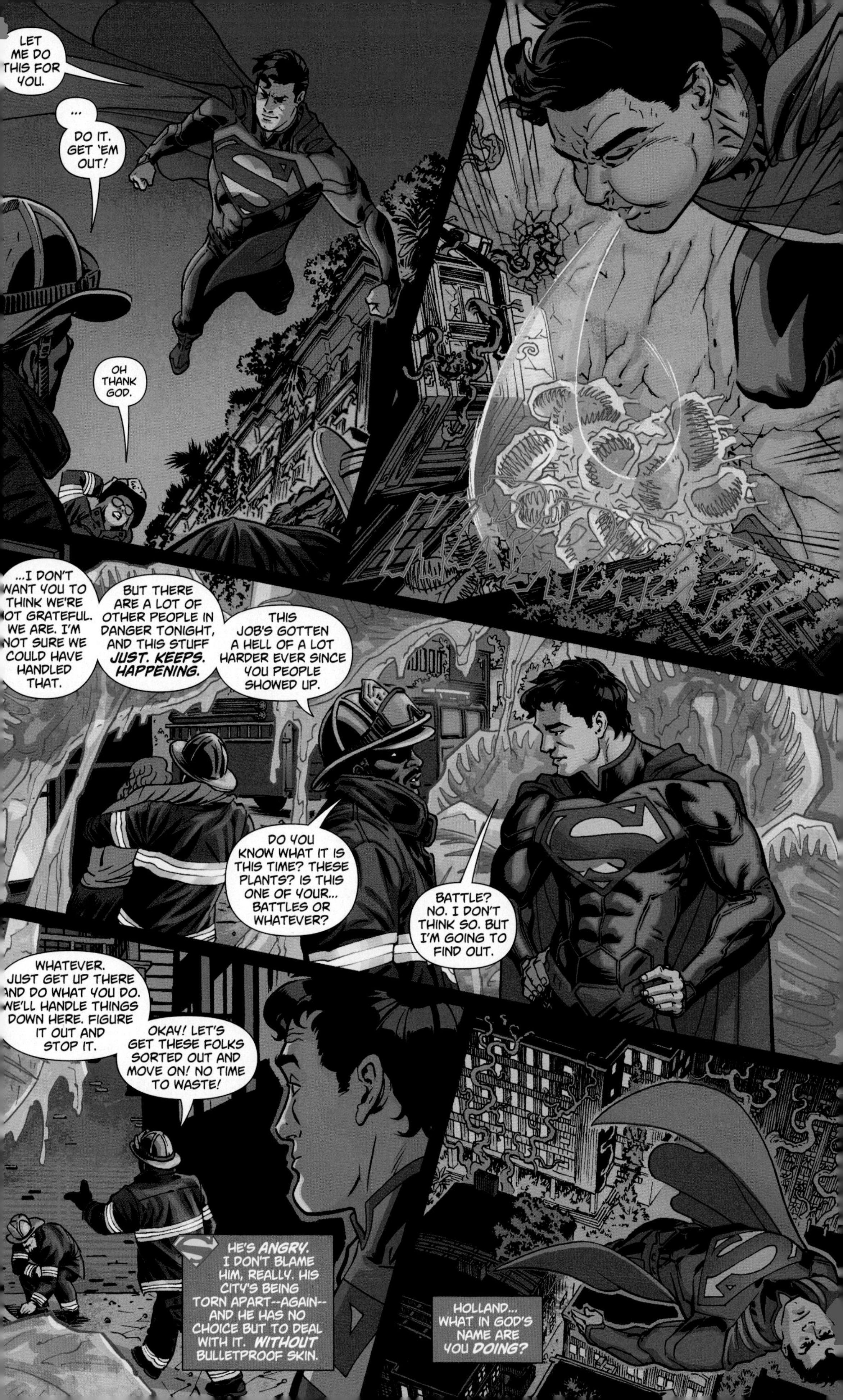
LET ME DO THIS FOR YOU.
...
DO IT. GET 'EM OUT!
OH THANK GOD.
...I DON'T WANT YOU TO THINK WE'RE NOT GRATEFUL. WE ARE. I'M NOT SURE WE COULD HAVE HANDLED THAT.
BUT THERE ARE A LOT OF OTHER PEOPLE IN DANGER TONIGHT, AND THIS STUFF JUST. KEEPS. HAPPENING.
THIS JOB'S GOTTEN A HELL OF A LOT HARDER EVER SINCE YOU PEOPLE SHOWED UP.
DO YOU KNOW WHAT IT IS THIS TIME? THESE PLANTS? IS THIS ONE OF YOUR... BATTLES OR WHATEVER?
BATTLE? NO. I DON'T THINK SO. BUT I'M GOING TO FIND OUT.
WHATEVER. JUST GET UP THERE AND DO WHAT YOU DO. WE'LL HANDLE THINGS DOWN HERE. FIGURE IT OUT AND STOP IT.
OKAY! LET'S GET THESE FOLKS SORTED OUT AND MOVE ON! NO TIME TO WASTE!
HE'S ANGRY. I DON'T BLAME HIM, REALLY. HIS CITY'S BEING TORN APART--AGAIN--AND HE HAS NO CHOICE BUT TO DEAL WITH IT. WITHOUT BULLETPROOF SKIN.
HOLLAND... WHAT IN GOD'S NAME ARE YOU DOING?

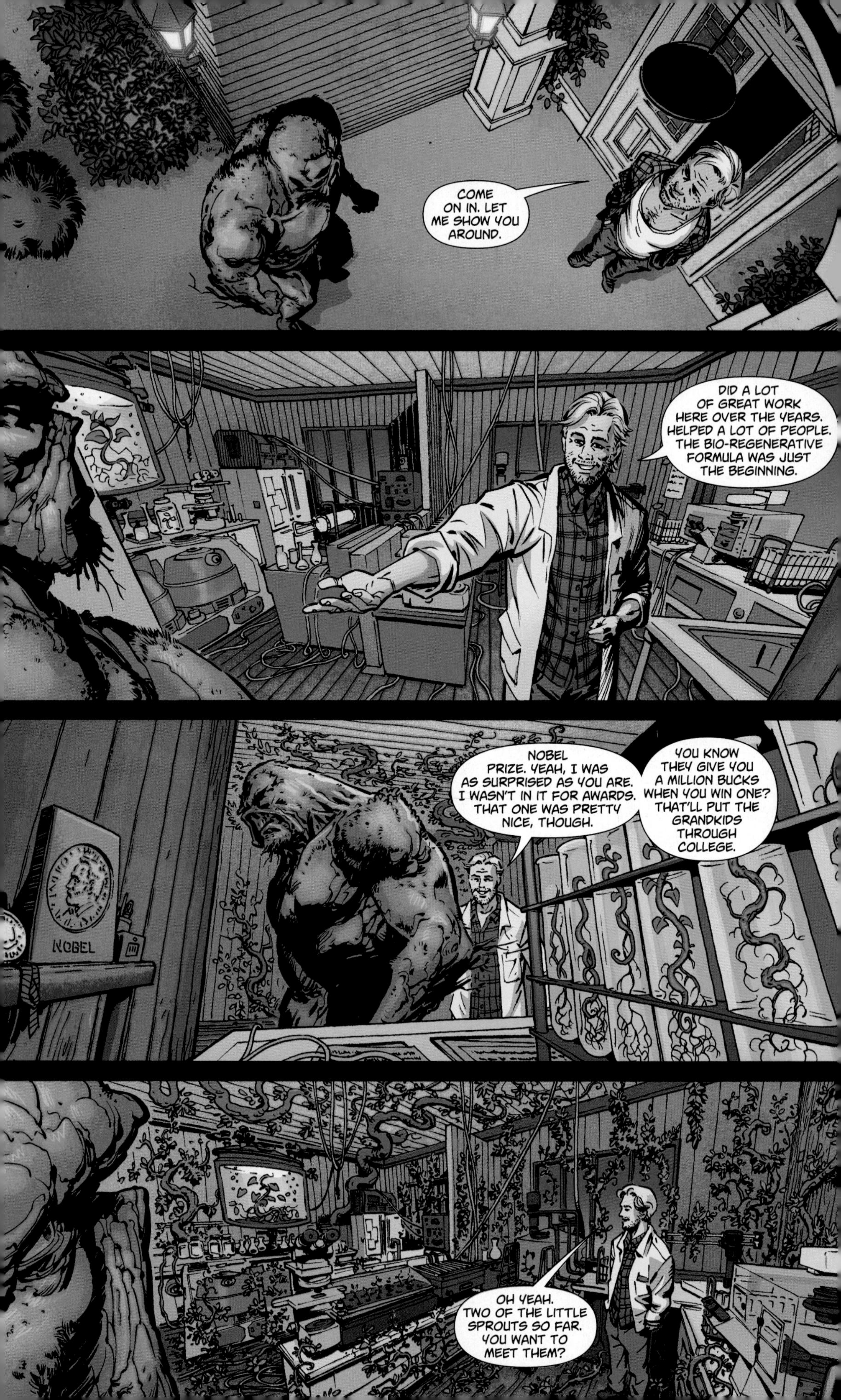
COME ON IN. LET ME SHOW YOU AROUND.
DID A LOT OF GREAT WORK HERE OVER THE YEARS. HELPED A LOT OF PEOPLE. THE BIO-REGENERATIVE FORMULA WAS JUST THE BEGINNING.
NOBEL PRIZE. YEAH, I WAS AS SURPRISED AS YOU ARE. I WASN'T IN IT FOR AWARDS. THAT ONE WAS PRETTY NICE, THOUGH.
YOU KNOW THEY GIVE YOU A MILLION BUCKS WHEN YOU WIN ONE? THAT'LL PUT THE GRANDKIDS THROUGH COLLEGE.
NOBEL
OH YEAH. TWO OF THE LITTLE SPROUTS SO FAR. YOU WANT TO MEET THEM?

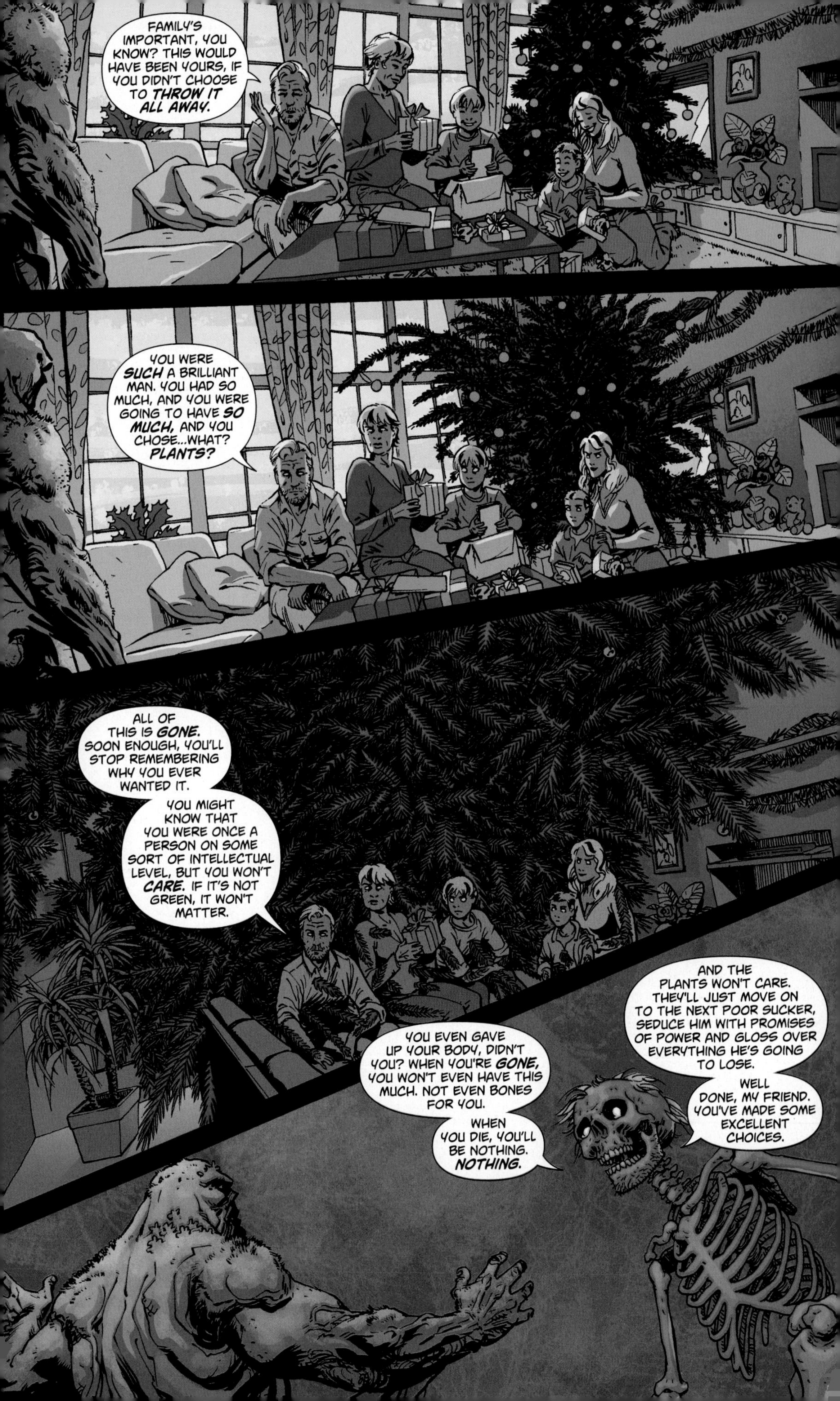
FAMILY'S IMPORTANT, YOU KNOW? THIS WOULD HAVE BEEN YOURS, IF YOU DIDN'T CHOOSE TO THROW IT ALL AWAY.
YOU WERE SUCH A BRILLIANT MAN. YOU HAD SO MUCH, AND YOU WERE GOING TO HAVE SO MUCH, AND YOU CHOSE...WHAT? PLANTS?
ALL OF THIS IS GONE. SOON ENOUGH, YOU'LL STOP REMEMBERING WHY YOU EVER WANTED IT.
YOU MIGHT KNOW THAT YOU WERE ONCE A PERSON ON SOME SORT OF INTELLECTUAL LEVEL, BUT YOU WON'T CARE. IF IT'S NOT GREEN, IT WON'T MATTER.
YOU EVEN GAVE UP YOUR BODY, DIDN'T YOU? WHEN YOU'RE GONE, YOU WON'T EVEN HAVE THIS MUCH. NOT EVEN BONES FOR YOU.
WHEN YOU DIE, YOU'LL BE NOTHING. NOTHING.
AND THE PLANTS WON'T CARE. THEY'LL JUST MOVE ON TO THE NEXT POOR SUCKER, SEDUCE HIM WITH PROMISES OF POWER AND GLOSS OVER EVERYTHING HE'S GOING TO LOSE.
WELL DONE, MY FRIEND. YOU'VE MADE SOME EXCELLENT CHOICES.

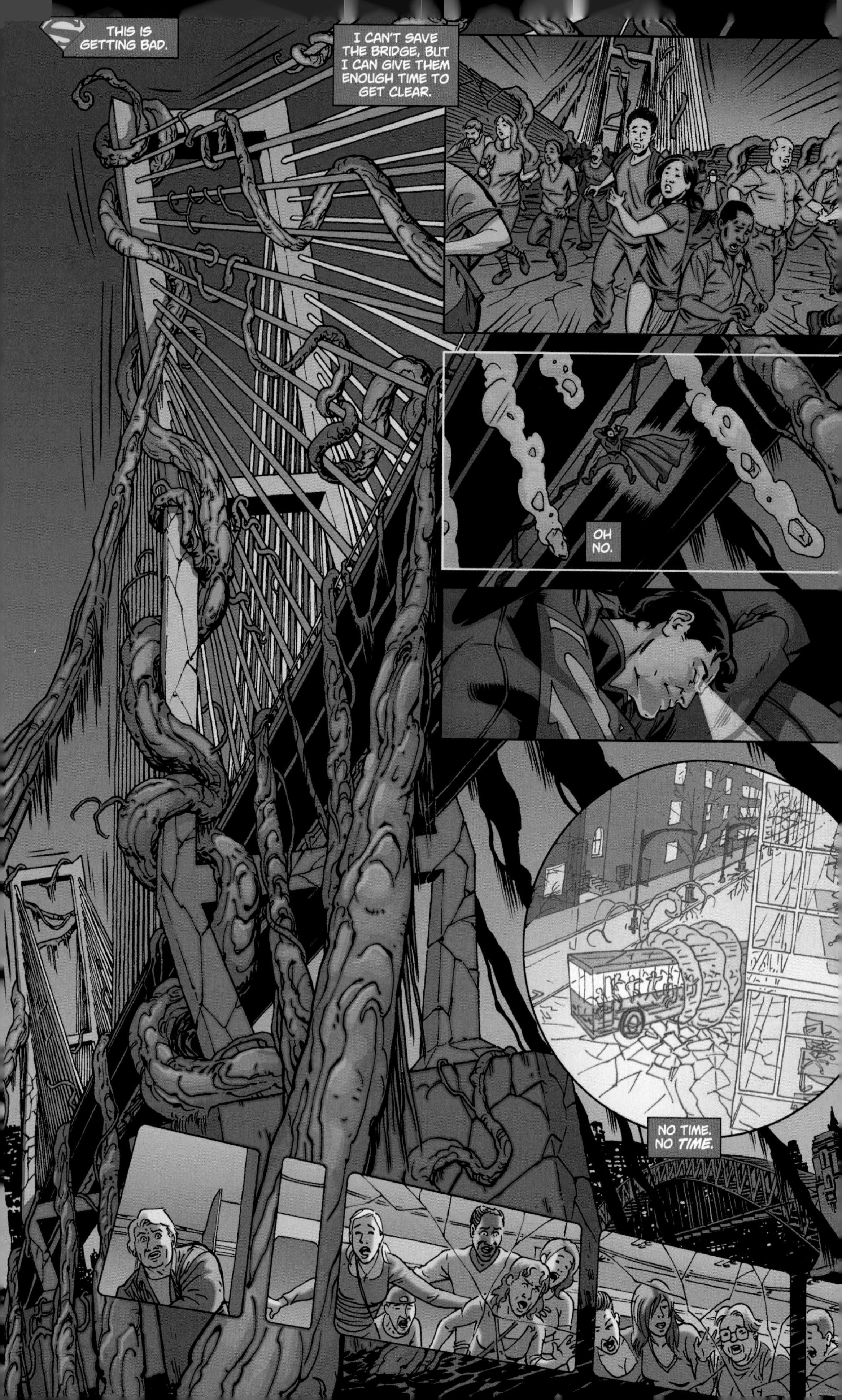
THIS IS GETTING BAD.
I CAN'T SAVE THE BRIDGE, BUT I CAN GIVE THEM ENOUGH TIME TO GET CLEAR.
OH NO.
NO TIME. NO *TIME*.

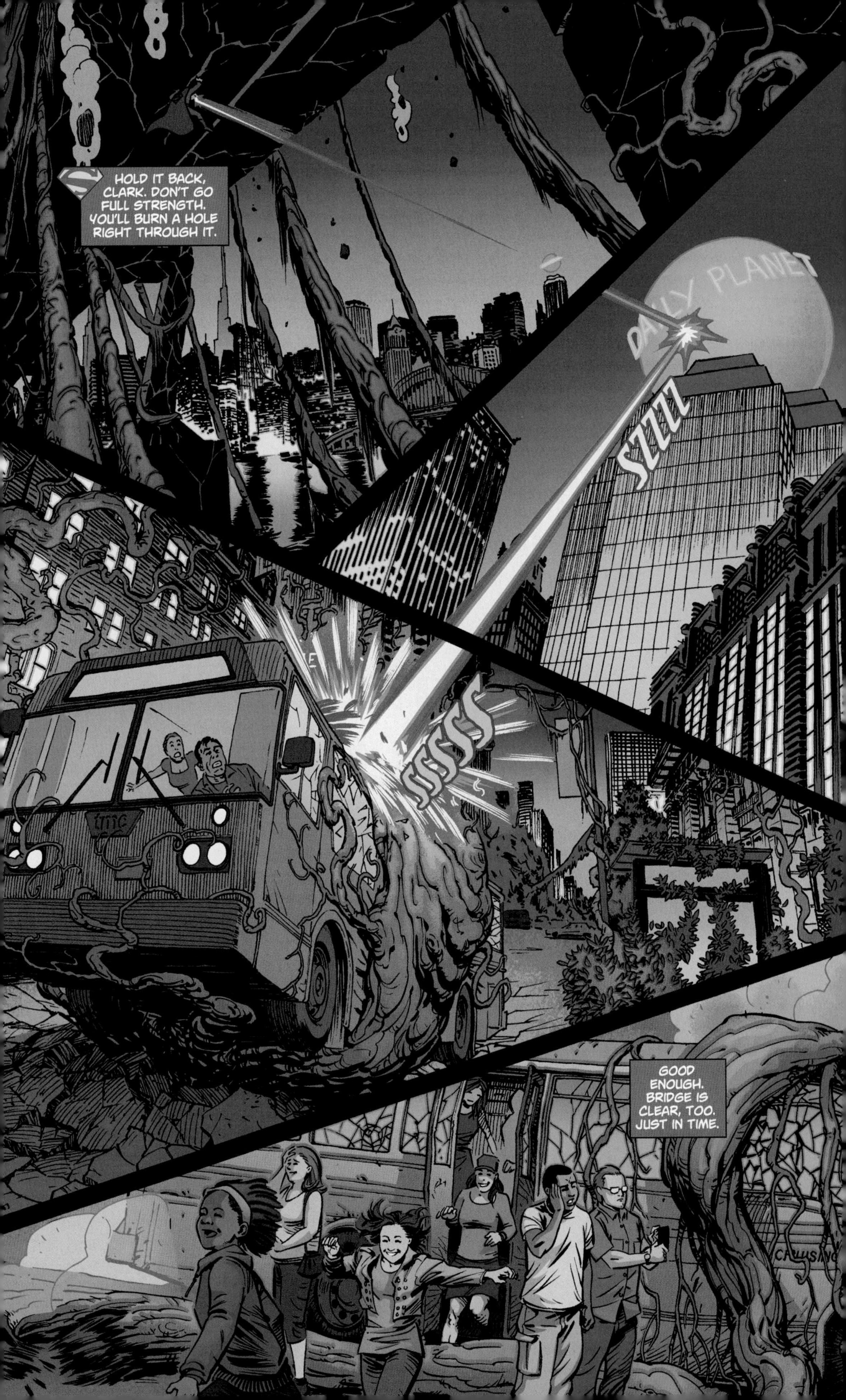
HOLD IT BACK, CLARK. DON'T GO FULL STRENGTH. YOU'LL BURN A HOLE RIGHT THROUGH IT.
DAILY PLANET
SZZZZ
SSSSS
GOOD ENOUGH. BRIDGE IS CLEAR, TOO. JUST IN TIME.

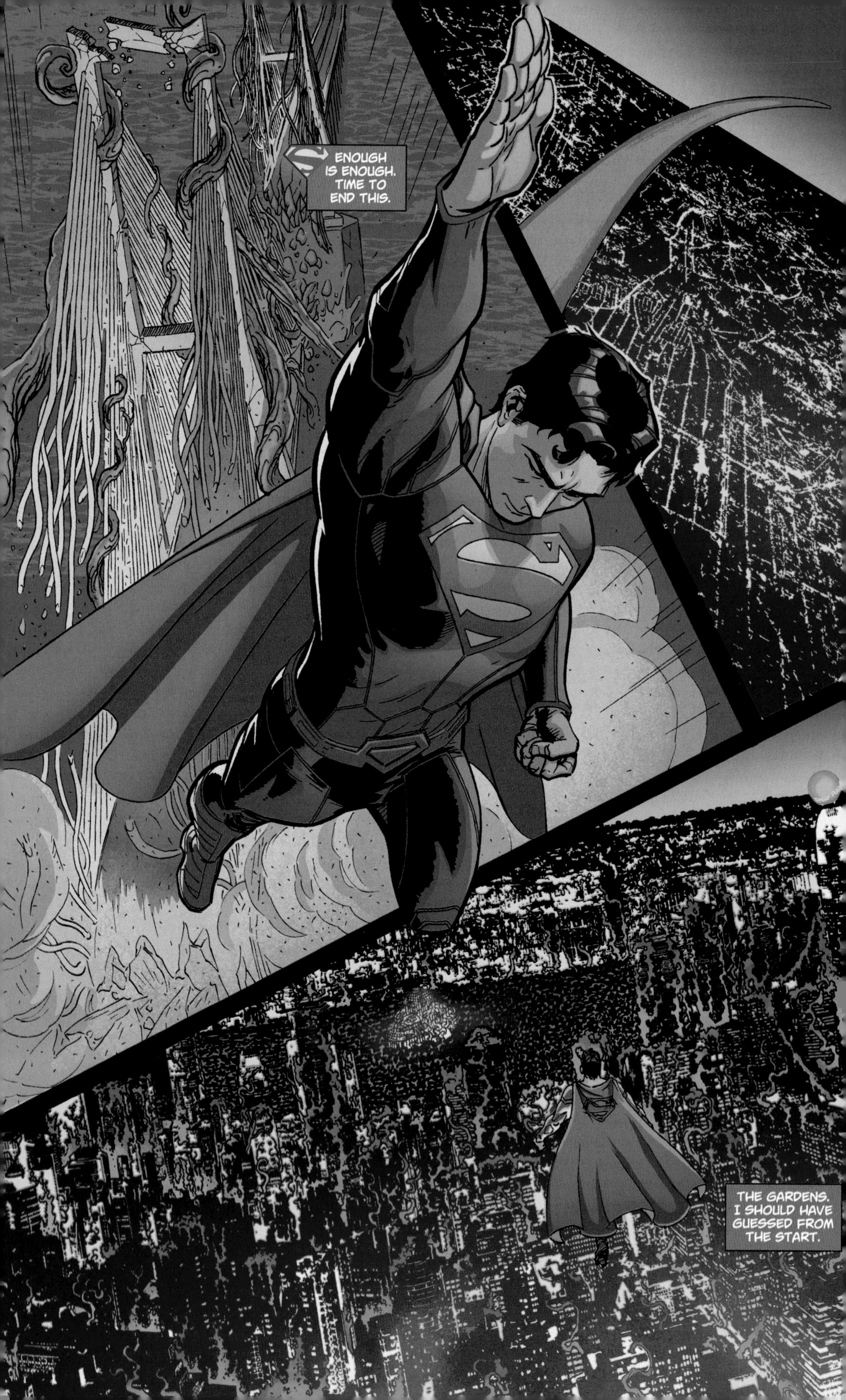
ENOUGH IS ENOUGH. TIME TO END THIS.
THE GARDENS. I SHOULD HAVE GUESSED FROM THE START.

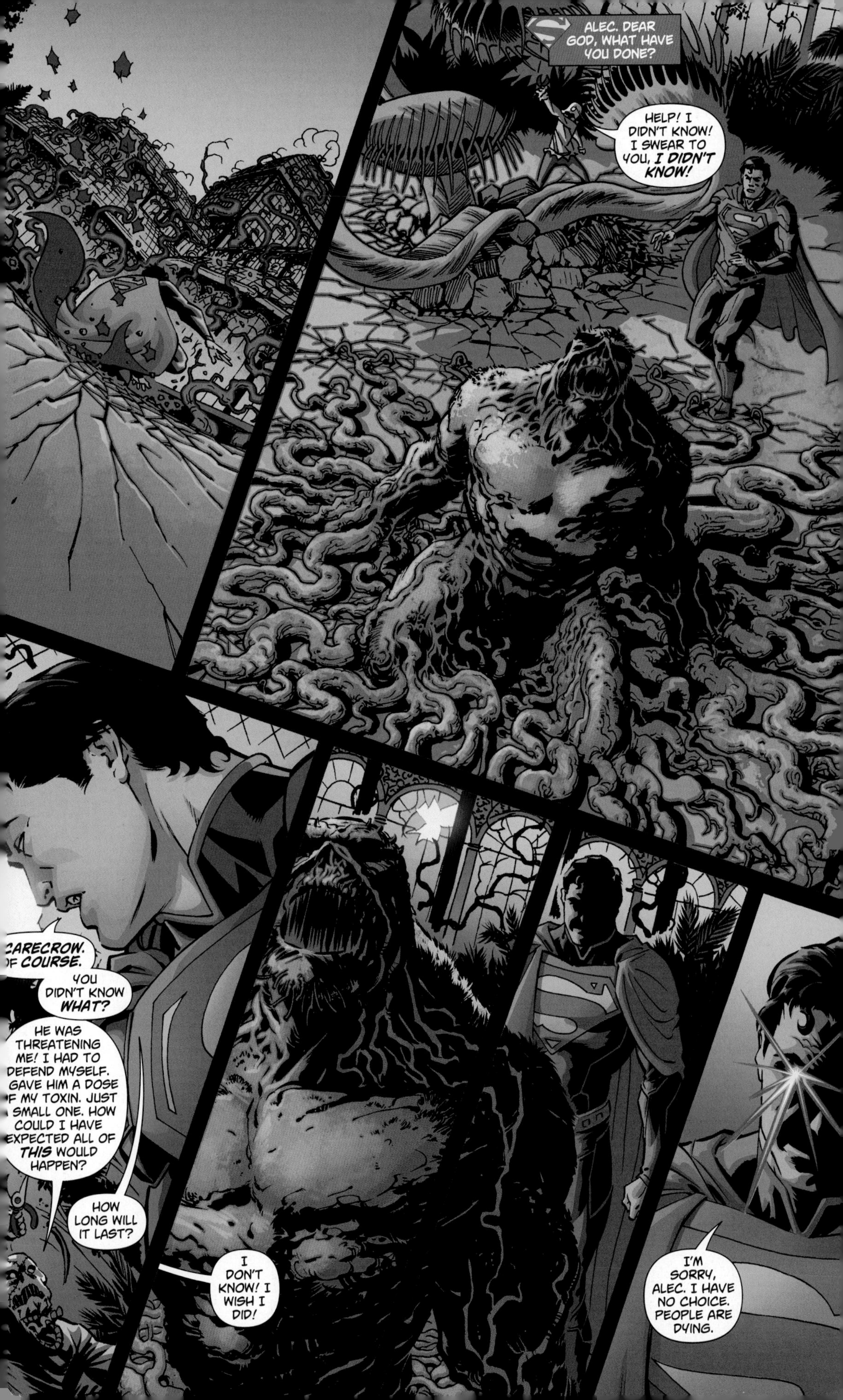
ALEC. DEAR GOD, WHAT HAVE YOU DONE?
HELP! I DIDN'T KNOW! I SWEAR TO YOU, I DIDN'T KNOW!
CARECROW. OF COURSE.
YOU DIDN'T KNOW WHAT?
HE WAS THREATENING ME! I HAD TO DEFEND MYSELF. GAVE HIM A DOSE OF MY TOXIN. JUST SMALL ONE. HOW COULD I HAVE EXPECTED ALL OF THIS WOULD HAPPEN?
HOW LONG WILL IT LAST?
I DON'T KNOW! I WISH I DID!
I'M SORRY, ALEC. I HAVE NO CHOICE. PEOPLE ARE DYING.

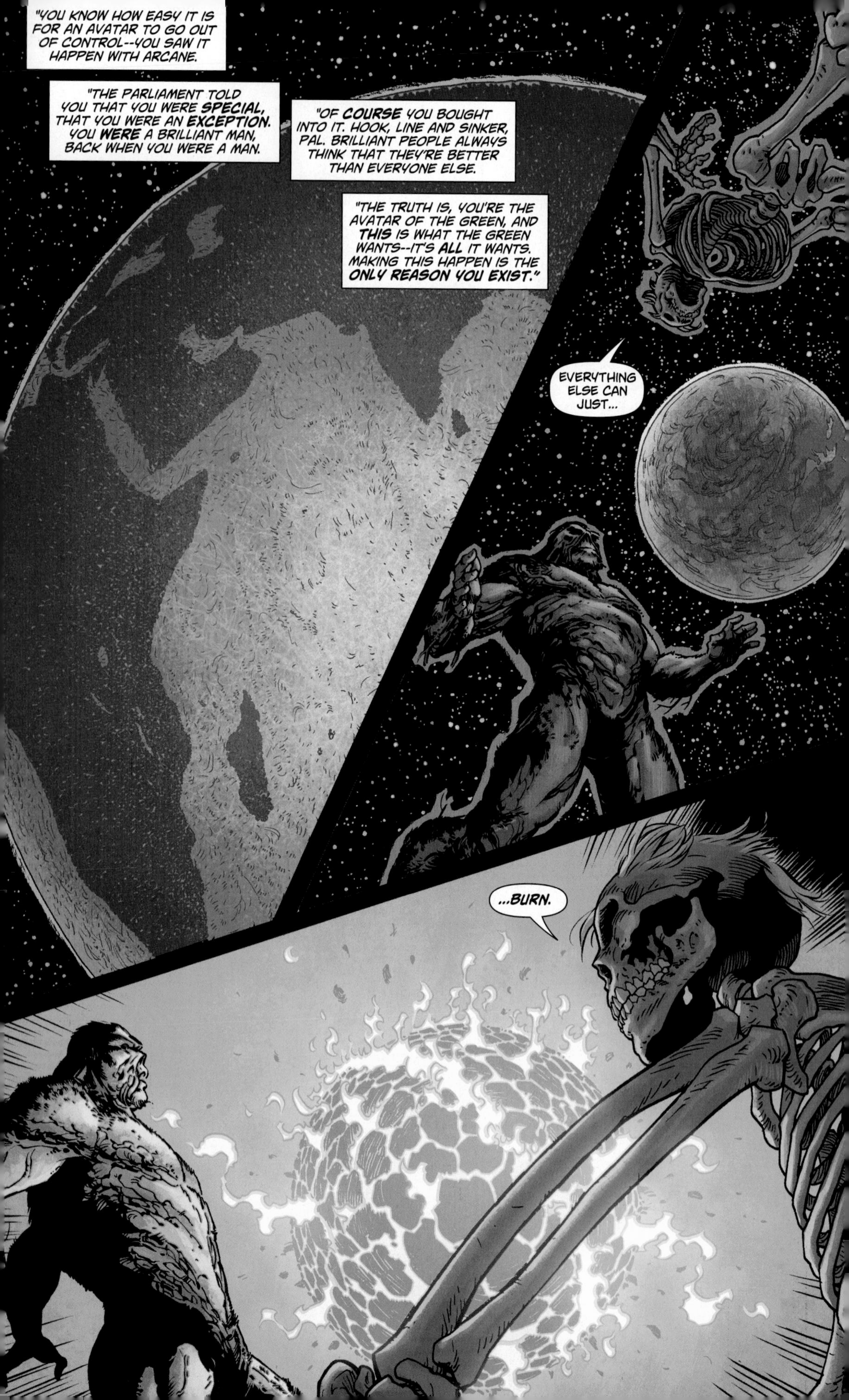
"YOU KNOW HOW EASY IT IS FOR AN AVATAR TO GO OUT OF CONTROL--YOU SAW IT HAPPEN WITH ARCANE.
"THE PARLIAMENT TOLD YOU THAT YOU WERE SPECIAL, THAT YOU WERE AN EXCEPTION. YOU WERE A BRILLIANT MAN, BACK WHEN YOU WERE A MAN.
"OF COURSE YOU BOUGHT INTO IT. HOOK, LINE AND SINKER, PAL. BRILLIANT PEOPLE ALWAYS THINK THAT THEY'RE BETTER THAN EVERYONE ELSE.
"THE TRUTH IS, YOU'RE THE AVATAR OF THE GREEN, AND THIS IS WHAT THE GREEN WANTS--IT'S ALL IT WANTS. MAKING THIS HAPPEN IS THE ONLY REASON YOU EXIST."
EVERYTHING ELSE CAN JUST...
...BURN.

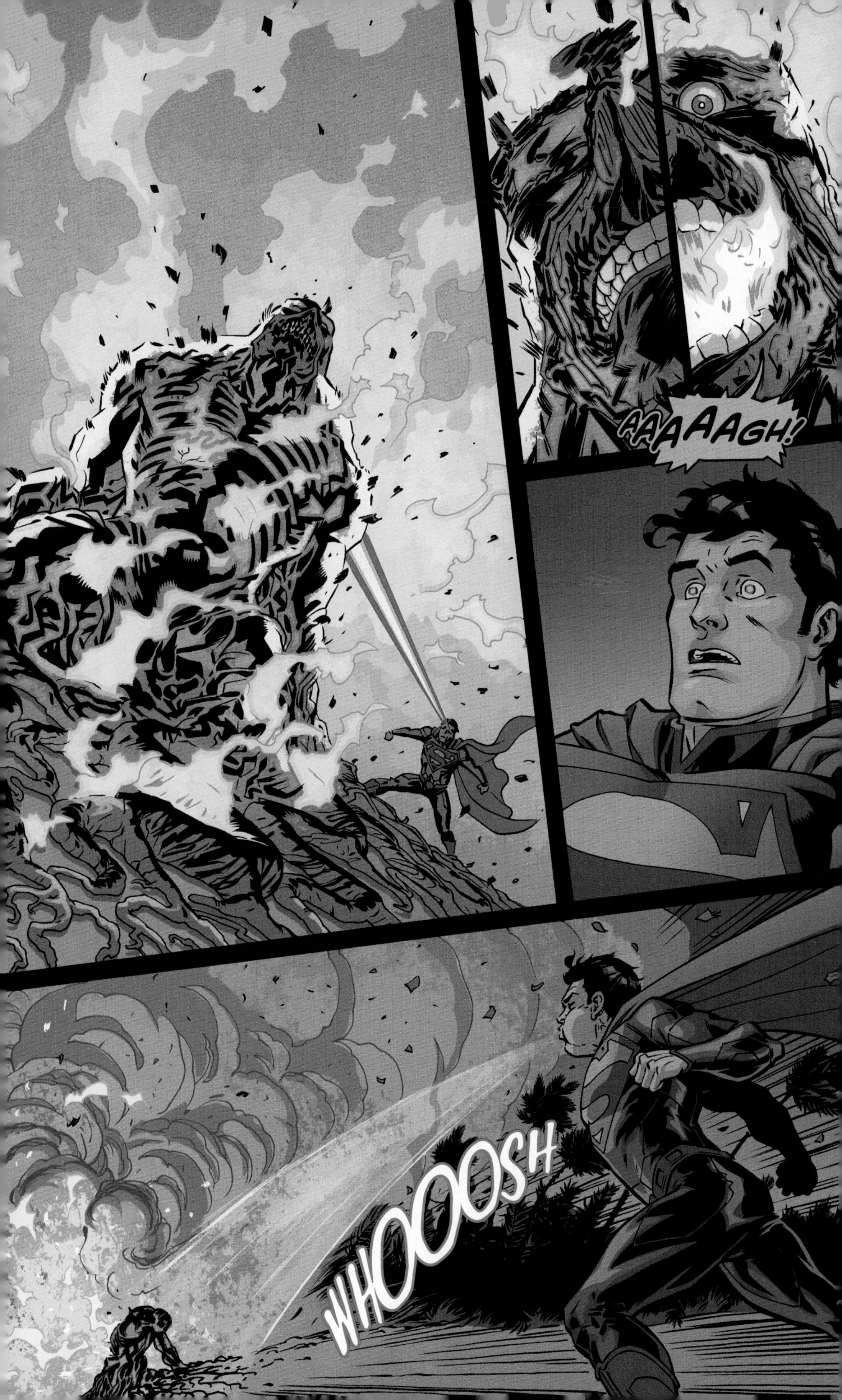
AAAAAAGH!
WHOOOOSH

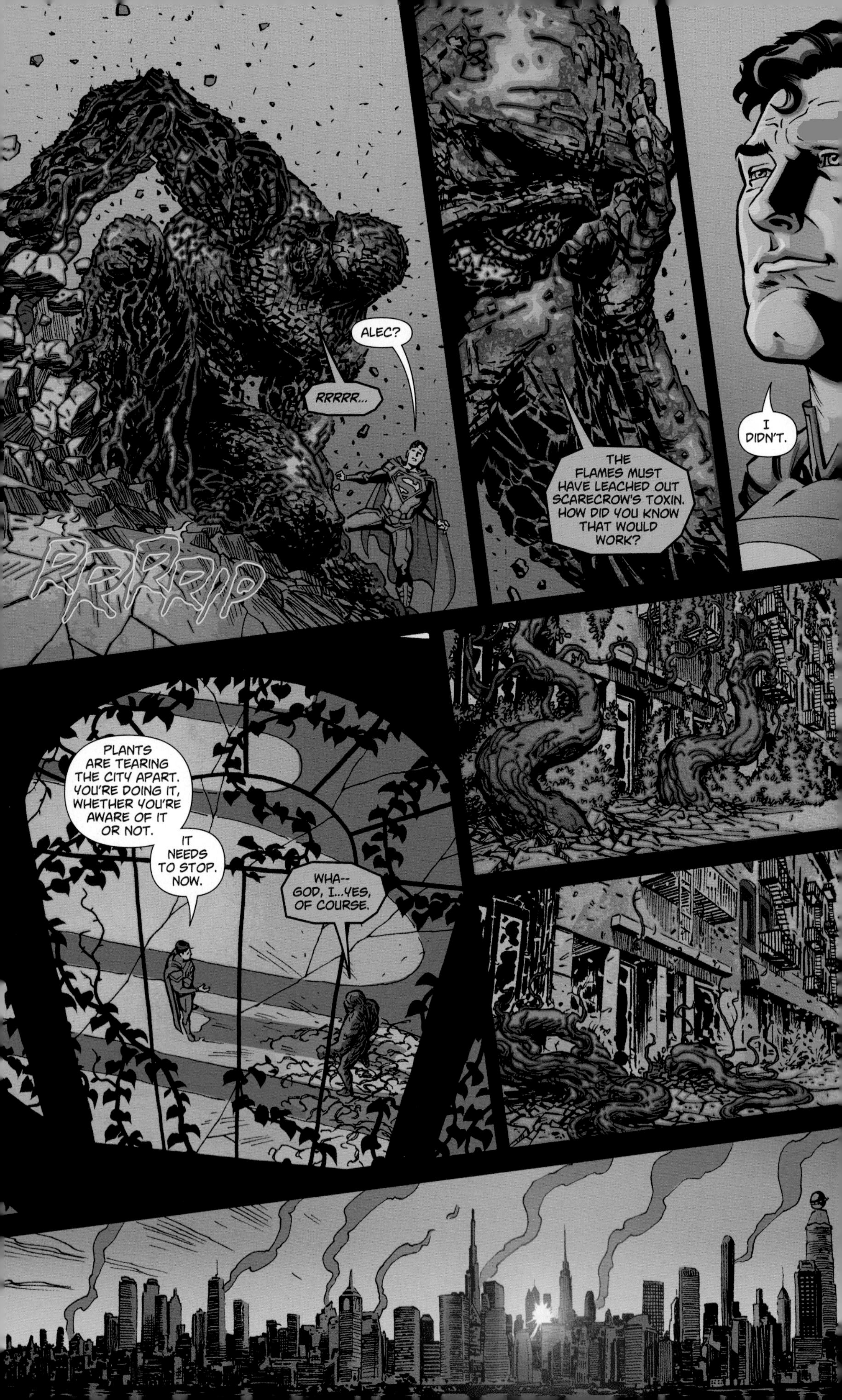
ALEC?
RRRRR...
RRRRRIP
THE FLAMES MUST HAVE LEACHED OUT SCARECROW'S TOXIN. HOW DID YOU KNOW THAT WOULD WORK?
I DIDN'T.
PLANTS ARE TEARING THE CITY APART. YOU'RE DOING IT, WHETHER YOU'RE AWARE OF IT OR NOT.
IT NEEDS TO STOP. NOW.
WHA-- GOD, I...YES, OF COURSE.

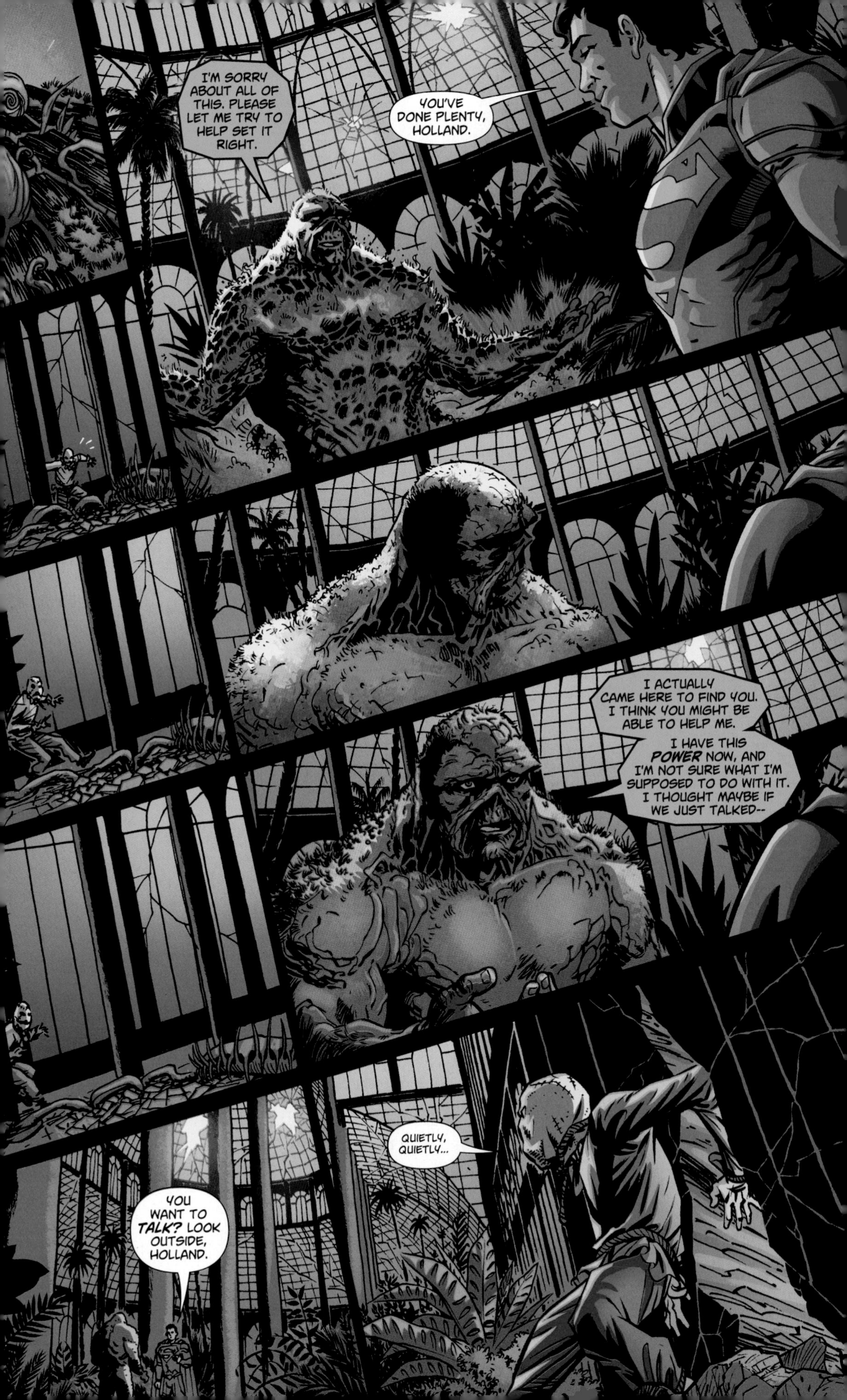
I'M SORRY ABOUT ALL OF THIS. PLEASE LET ME TRY TO HELP SET IT RIGHT.
YOU'VE DONE PLENTY, HOLLAND.
I ACTUALLY CAME HERE TO FIND YOU. I THINK YOU MIGHT BE ABLE TO HELP ME.
I HAVE THIS POWER NOW, AND I'M NOT SURE WHAT I'M SUPPOSED TO DO WITH IT. I THOUGHT MAYBE IF WE JUST TALKED--
QUIETLY, QUIETLY...
YOU WANT TO TALK? LOOK OUTSIDE, HOLLAND.

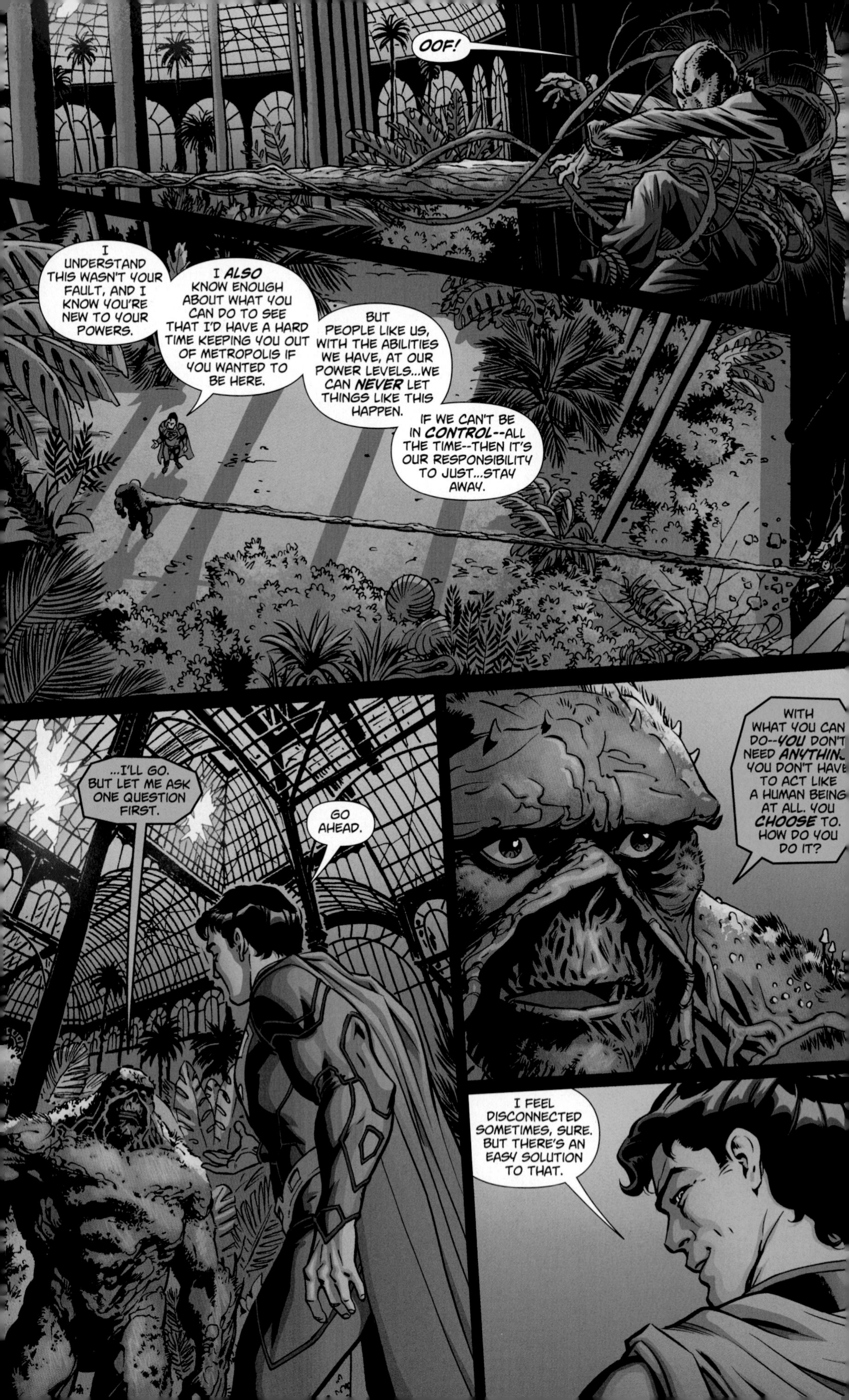
OOF!
I UNDERSTAND THIS WASN'T YOUR FAULT, AND I KNOW YOU'RE NEW TO YOUR POWERS.
I ALSO KNOW ENOUGH ABOUT WHAT YOU CAN DO TO SEE THAT I'D HAVE A HARD TIME KEEPING YOU OUT OF METROPOLIS IF YOU WANTED TO BE HERE.
BUT PEOPLE LIKE US, WITH THE ABILITIES WE HAVE, AT OUR POWER LEVELS...WE CAN NEVER LET THINGS LIKE THIS HAPPEN.
IF WE CAN'T BE IN CONTROL--ALL THE TIME--THEN IT'S OUR RESPONSIBILITY TO JUST...STAY AWAY.
...I'LL GO. BUT LET ME ASK ONE QUESTION FIRST.
GO AHEAD.
WITH WHAT YOU CAN DO--YOU DON'T NEED ANYTHING. YOU DON'T HAVE TO ACT LIKE A HUMAN BEING AT ALL. YOU CHOOSE TO. HOW DO YOU DO IT?
I FEEL DISCONNECTED SOMETIMES, SURE. BUT THERE'S AN EASY SOLUTION TO THAT.

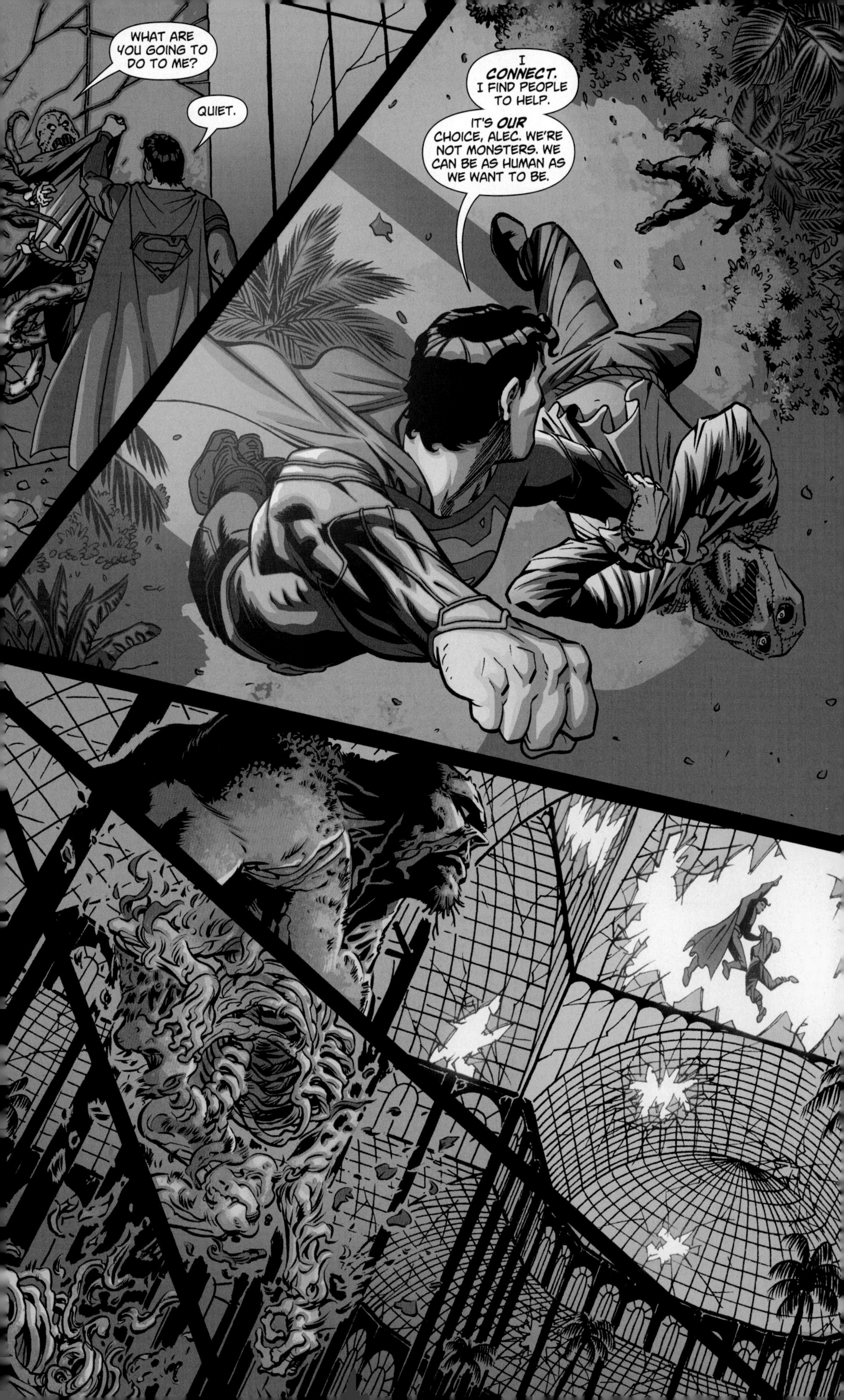
WHAT ARE YOU GOING TO DO TO ME?
QUIET.
I CONNECT. I FIND PEOPLE TO HELP.
IT'S OUR CHOICE, ALEC. WE'RE NOT MONSTERS. WE CAN BE AS HUMAN AS WE WANT TO BE.

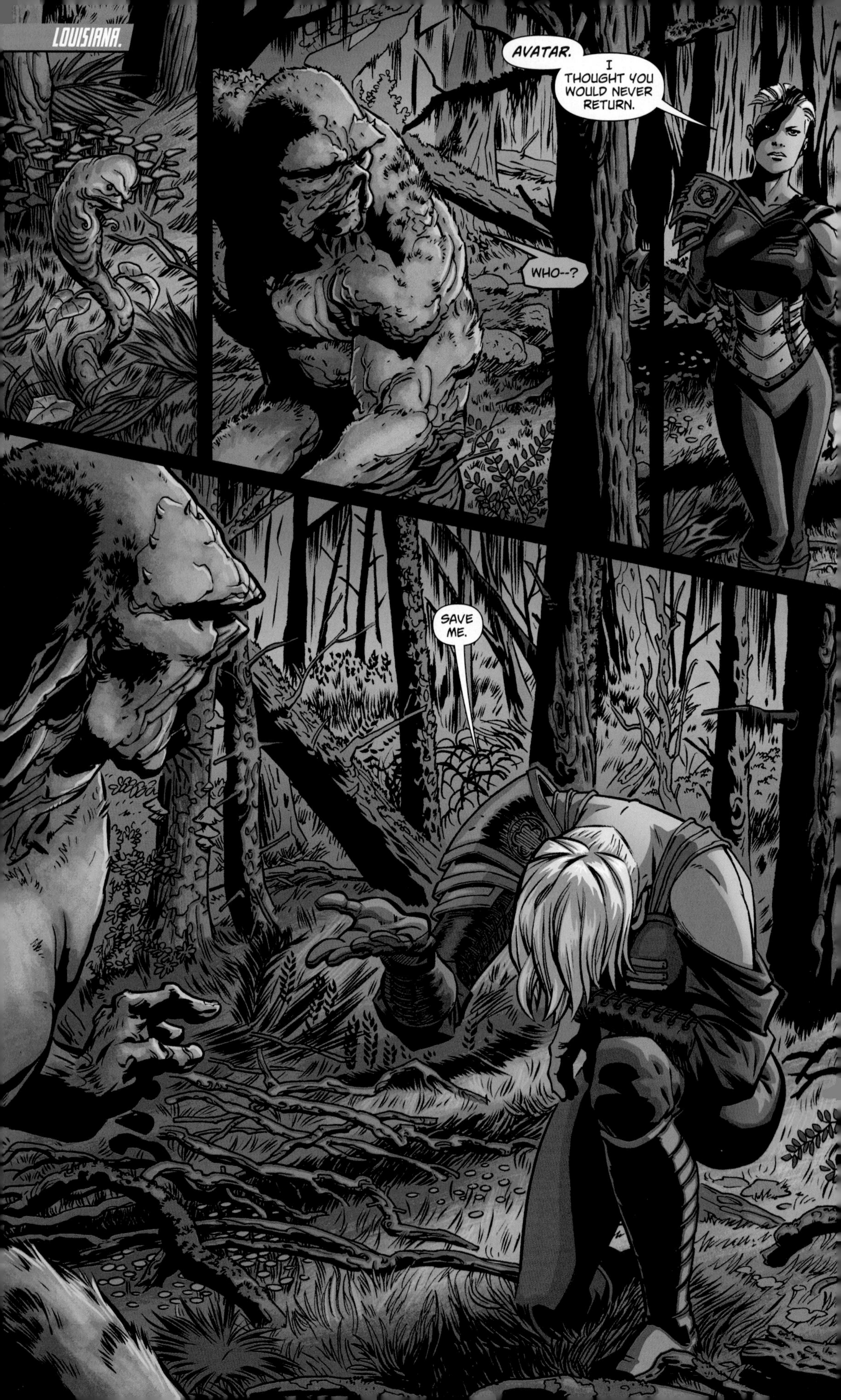
LOUISIANA.
AVATAR.
I THOUGHT YOU WOULD NEVER RETURN.
WHO--?
SAVE ME.

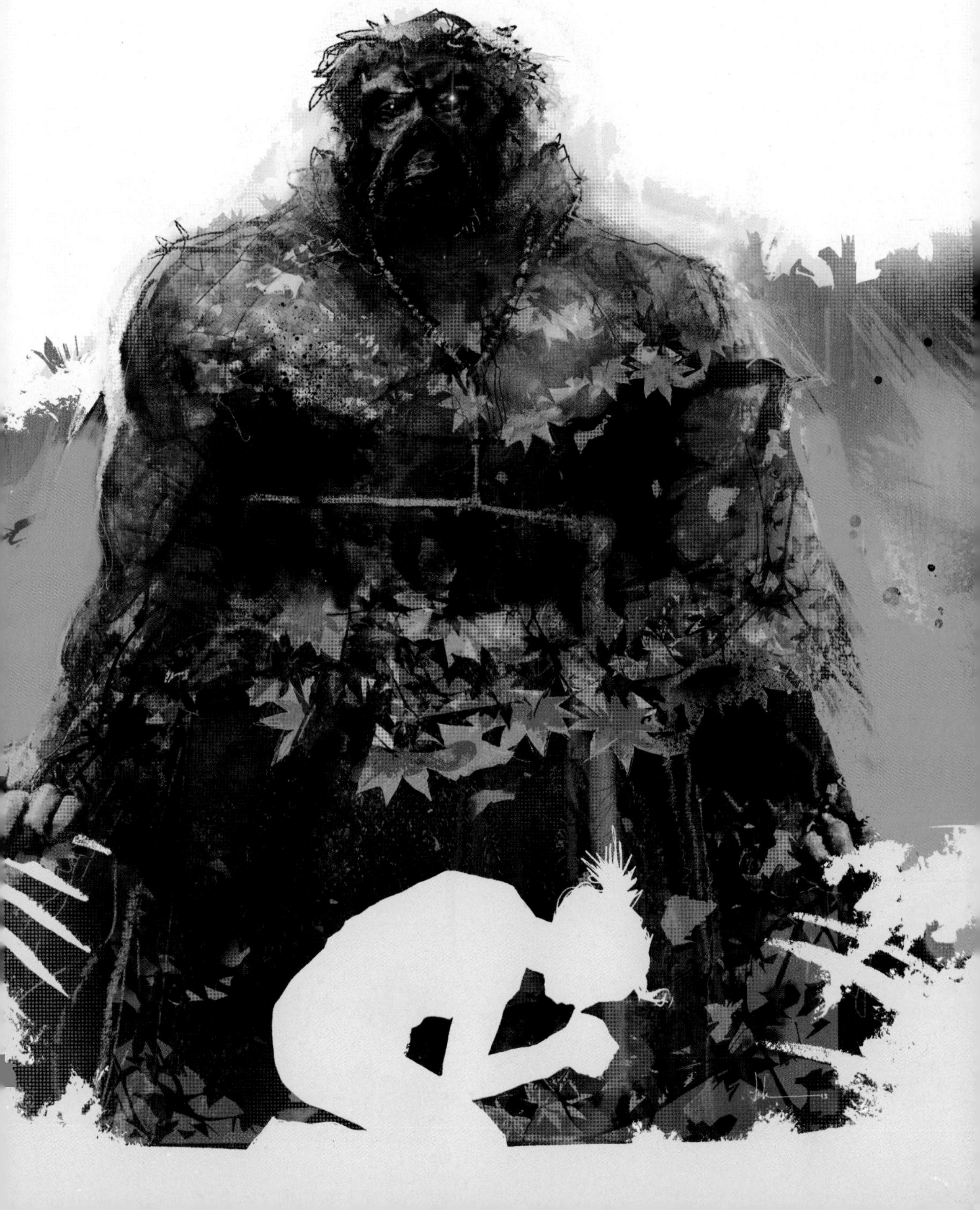

## THE MURDER POET

**CHARLES SOULE** writer **JESUS SAIZ** artist cover art by **JOCK**

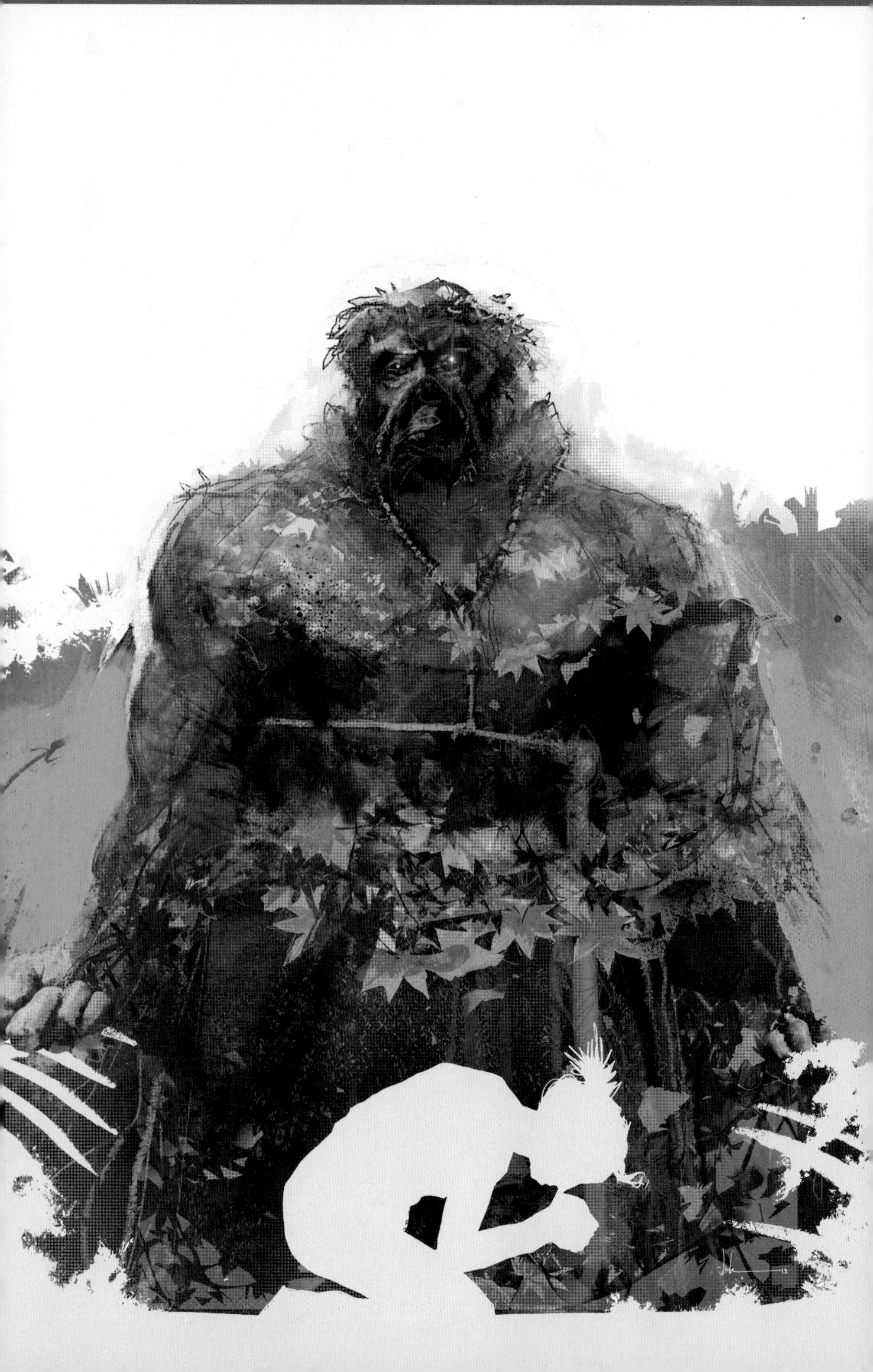

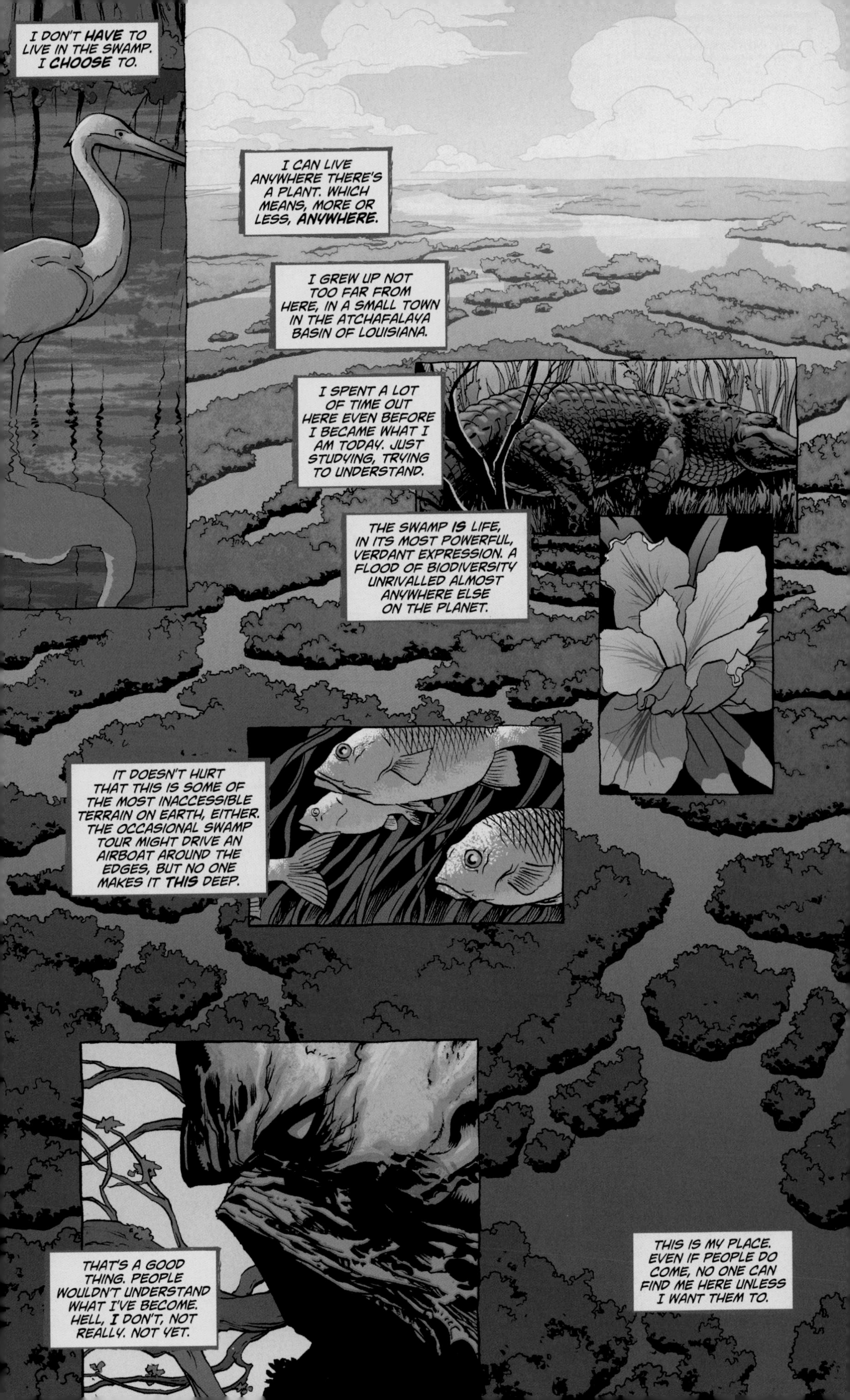
I DON'T HAVE TO LIVE IN THE SWAMP. I CHOOSE TO.
I CAN LIVE ANYWHERE THERE'S A PLANT. WHICH MEANS, MORE OR LESS, ANYWHERE.
I GREW UP NOT TOO FAR FROM HERE, IN A SMALL TOWN IN THE ATCHAFALAYA BASIN OF LOUISIANA.
I SPENT A LOT OF TIME OUT HERE EVEN BEFORE I BECAME WHAT I AM TODAY. JUST STUDYING, TRYING TO UNDERSTAND.
THE SWAMP IS LIFE, IN ITS MOST POWERFUL, VERDANT EXPRESSION. A FLOOD OF BIODIVERSITY UNRIVALLED ALMOST ANYWHERE ELSE ON THE PLANET.
IT DOESN'T HURT THAT THIS IS SOME OF THE MOST INACCESSIBLE TERRAIN ON EARTH, EITHER. THE OCCASIONAL SWAMP TOUR MIGHT DRIVE AN AIRBOAT AROUND THE EDGES, BUT NO ONE MAKES IT THIS DEEP.
THAT'S A GOOD THING. PEOPLE WOULDN'T UNDERSTAND WHAT I'VE BECOME. HELL, I DON'T, NOT REALLY. NOT YET.
THIS IS MY PLACE. EVEN IF PEOPLE DO COME, NO ONE CAN FIND ME HERE UNLESS I WANT THEM TO.

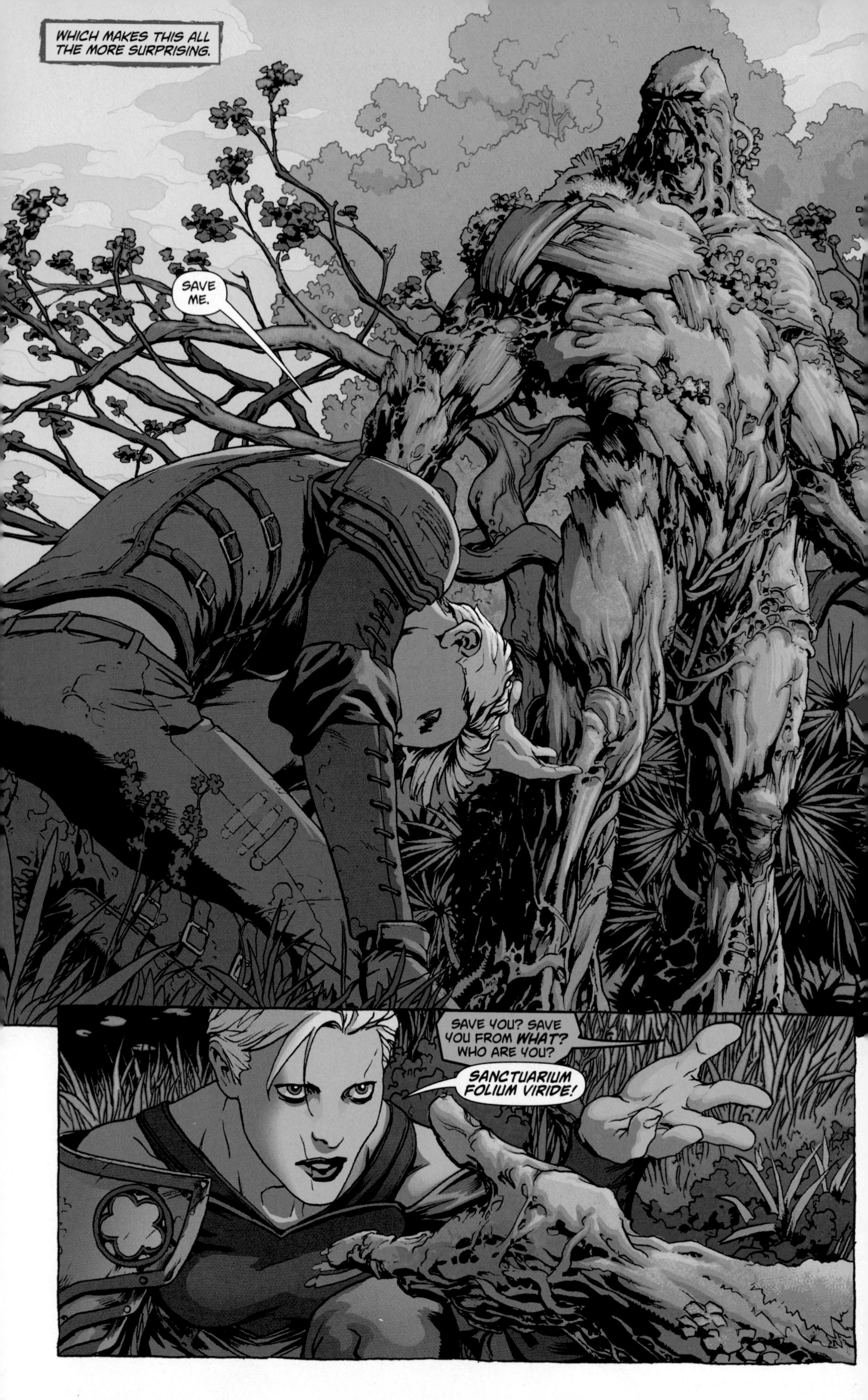
WHICH MAKES THIS ALL THE MORE SURPRISING.
SAVE ME.
SAVE YOU? SAVE YOU FROM WHAT? WHO ARE YOU?
SANCTUARIUM FOLIUM VIRIDE!

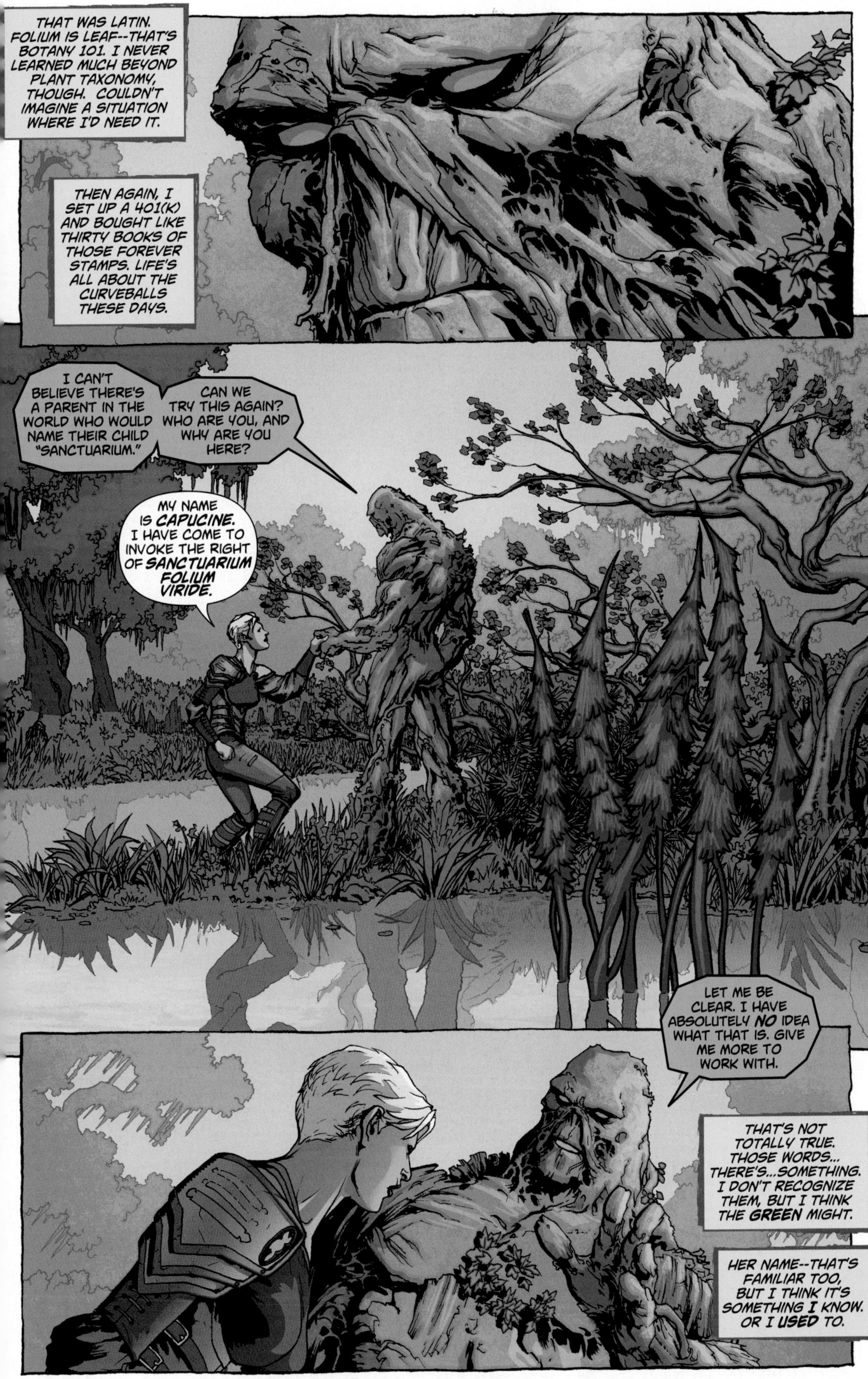
THAT WAS LATIN. FOLIUM IS LEAF--THAT'S BOTANY 101. I NEVER LEARNED MUCH BEYOND PLANT TAXONOMY, THOUGH. COULDN'T IMAGINE A SITUATION WHERE I'D NEED IT.
THEN AGAIN, I SET UP A 401(K) AND BOUGHT LIKE THIRTY BOOKS OF THOSE FOREVER STAMPS. LIFE'S ALL ABOUT THE CURVEBALLS THESE DAYS.
I CAN'T BELIEVE THERE'S A PARENT IN THE WORLD WHO WOULD NAME THEIR CHILD "SANCTUARIUM."
CAN WE TRY THIS AGAIN? WHO ARE YOU, AND WHY ARE YOU HERE?
MY NAME IS CAPUCINE. I HAVE COME TO INVOKE THE RIGHT OF SANCTUARIUM FOLIUM VIRIDE.
LET ME BE CLEAR. I HAVE ABSOLUTELY NO IDEA WHAT THAT IS. GIVE ME MORE TO WORK WITH.
THAT'S NOT TOTALLY TRUE. THOSE WORDS... THERE'S...SOMETHING. I DON'T RECOGNIZE THEM, BUT I THINK THE GREEN MIGHT.
HER NAME--THAT'S FAMILIAR TOO, BUT I THINK IT'S SOMETHING I KNOW. OR I USED TO.

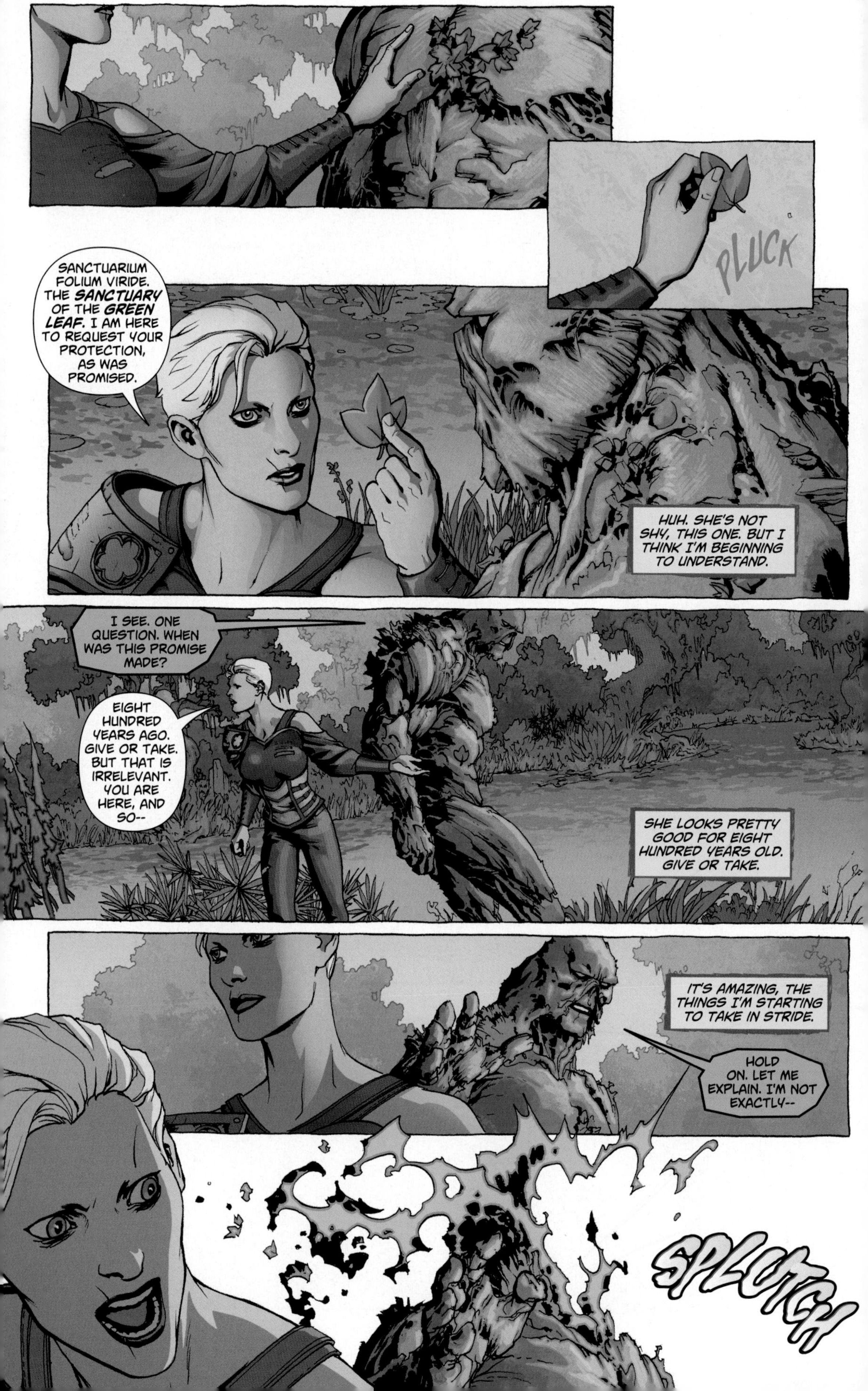
PLUCK
SANCTUARIUM FOLIUM VIRIDE. THE SANCTUARY OF THE GREEN LEAF. I AM HERE TO REQUEST YOUR PROTECTION, AS WAS PROMISED.
HUH. SHE'S NOT SHY, THIS ONE. BUT I THINK I'M BEGINNING TO UNDERSTAND.
I SEE. ONE QUESTION. WHEN WAS THIS PROMISE MADE?
EIGHT HUNDRED YEARS AGO. GIVE OR TAKE. BUT THAT IS IRRELEVANT. YOU ARE HERE, AND SO--
SHE LOOKS PRETTY GOOD FOR EIGHT HUNDRED YEARS OLD. GIVE OR TAKE.
IT'S AMAZING, THE THINGS I'M STARTING TO TAKE IN STRIDE.
HOLD ON. LET ME EXPLAIN. I'M NOT EXACTLY--
SPLOTCH

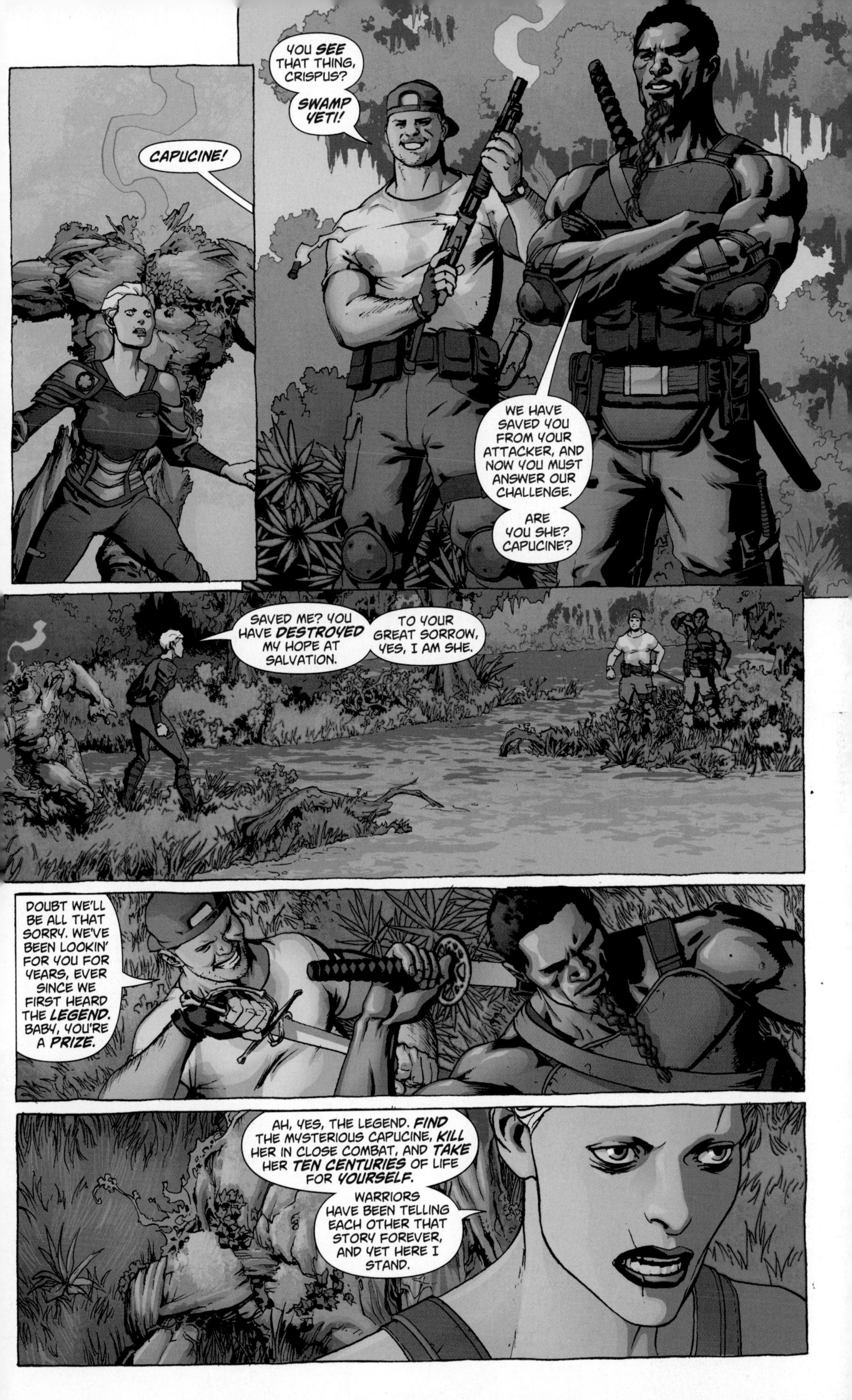
CAPUCINE!
YOU SEE THAT THING, CRISPUS?
SWAMP YETI!
WE HAVE SAVED YOU FROM YOUR ATTACKER, AND NOW YOU MUST ANSWER OUR CHALLENGE.
ARE YOU SHE? CAPUCINE?
SAVED ME? YOU HAVE DESTROYED MY HOPE AT SALVATION.
TO YOUR GREAT SORROW, YES, I AM SHE.
DOUBT WE'LL BE ALL THAT SORRY. WE'VE BEEN LOOKIN' FOR YOU FOR YEARS, EVER SINCE WE FIRST HEARD THE LEGEND. BABY, YOU'RE A PRIZE.
AH, YES, THE LEGEND. FIND THE MYSTERIOUS CAPUCINE, KILL HER IN CLOSE COMBAT, AND TAKE HER TEN CENTURIES OF LIFE FOR YOURSELF.
WARRIORS HAVE BEEN TELLING EACH OTHER THAT STORY FOREVER, AND YET HERE I STAND.

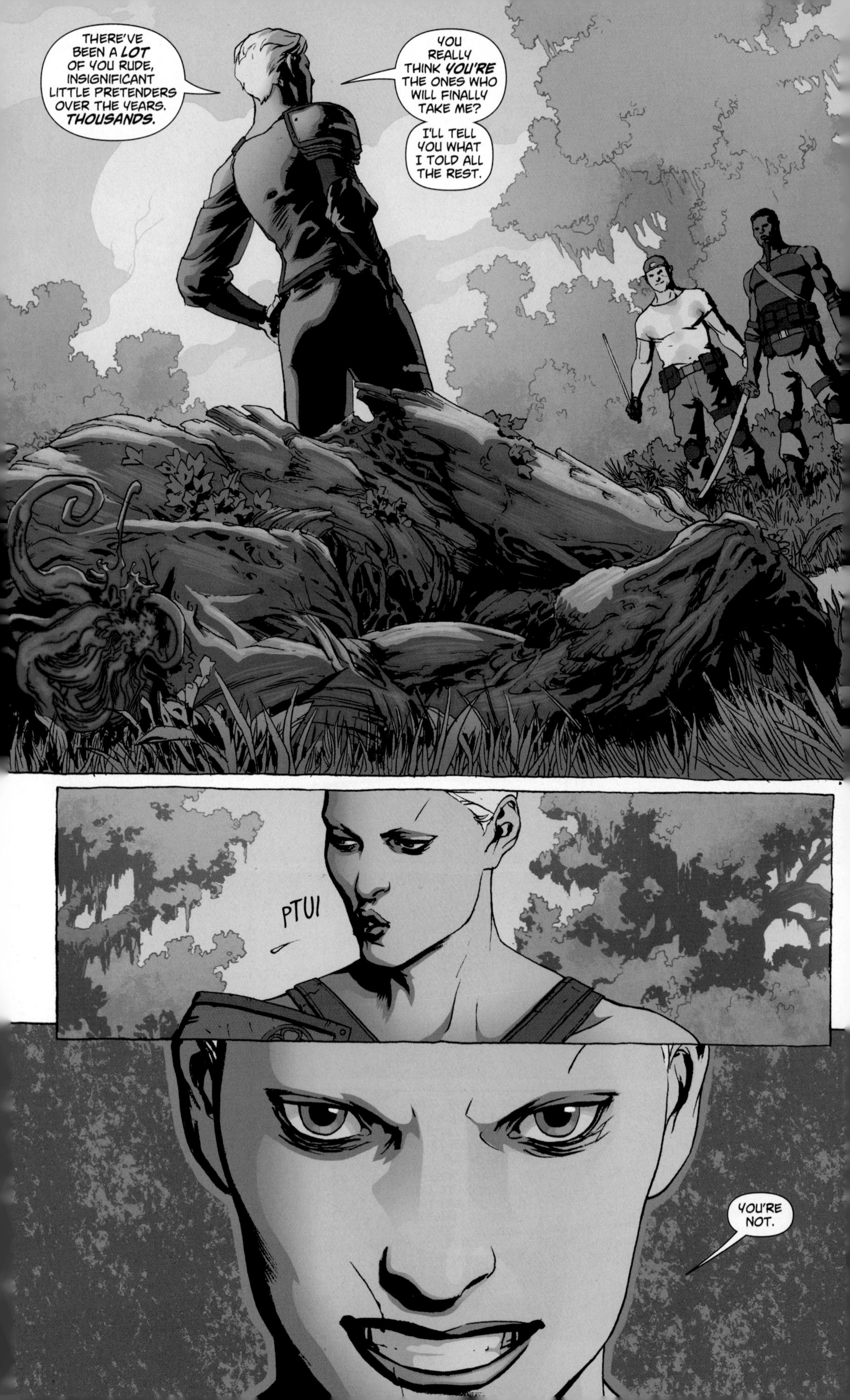
THERE'VE BEEN A LOT OF YOU RUDE, INSIGNIFICANT LITTLE PRETENDERS OVER THE YEARS. THOUSANDS.
YOU REALLY THINK YOU'RE THE ONES WHO WILL FINALLY TAKE ME?
I'LL TELL YOU WHAT I TOLD ALL THE REST.
PTUI
YOU'RE NOT.

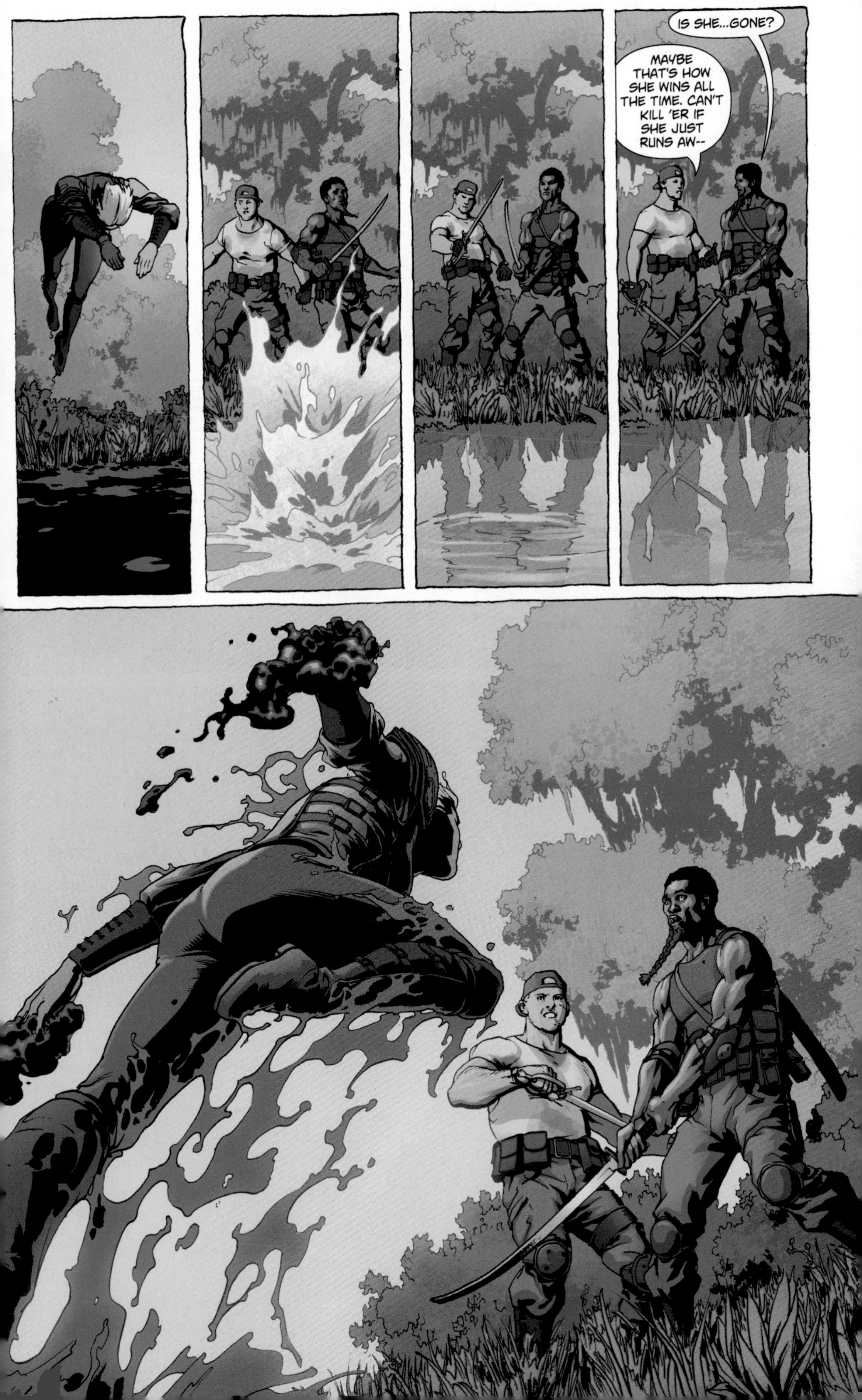
IS SHE...GONE?
MAYBE THAT'S HOW SHE WINS ALL THE TIME. CAN'T KILL 'ER IF SHE JUST RUNS AW--

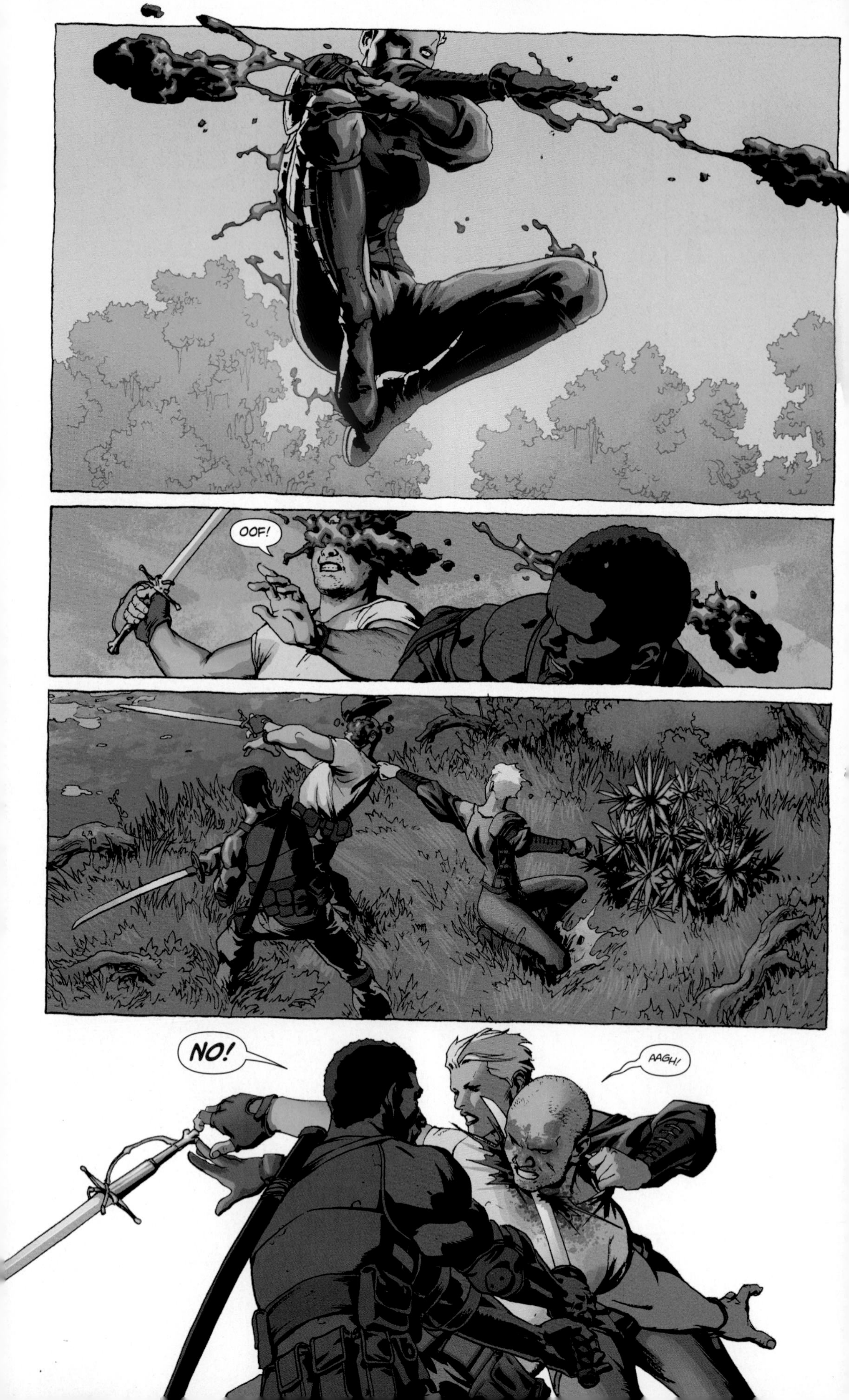
OOF!
NO!
AAGH!

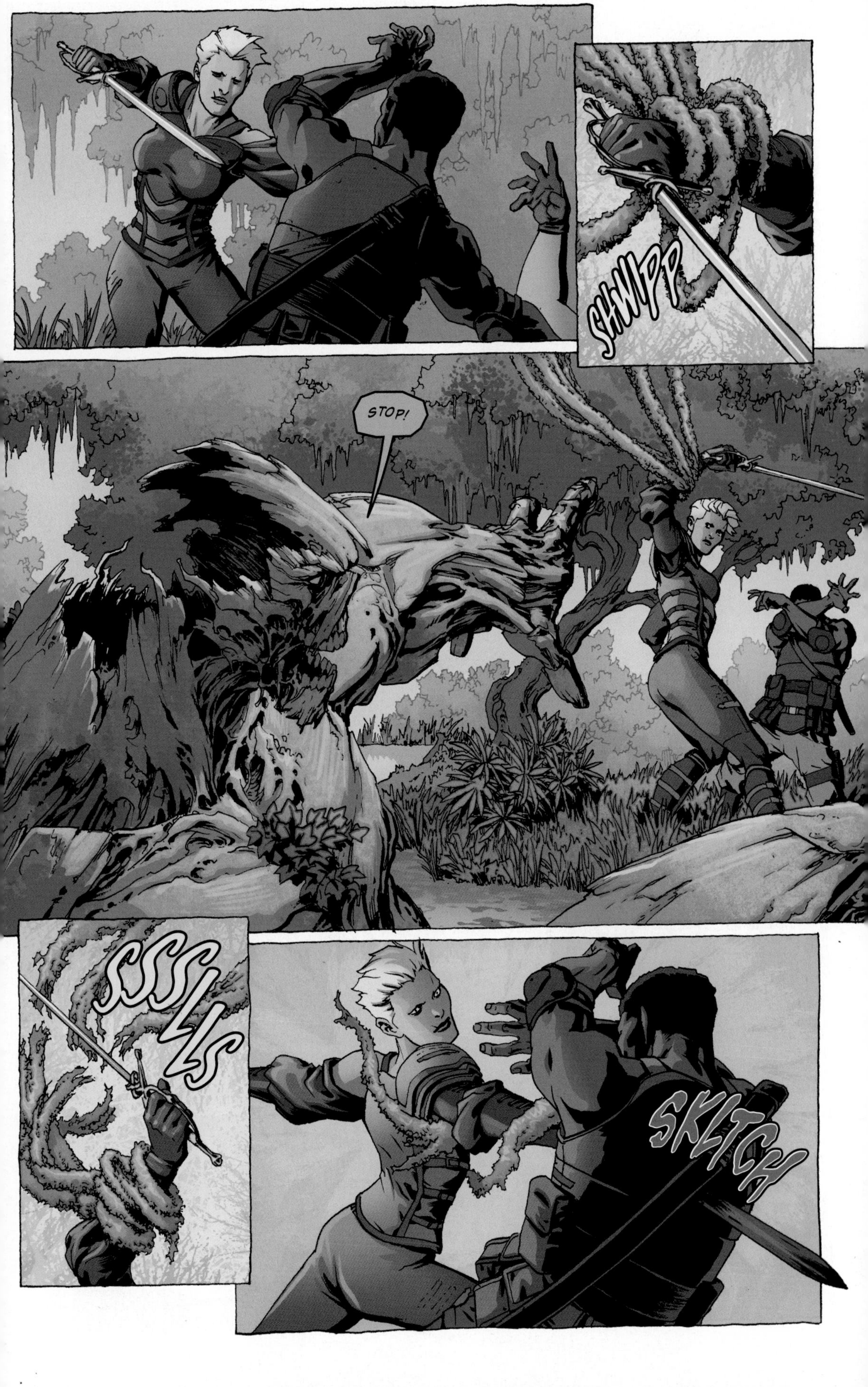
SHWIPP
STOP!
SSSLSS
SKLTCH

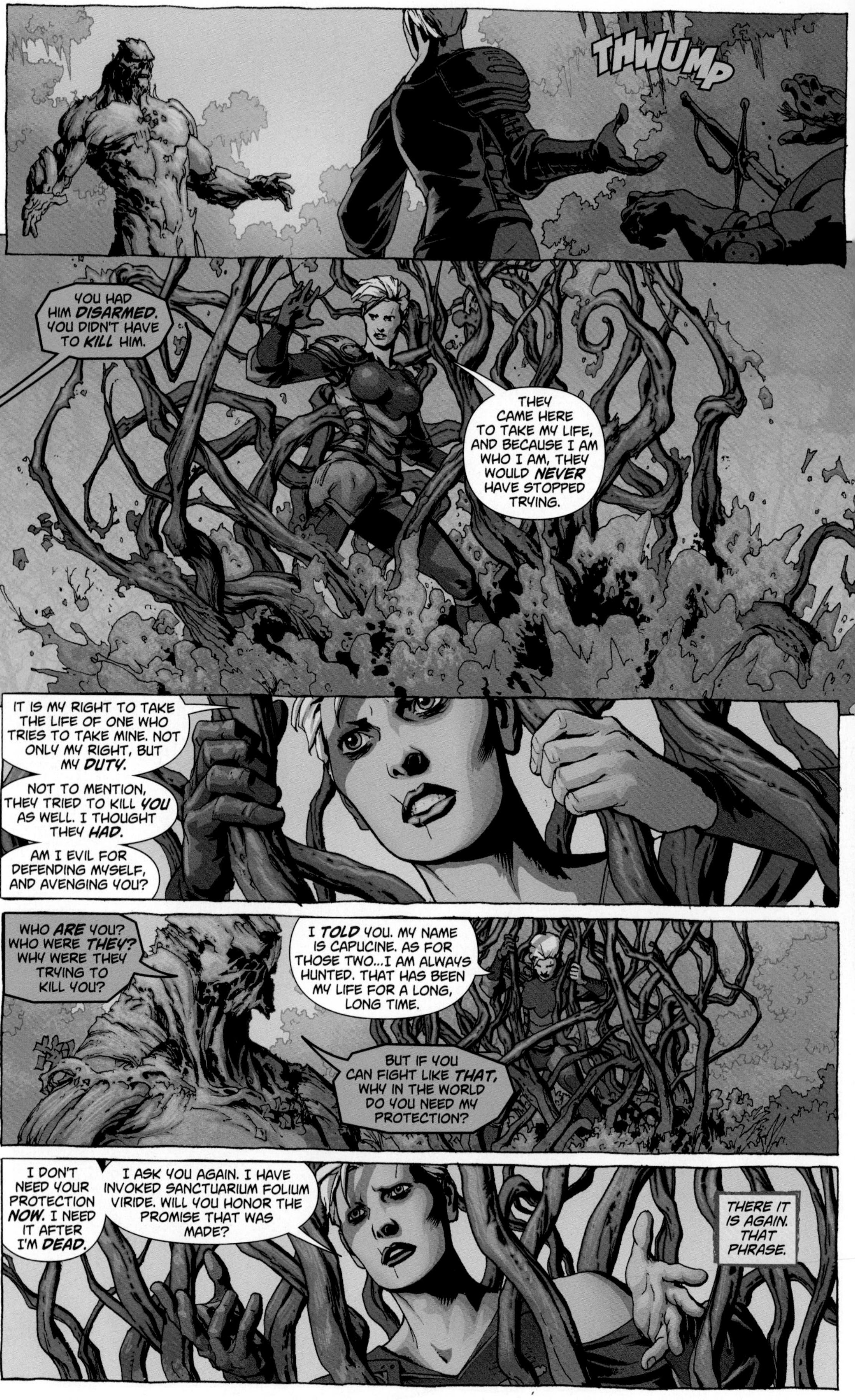
THWUMP
YOU HAD HIM DISARMED. YOU DIDN'T HAVE TO KILL HIM.
THEY CAME HERE TO TAKE MY LIFE, AND BECAUSE I AM WHO I AM, THEY WOULD NEVER HAVE STOPPED TRYING.
IT IS MY RIGHT TO TAKE THE LIFE OF ONE WHO TRIES TO TAKE MINE. NOT ONLY MY RIGHT, BUT MY DUTY.
NOT TO MENTION, THEY TRIED TO KILL YOU AS WELL. I THOUGHT THEY HAD.
AM I EVIL FOR DEFENDING MYSELF, AND AVENGING YOU?
WHO ARE YOU? WHO WERE THEY? WHY WERE THEY TRYING TO KILL YOU?
I TOLD YOU. MY NAME IS CAPUCINE. AS FOR THOSE TWO...I AM ALWAYS HUNTED. THAT HAS BEEN MY LIFE FOR A LONG, LONG TIME.
BUT IF YOU CAN FIGHT LIKE THAT, WHY IN THE WORLD DO YOU NEED MY PROTECTION?
I DON'T NEED YOUR PROTECTION NOW. I NEED IT AFTER I'M DEAD.
I ASK YOU AGAIN. I HAVE INVOKED SANCTUARIUM FOLIUM VIRIDE. WILL YOU HONOR THE PROMISE THAT WAS MADE?
THERE IT IS AGAIN. THAT PHRASE.

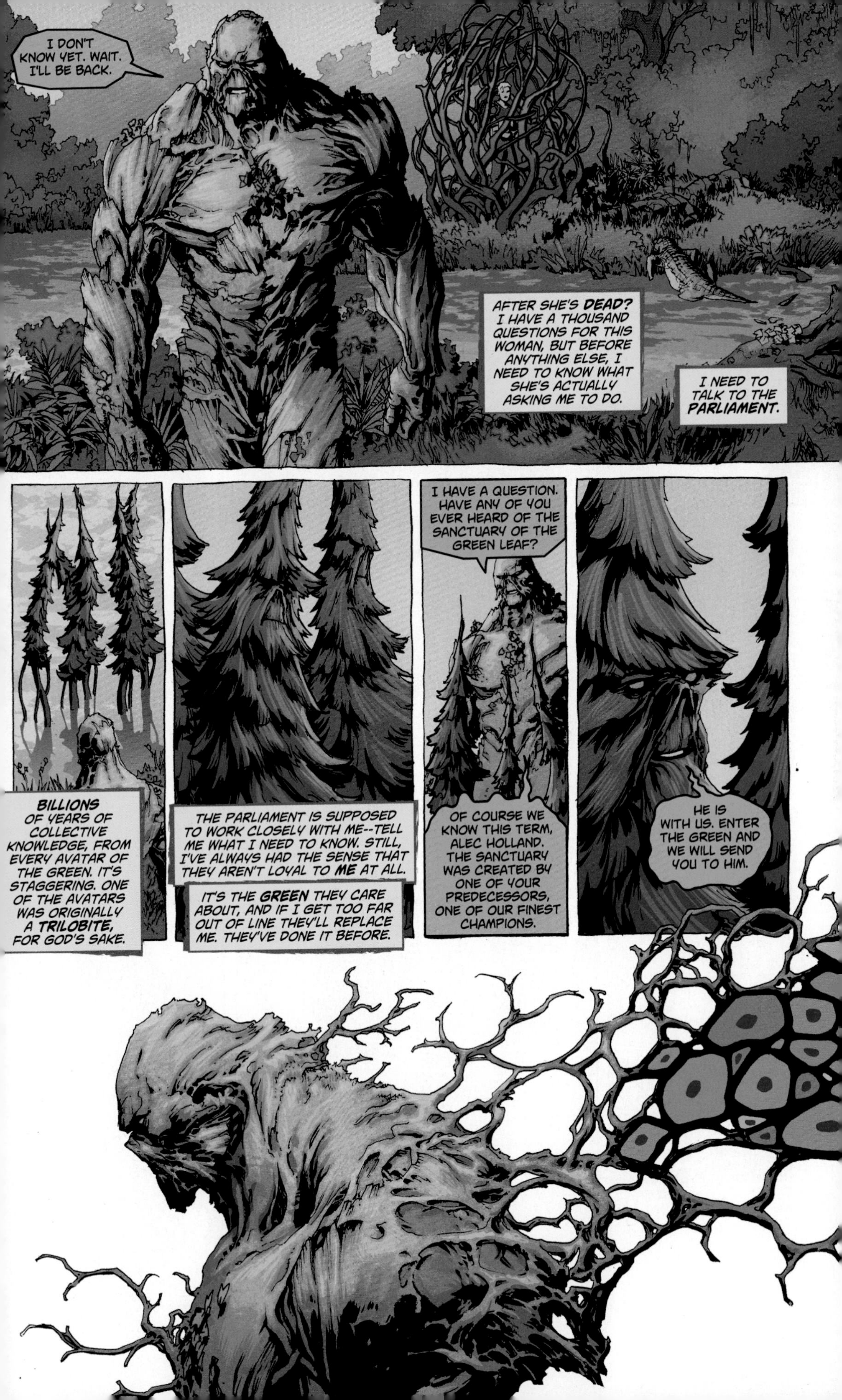
I DON'T KNOW YET. WAIT. I'LL BE BACK.
AFTER SHE'S DEAD? I HAVE A THOUSAND QUESTIONS FOR THIS WOMAN, BUT BEFORE ANYTHING ELSE, I NEED TO KNOW WHAT SHE'S ACTUALLY ASKING ME TO DO.
I NEED TO TALK TO THE PARLIAMENT.
BILLIONS OF YEARS OF COLLECTIVE KNOWLEDGE, FROM EVERY AVATAR OF THE GREEN. IT'S STAGGERING. ONE OF THE AVATARS WAS ORIGINALLY A TRILOBITE, FOR GOD'S SAKE.
THE PARLIAMENT IS SUPPOSED TO WORK CLOSELY WITH ME--TELL ME WHAT I NEED TO KNOW. STILL, I'VE ALWAYS HAD THE SENSE THAT THEY AREN'T LOYAL TO ME AT ALL.
IT'S THE GREEN THEY CARE ABOUT, AND IF I GET TOO FAR OUT OF LINE THEY'LL REPLACE ME. THEY'VE DONE IT BEFORE.
I HAVE A QUESTION. HAVE ANY OF YOU EVER HEARD OF THE SANCTUARY OF THE GREEN LEAF?
OF COURSE WE KNOW THIS TERM, ALEC HOLLAND. THE SANCTUARY WAS CREATED BY ONE OF YOUR PREDECESSORS, ONE OF OUR FINEST CHAMPIONS.
HE IS WITH US. ENTER THE GREEN AND WE WILL SEND YOU TO HIM.

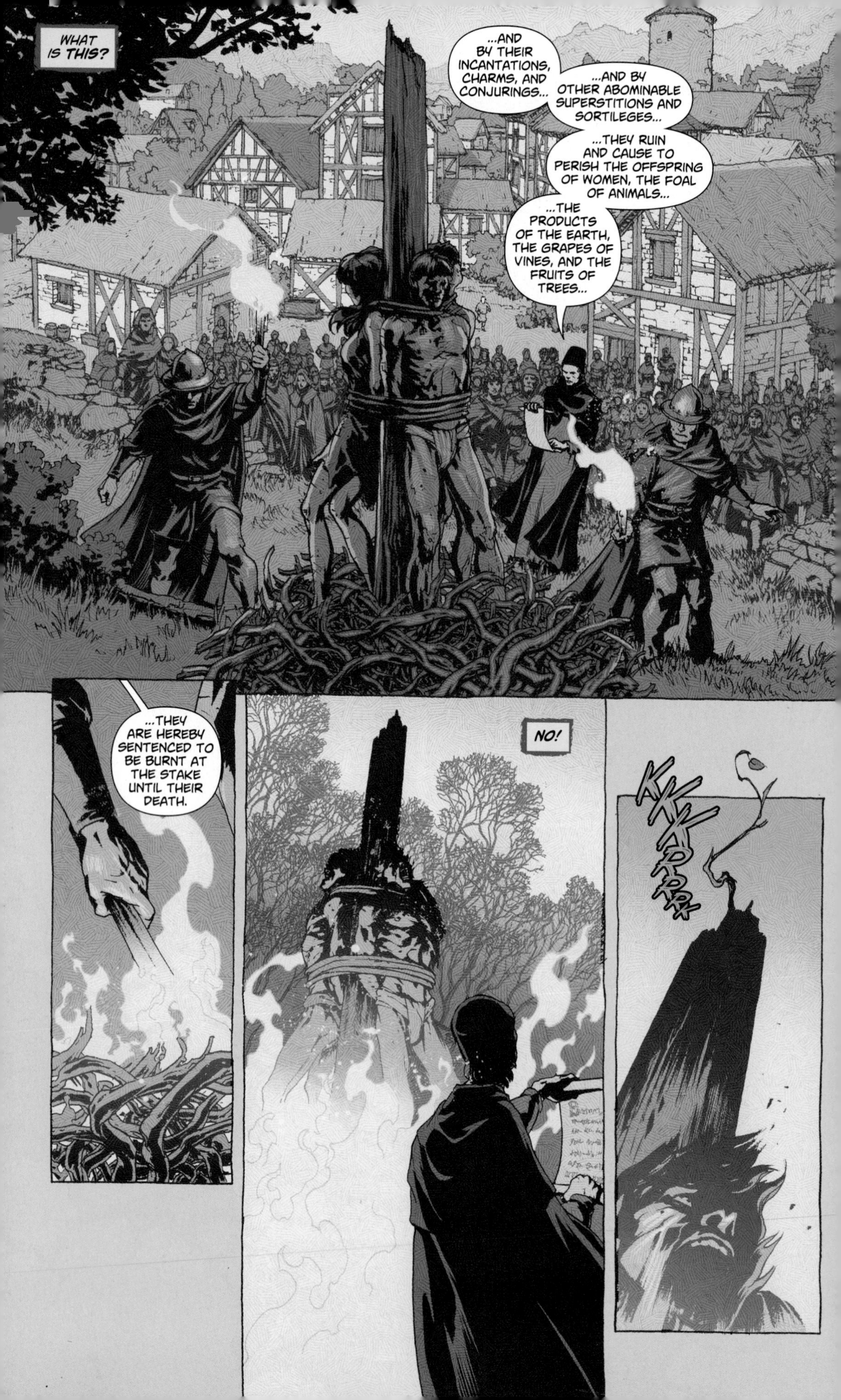
WHAT IS THIS?
...AND BY THEIR INCANTATIONS, CHARMS, AND CONJURINGS...
...AND BY OTHER ABOMINABLE SUPERSTITIONS AND SORTILEGES...
...THEY RUIN AND CAUSE TO PERISH THE OFFSPRING OF WOMEN, THE FOAL OF ANIMALS...
...THE PRODUCTS OF THE EARTH, THE GRAPES OF VINES, AND THE FRUITS OF TREES...
...THEY ARE HEREBY SENTENCED TO BE BURNT AT THE STAKE UNTIL THEIR DEATH.
NO!
KKKKRRRK

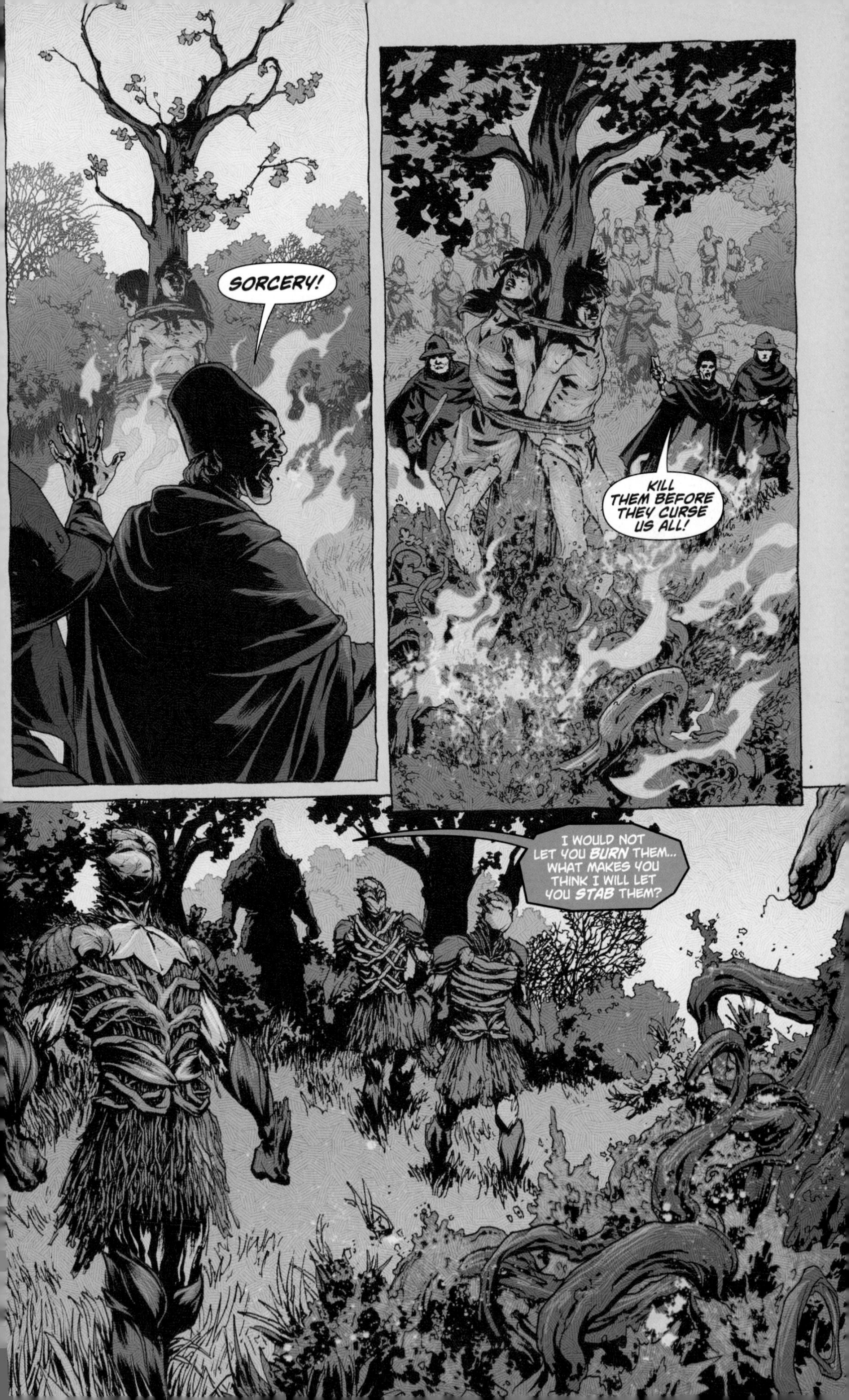
SORCERY!
KILL THEM BEFORE THEY CURSE US ALL!
I WOULD NOT LET YOU BURN THEM... WHAT MAKES YOU THINK I WILL LET YOU STAB THEM?

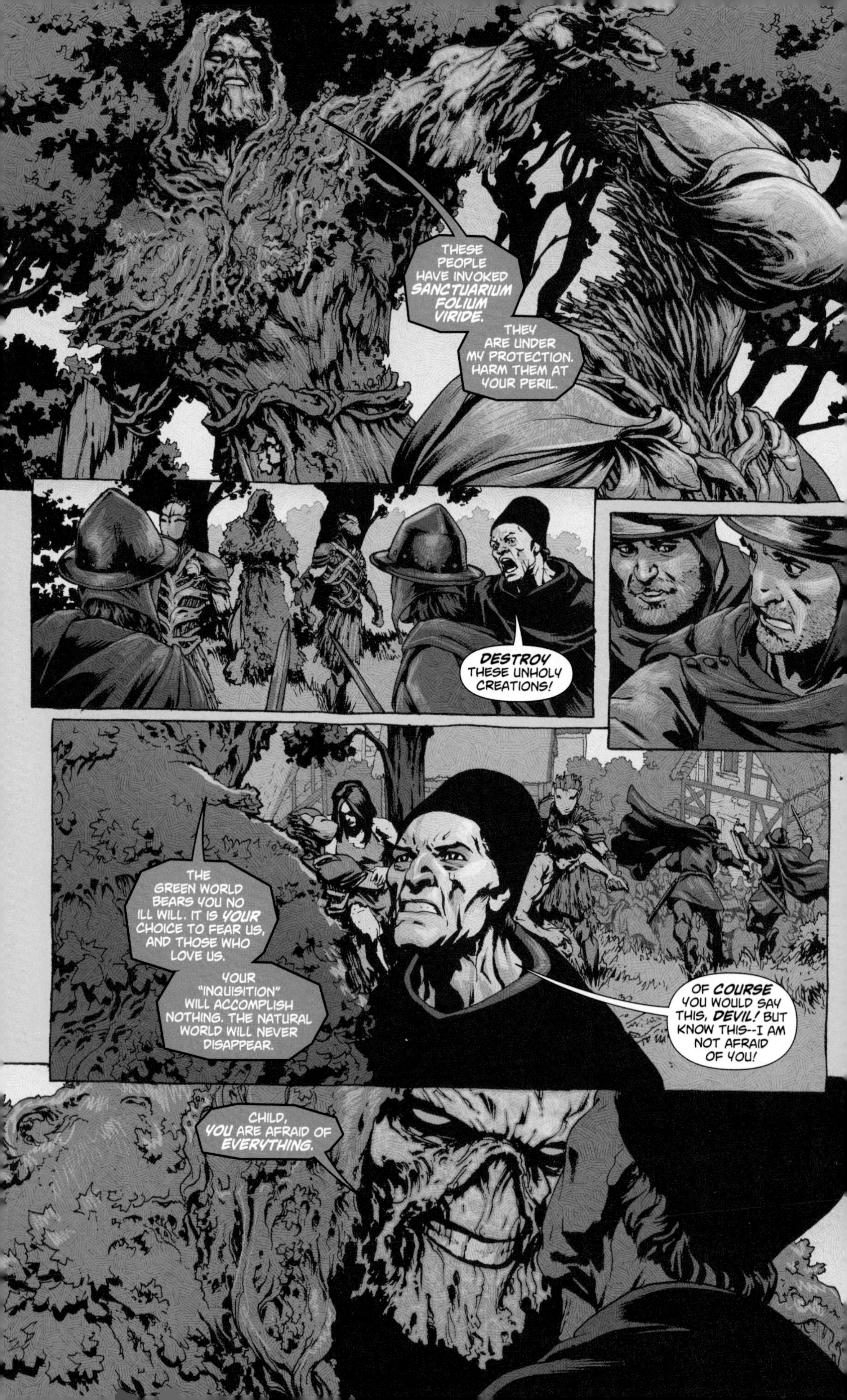

THESE PEOPLE HAVE INVOKED SANCTUARIUM FOLIUM VIRIDE.
THEY ARE UNDER MY PROTECTION. HARM THEM AT YOUR PERIL.
DESTROY THESE UNHOLY CREATIONS!
THE GREEN WORLD BEARS YOU NO ILL WILL. IT IS YOUR CHOICE TO FEAR US, AND THOSE WHO LOVE US.
YOUR "INQUISITION" WILL ACCOMPLISH NOTHING. THE NATURAL WORLD WILL NEVER DISAPPEAR.
OF COURSE YOU WOULD SAY THIS, DEVIL! BUT KNOW THIS--I AM NOT AFRAID OF YOU!
CHILD, YOU ARE AFRAID OF EVERYTHING.

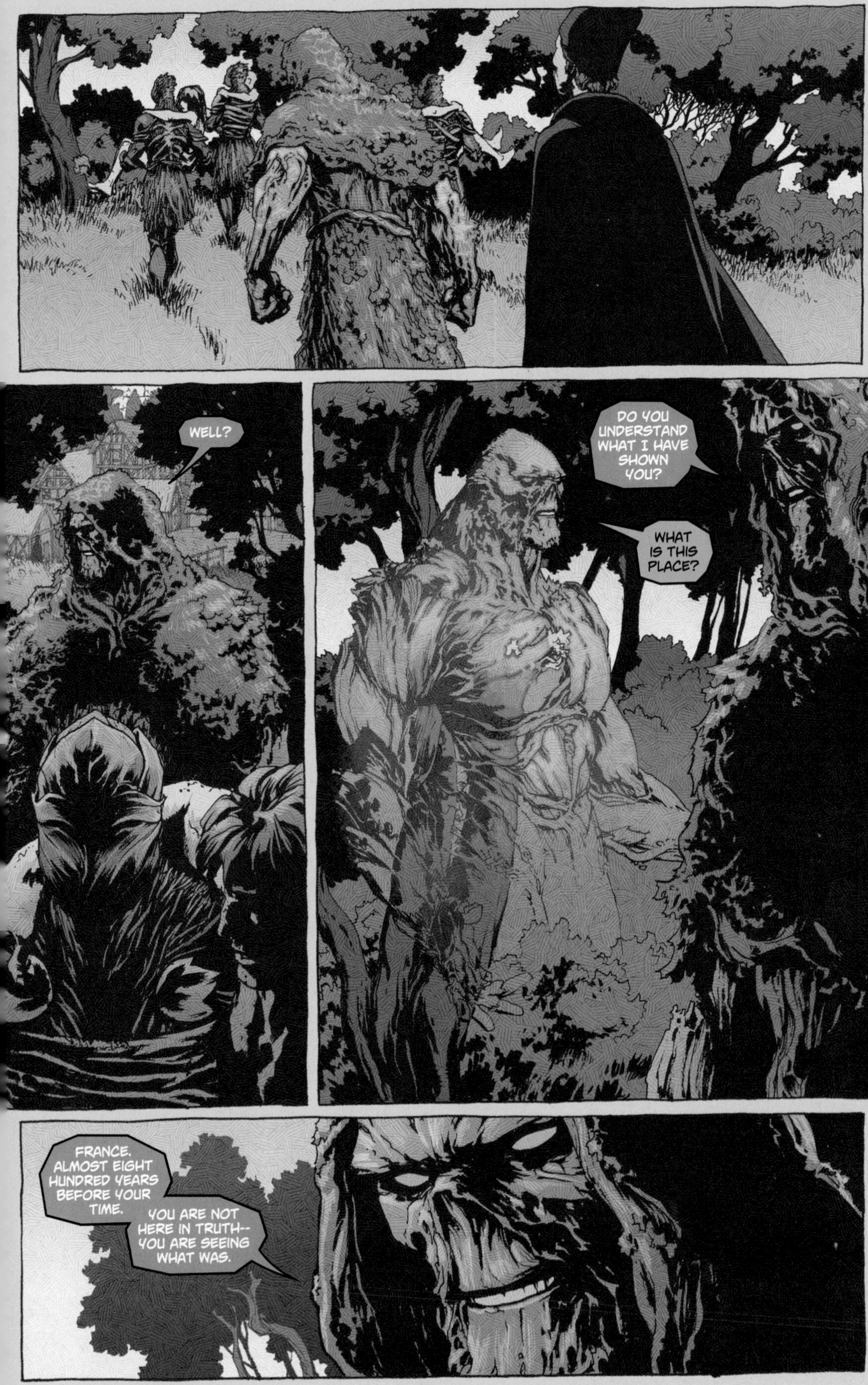
WELL?
DO YOU UNDERSTAND WHAT I HAVE SHOWN YOU?
WHAT IS THIS PLACE?
FRANCE. ALMOST EIGHT HUNDRED YEARS BEFORE YOUR TIME.
YOU ARE NOT HERE IN TRUTH-- YOU ARE SEEING WHAT WAS.

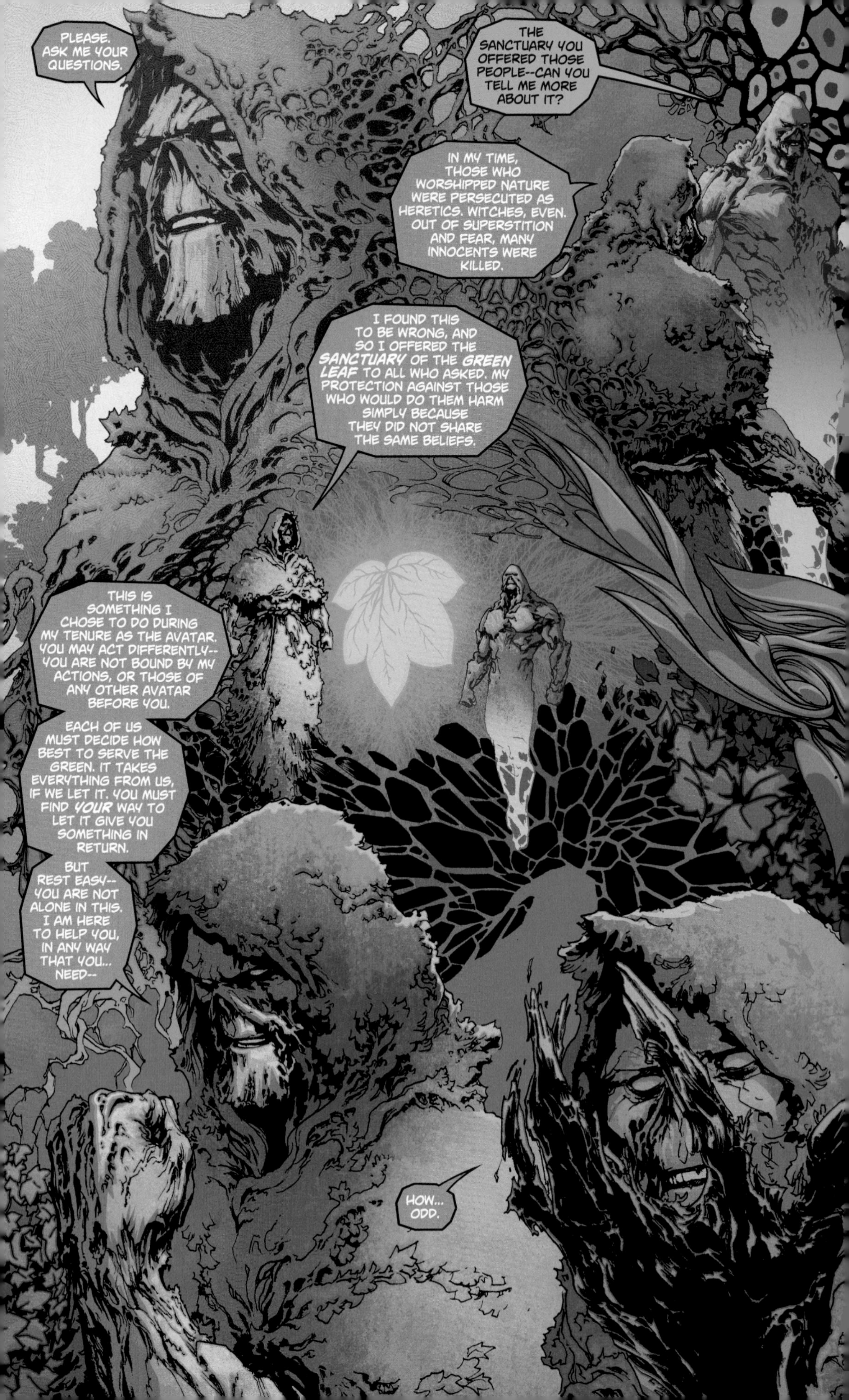
PLEASE. ASK ME YOUR QUESTIONS.
THE SANCTUARY YOU OFFERED THOSE PEOPLE--CAN YOU TELL ME MORE ABOUT IT?
IN MY TIME, THOSE WHO WORSHIPPED NATURE WERE PERSECUTED AS HERETICS. WITCHES, EVEN. OUT OF SUPERSTITION AND FEAR, MANY INNOCENTS WERE KILLED.
I FOUND THIS TO BE WRONG, AND SO I OFFERED THE SANCTUARY OF THE GREEN LEAF TO ALL WHO ASKED. MY PROTECTION AGAINST THOSE WHO WOULD DO THEM HARM SIMPLY BECAUSE THEY DID NOT SHARE THE SAME BELIEFS.
THIS IS SOMETHING I CHOSE TO DO DURING MY TENURE AS THE AVATAR. YOU MAY ACT DIFFERENTLY--YOU ARE NOT BOUND BY MY ACTIONS, OR THOSE OF ANY OTHER AVATAR BEFORE YOU.
EACH OF US MUST DECIDE HOW BEST TO SERVE THE GREEN. IT TAKES EVERYTHING FROM US, IF WE LET IT. YOU MUST FIND YOUR WAY TO LET IT GIVE YOU SOMETHING IN RETURN.
BUT REST EASY--YOU ARE NOT ALONE IN THIS. I AM HERE TO HELP YOU, IN ANY WAY THAT YOU... NEED--
HOW... ODD.

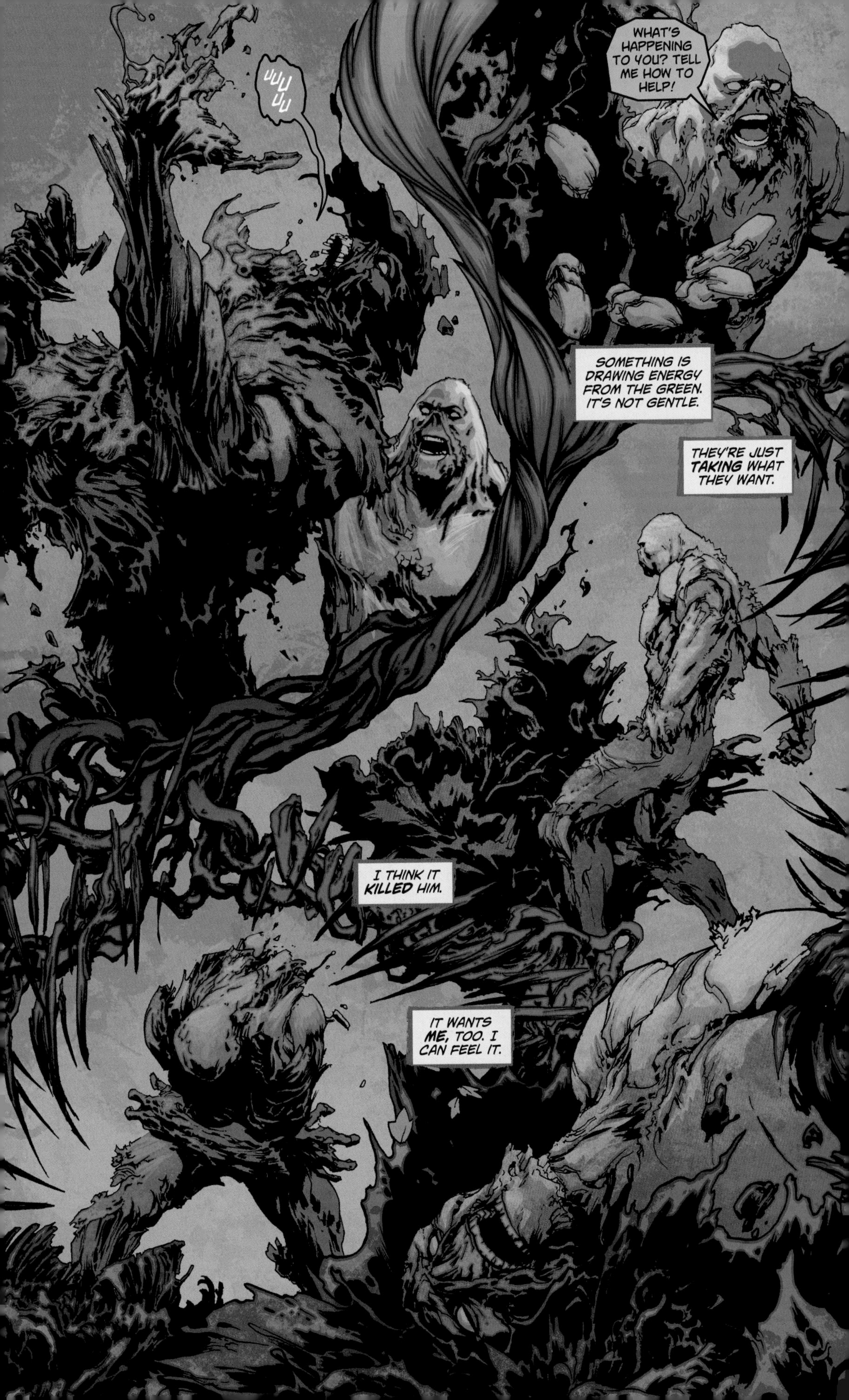
UUU
UU
WHAT'S HAPPENING TO YOU? TELL ME HOW TO HELP!
SOMETHING IS DRAWING ENERGY FROM THE GREEN. IT'S NOT GENTLE.
THEY'RE JUST TAKING WHAT THEY WANT.
I THINK IT KILLED HIM.
IT WANTS ME, TOO. I CAN FEEL IT.

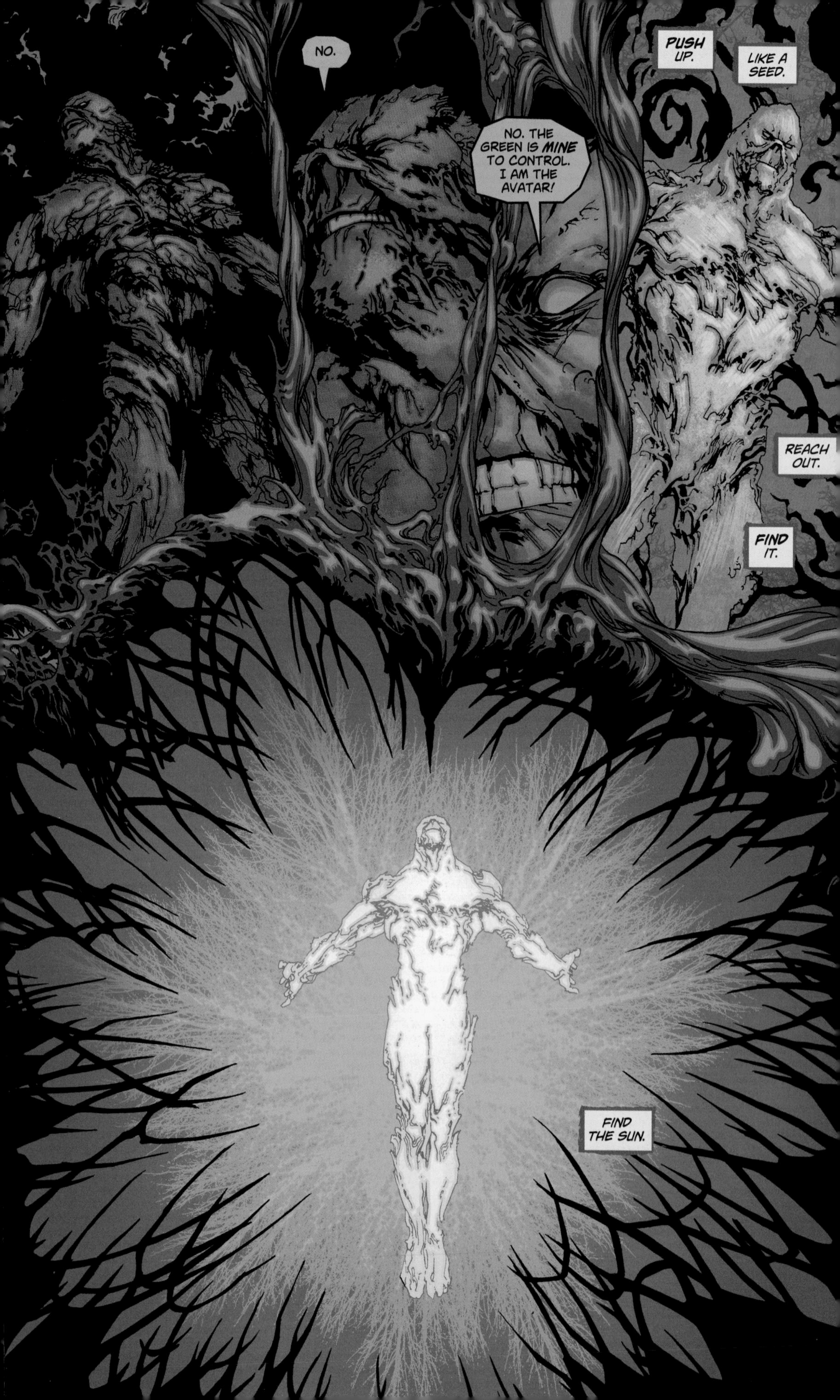
NO.
NO. THE GREEN IS MINE TO CONTROL. I AM THE AVATAR!
PUSH UP.
LIKE A SEED.
REACH OUT.
FIND IT.
FIND THE SUN.

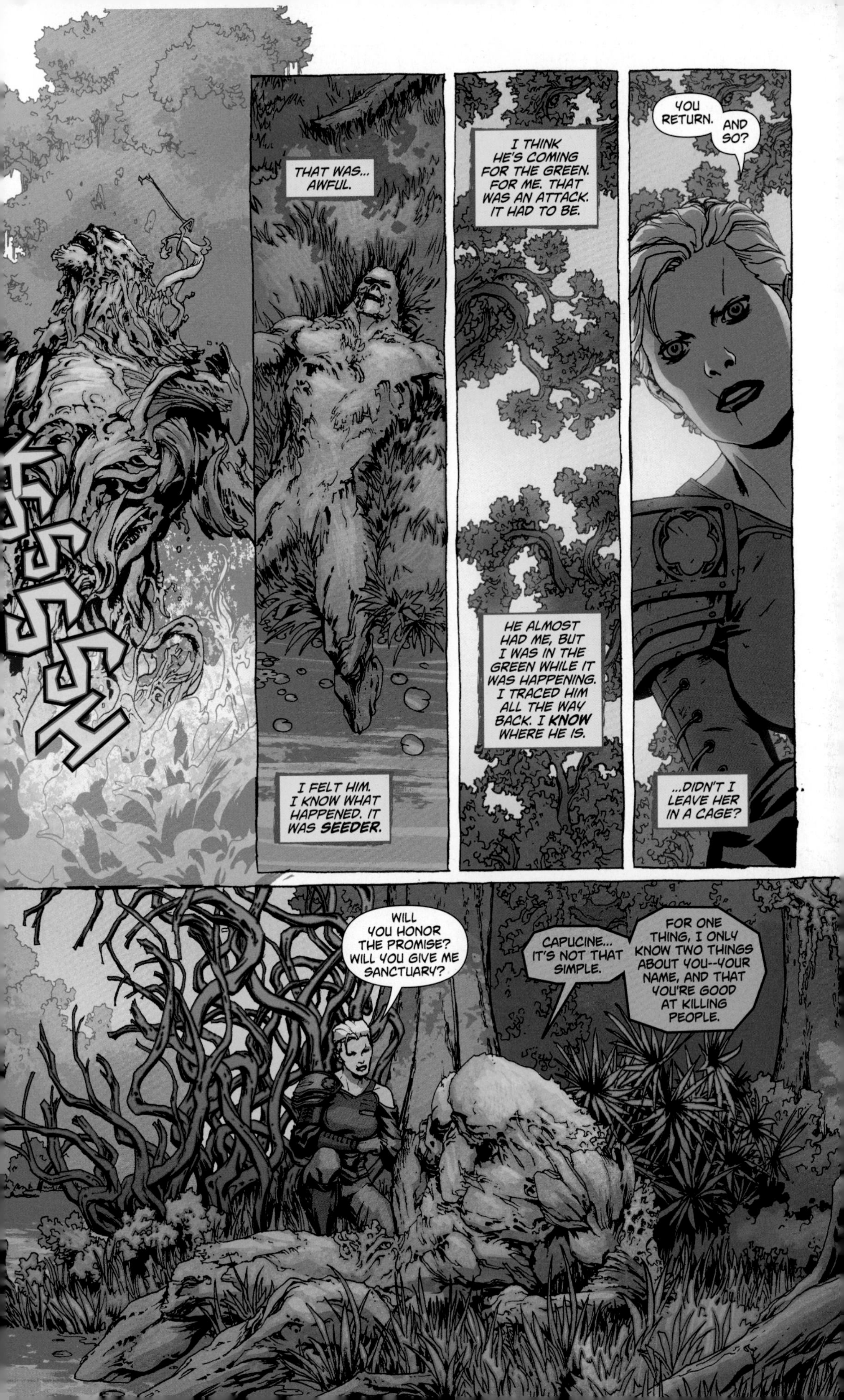
KSSSH
THAT WAS... AWFUL.
I FELT HIM. I KNOW WHAT HAPPENED. IT WAS SEEDER.
I THINK HE'S COMING FOR THE GREEN. FOR ME. THAT WAS AN ATTACK. IT HAD TO BE.
HE ALMOST HAD ME, BUT I WAS IN THE GREEN WHILE IT WAS HAPPENING. I TRACED HIM ALL THE WAY BACK. I KNOW WHERE HE IS.
YOU RETURN.
AND SO?
...DIDN'T I LEAVE HER IN A CAGE?
WILL YOU HONOR THE PROMISE? WILL YOU GIVE ME SANCTUARY?
CAPUCINE... IT'S NOT THAT SIMPLE.
FOR ONE THING, I ONLY KNOW TWO THINGS ABOUT YOU--YOUR NAME, AND THAT YOU'RE GOOD AT KILLING PEOPLE.

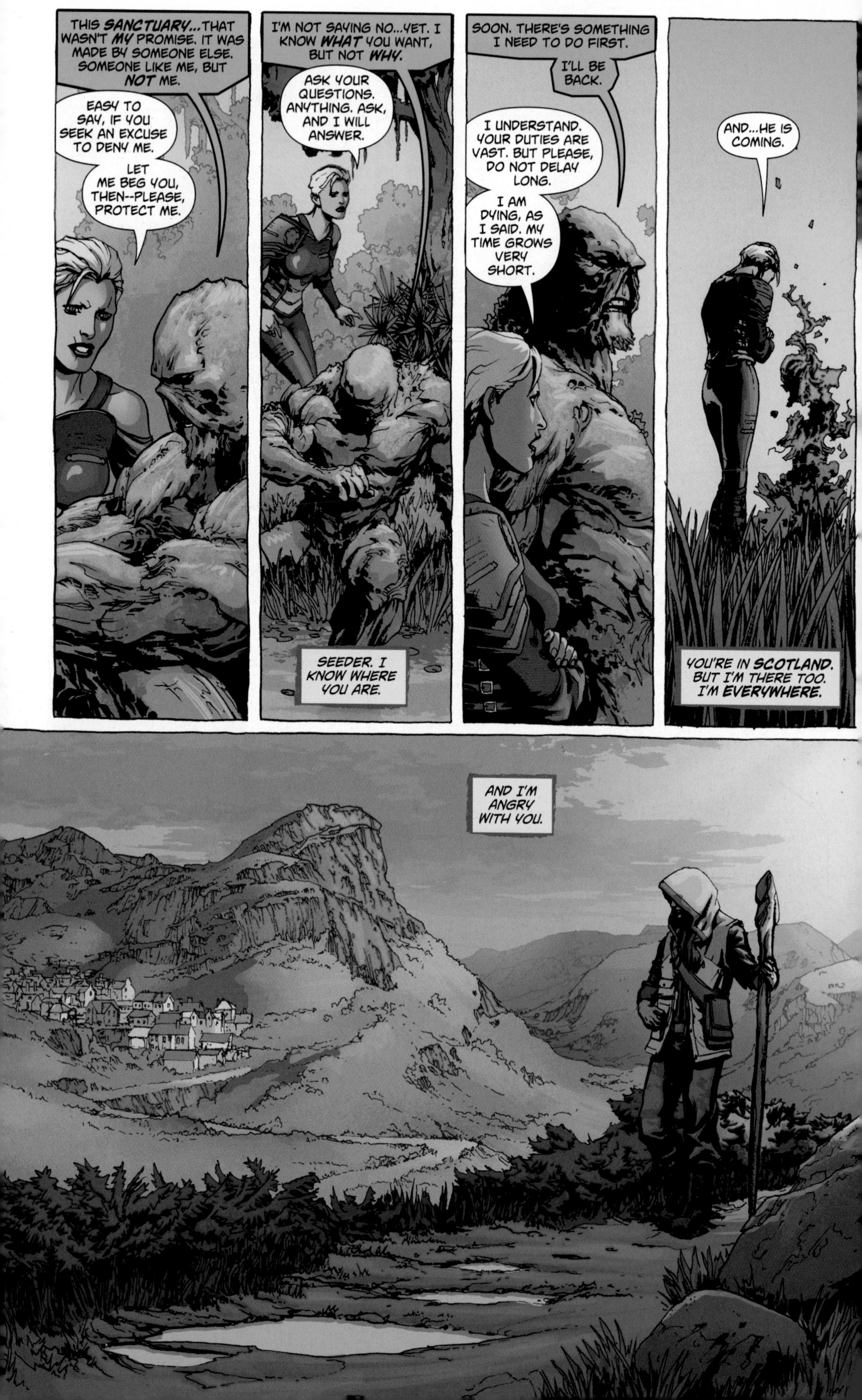
THIS SANCTUARY...THAT WASN'T MY PROMISE. IT WAS MADE BY SOMEONE ELSE. SOMEONE LIKE ME, BUT NOT ME.
EASY TO SAY, IF YOU SEEK AN EXCUSE TO DENY ME.
LET ME BEG YOU, THEN--PLEASE, PROTECT ME.
I'M NOT SAYING NO...YET. I KNOW WHAT YOU WANT, BUT NOT WHY.
ASK YOUR QUESTIONS. ANYTHING. ASK, AND I WILL ANSWER.
SEEDER. I KNOW WHERE YOU ARE.
SOON. THERE'S SOMETHING I NEED TO DO FIRST.
I'LL BE BACK.
I UNDERSTAND. YOUR DUTIES ARE VAST. BUT PLEASE, DO NOT DELAY LONG.
I AM DYING, AS I SAID. MY TIME GROWS VERY SHORT.
AND...HE IS COMING.
YOU'RE IN SCOTLAND. BUT I'M THERE TOO. I'M EVERYWHERE.
AND I'M ANGRY WITH YOU.

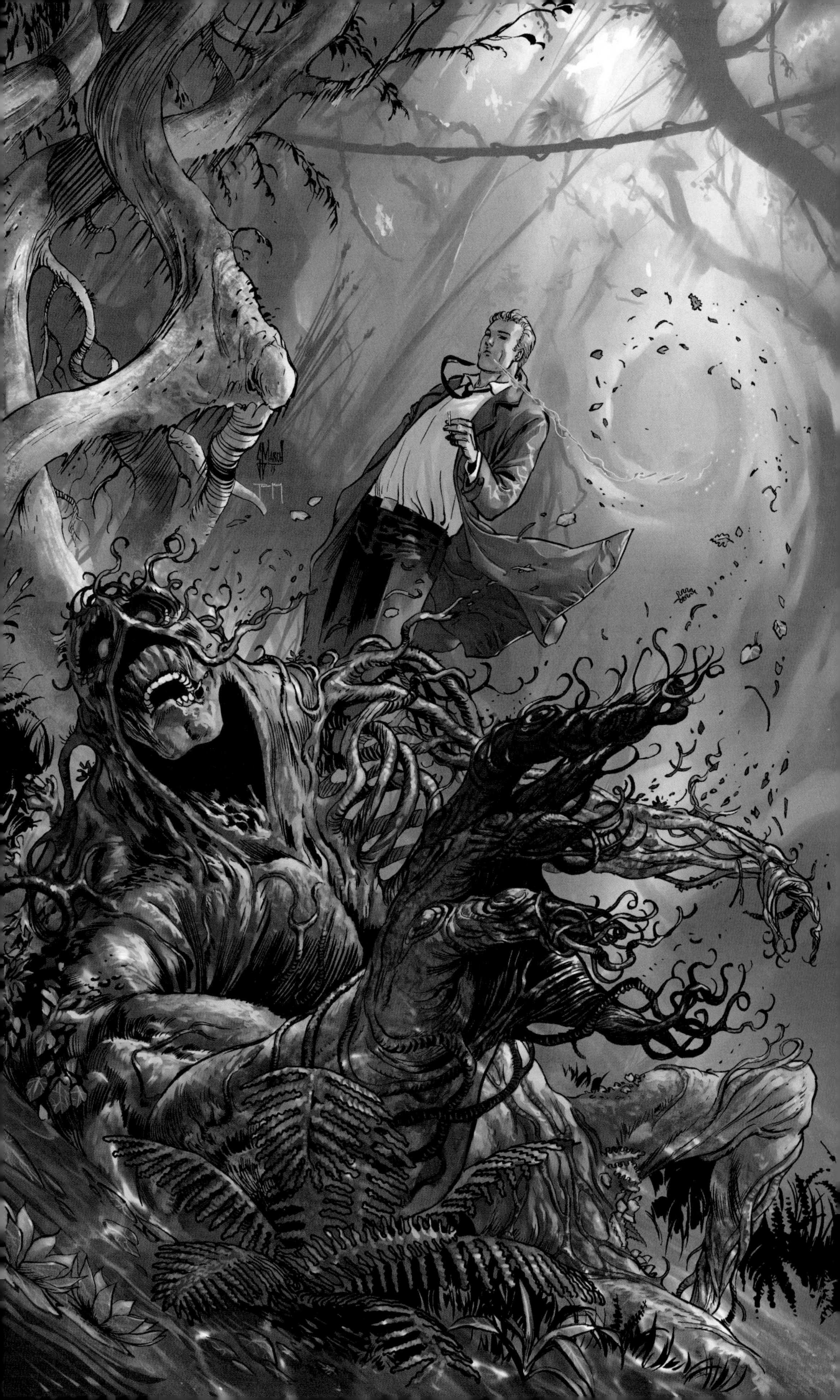

## THE WHISKEY TREE: PART 1

CHARLES SOULE writer KANO penciller KANO & ALVARO LOPEZ inkers cover art by GUILLEM MARCH & TOMEU MOREY

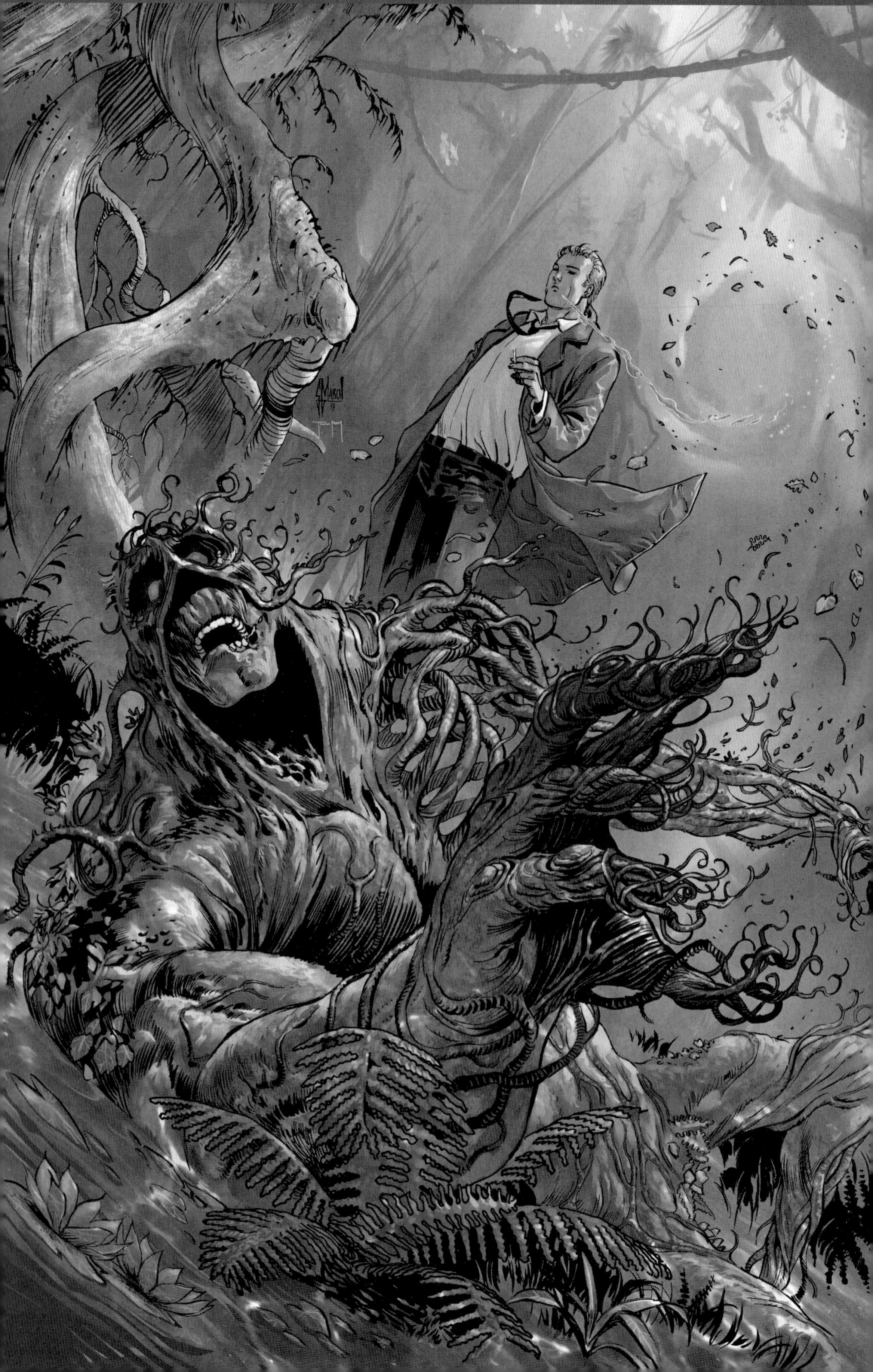

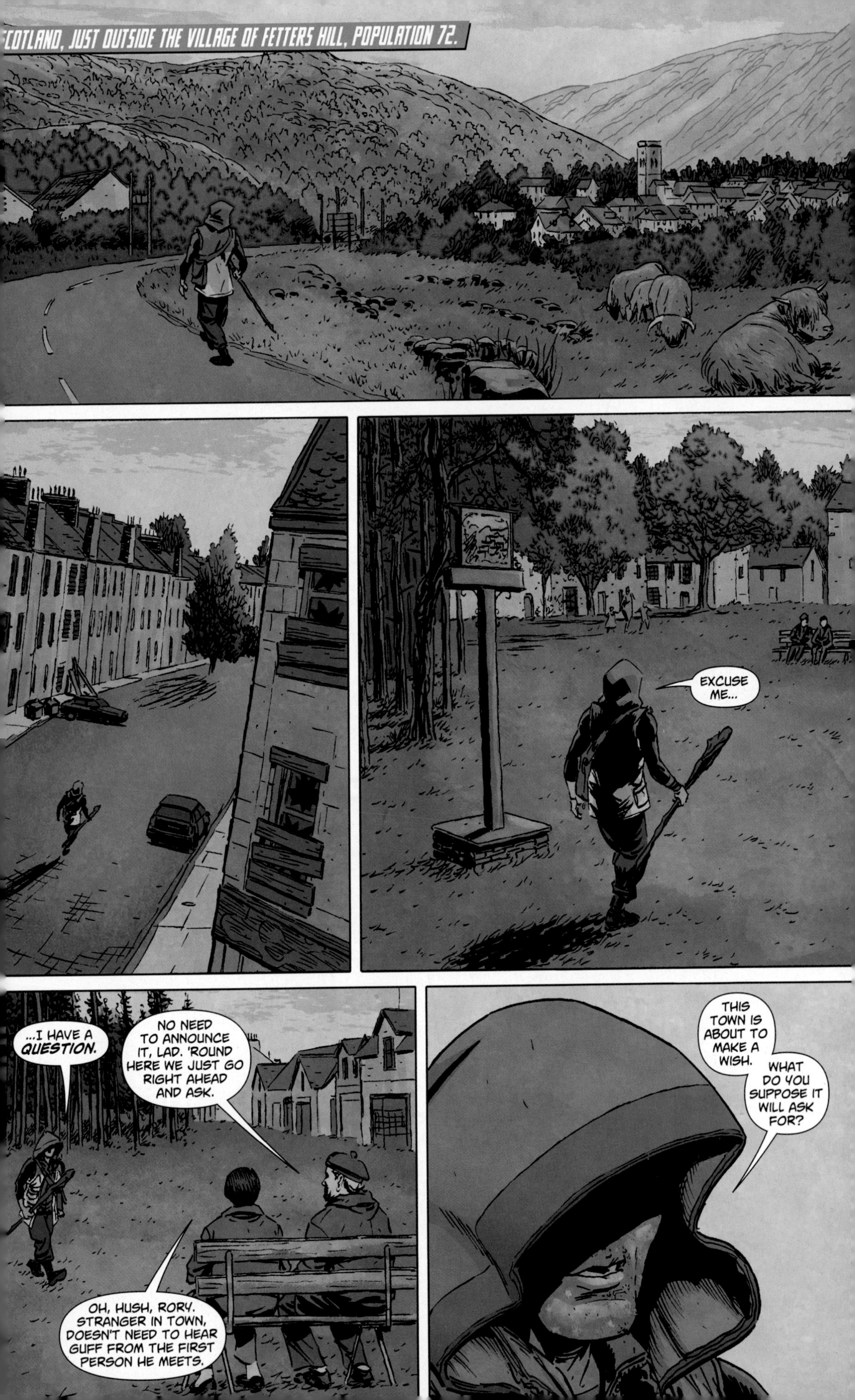

SCOTLAND, JUST OUTSIDE THE VILLAGE OF FETTERS HILL, POPULATION 72.
EXCUSE ME...
...I HAVE A QUESTION.
NO NEED TO ANNOUNCE IT, LAD. 'ROUND HERE WE JUST GO RIGHT AHEAD AND ASK.
OH, HUSH, RORY. STRANGER IN TOWN, DOESN'T NEED TO HEAR GUFF FROM THE FIRST PERSON HE MEETS.
THIS TOWN IS ABOUT TO MAKE A WISH.
WHAT DO YOU SUPPOSE IT WILL ASK FOR?

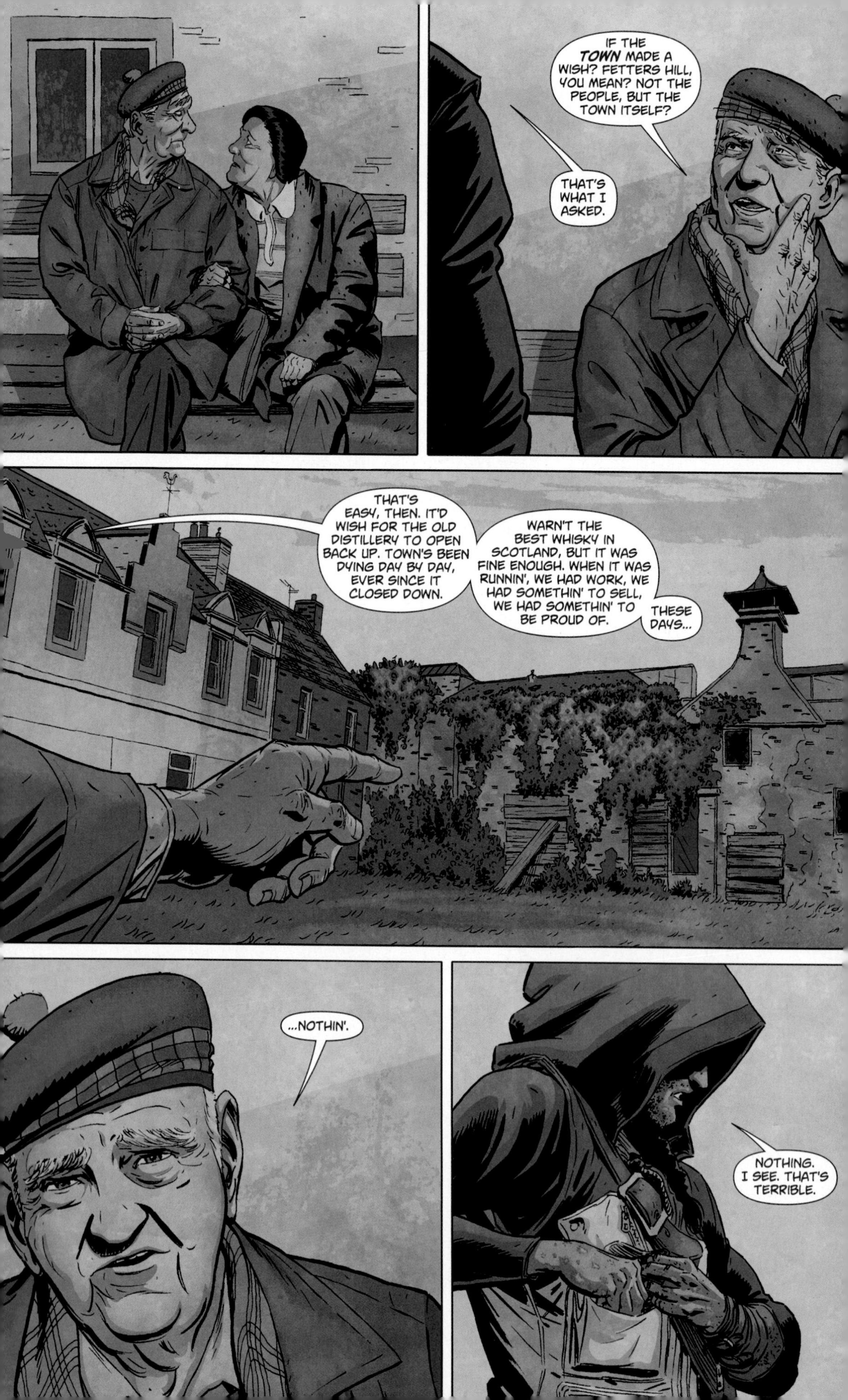
IF THE *TOWN* MADE A WISH? FETTERS HILL, YOU MEAN? NOT THE PEOPLE, BUT THE TOWN ITSELF?
THAT'S WHAT I ASKED.
THAT'S EASY, THEN. IT'D WISH FOR THE OLD DISTILLERY TO OPEN BACK UP. TOWN'S BEEN DYING DAY BY DAY, EVER SINCE IT CLOSED DOWN.
WARN'T THE BEST WHISKY IN SCOTLAND, BUT IT WAS FINE ENOUGH. WHEN IT WAS RUNNIN', WE HAD WORK, WE HAD SOMETHIN' TO SELL, WE HAD SOMETHIN' TO BE PROUD OF.
THESE DAYS...
...NOTHIN'.
NOTHING. I SEE. THAT'S TERRIBLE.

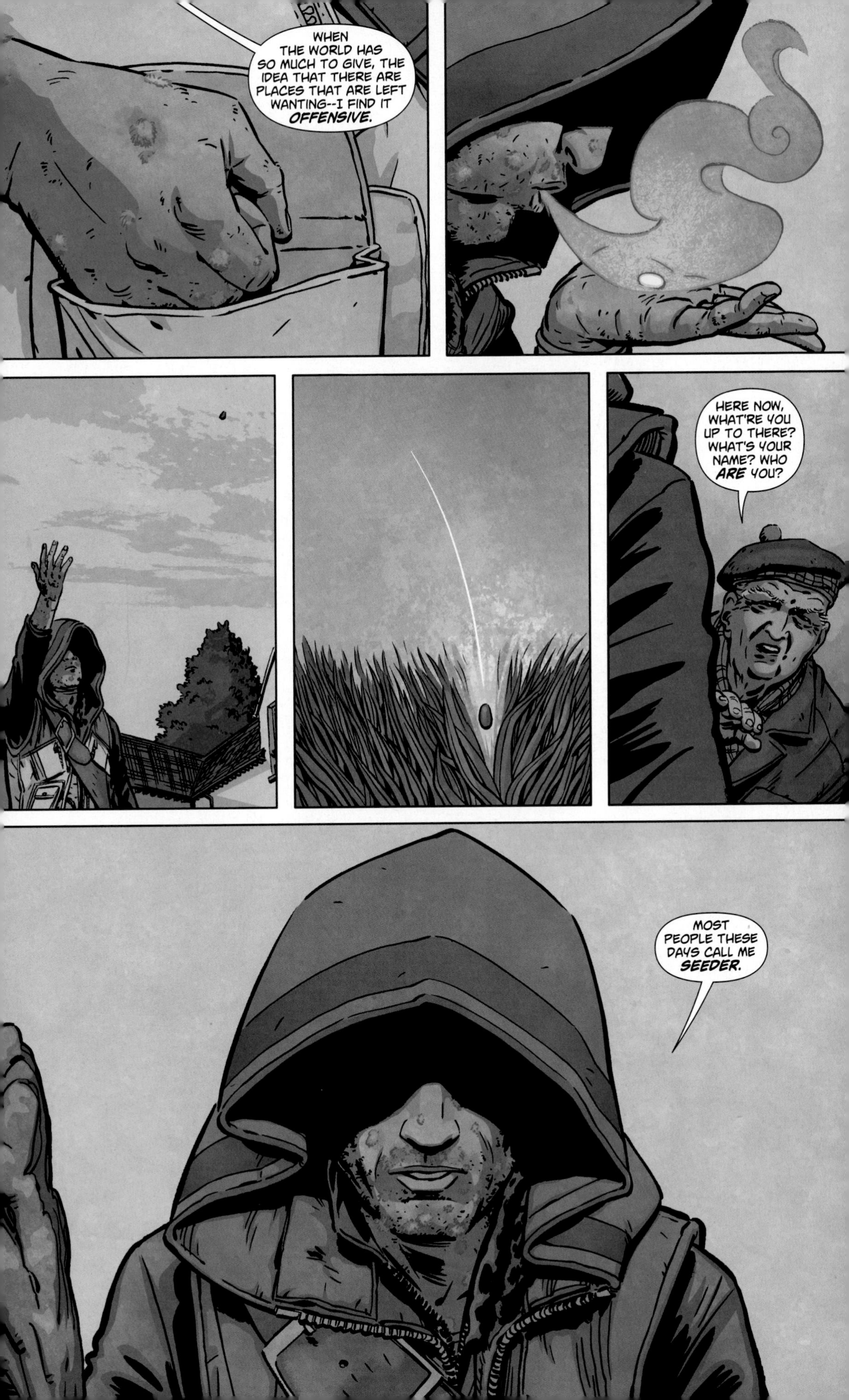
WHEN THE WORLD HAS SO MUCH TO GIVE, THE IDEA THAT THERE ARE PLACES THAT ARE LEFT WANTING--I FIND IT *OFFENSIVE.*
HERE NOW, WHAT'RE YOU UP TO THERE? WHAT'S YOUR NAME? WHO *ARE* YOU?
MOST PEOPLE THESE DAYS CALL ME *SEEDER.*

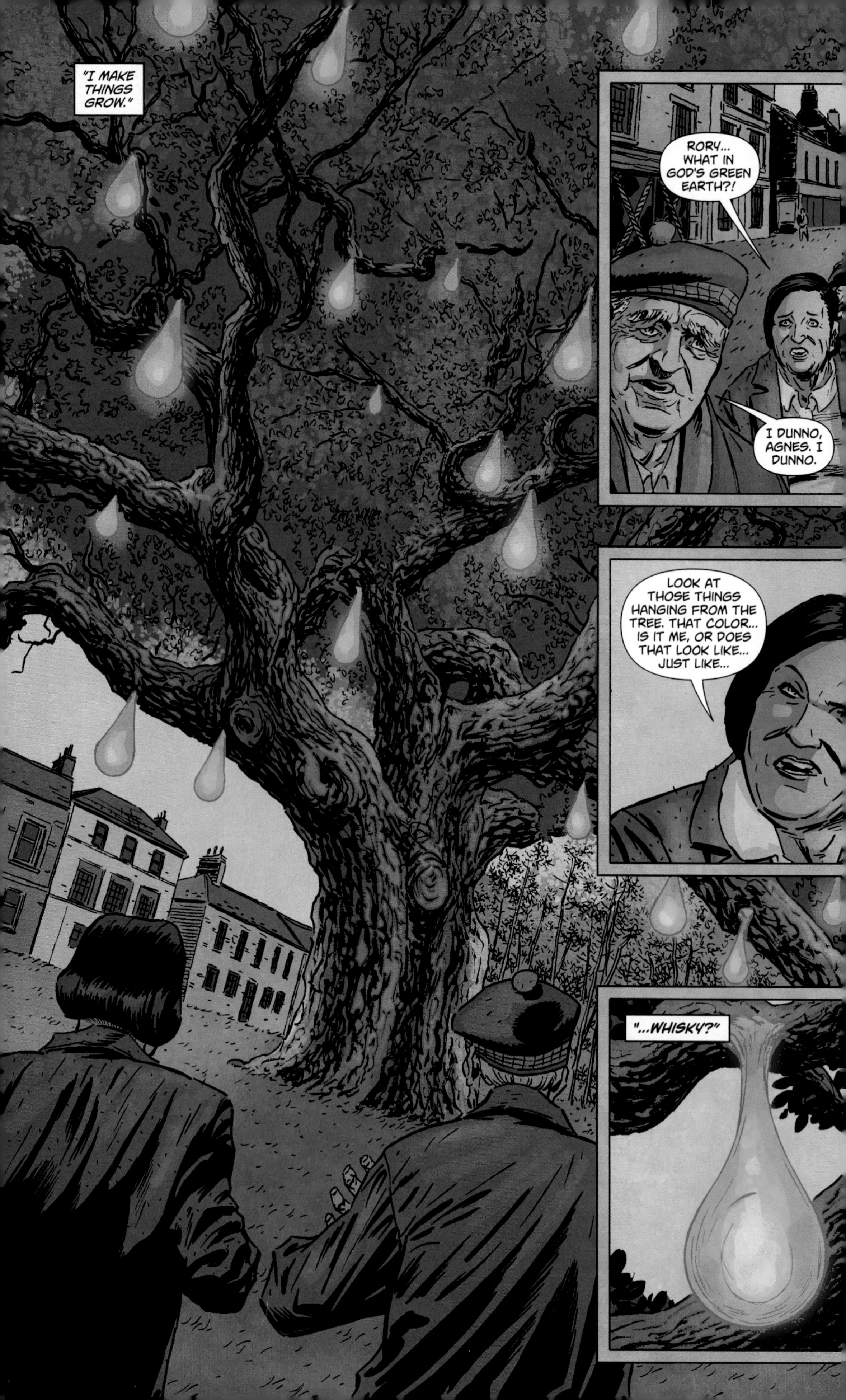
"I MAKE THINGS GROW."
RORY... WHAT IN GOD'S GREEN EARTH?!
I DUNNO, AGNES. I DUNNO.
LOOK AT THOSE THINGS HANGING FROM THE TREE. THAT COLOR... IS IT ME, OR DOES THAT LOOK LIKE... JUST LIKE...
"...WHISKY?"

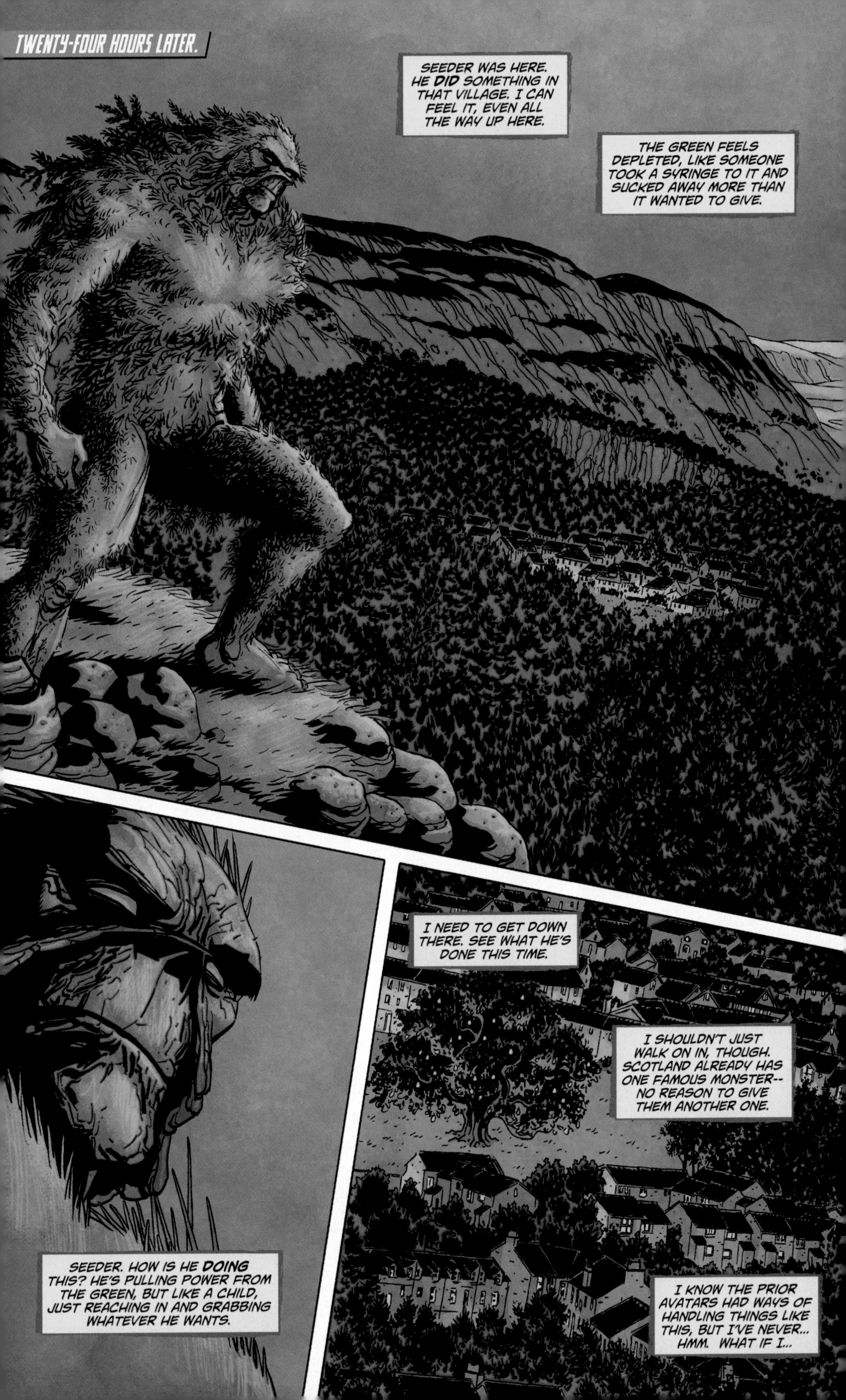
TWENTY-FOUR HOURS LATER.
SEEDER WAS HERE. HE DID SOMETHING IN THAT VILLAGE. I CAN FEEL IT, EVEN ALL THE WAY UP HERE.
THE GREEN FEELS DEPLETED, LIKE SOMEONE TOOK A SYRINGE TO IT AND SUCKED AWAY MORE THAN IT WANTED TO GIVE.
SEEDER. HOW IS HE DOING THIS? HE'S PULLING POWER FROM THE GREEN, BUT LIKE A CHILD, JUST REACHING IN AND GRABBING WHATEVER HE WANTS.
I NEED TO GET DOWN THERE. SEE WHAT HE'S DONE THIS TIME.
I SHOULDN'T JUST WALK ON IN, THOUGH. SCOTLAND ALREADY HAS ONE FAMOUS MONSTER-- NO REASON TO GIVE THEM ANOTHER ONE.
I KNOW THE PRIOR AVATARS HAD WAYS OF HANDLING THINGS LIKE THIS, BUT I'VE NEVER... HMM. WHAT IF I...

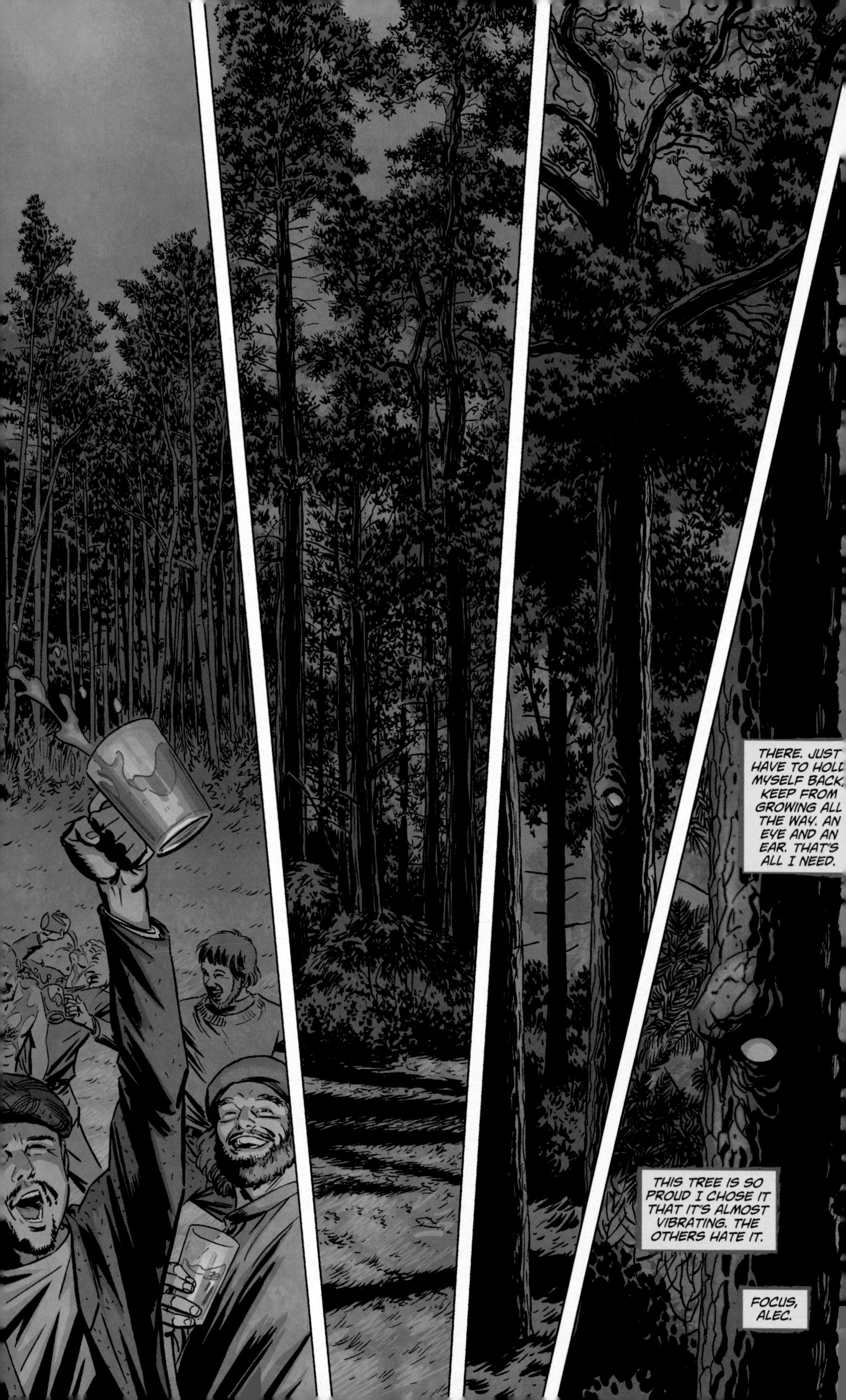
THERE. JUST HAVE TO HOLD MYSELF BACK, KEEP FROM GROWING ALL THE WAY. AN EYE AND AN EAR. THAT'S ALL I NEED.
THIS TREE IS SO PROUD I CHOSE IT THAT IT'S ALMOST VIBRATING. THE OTHERS HATE IT.
FOCUS, ALEC.

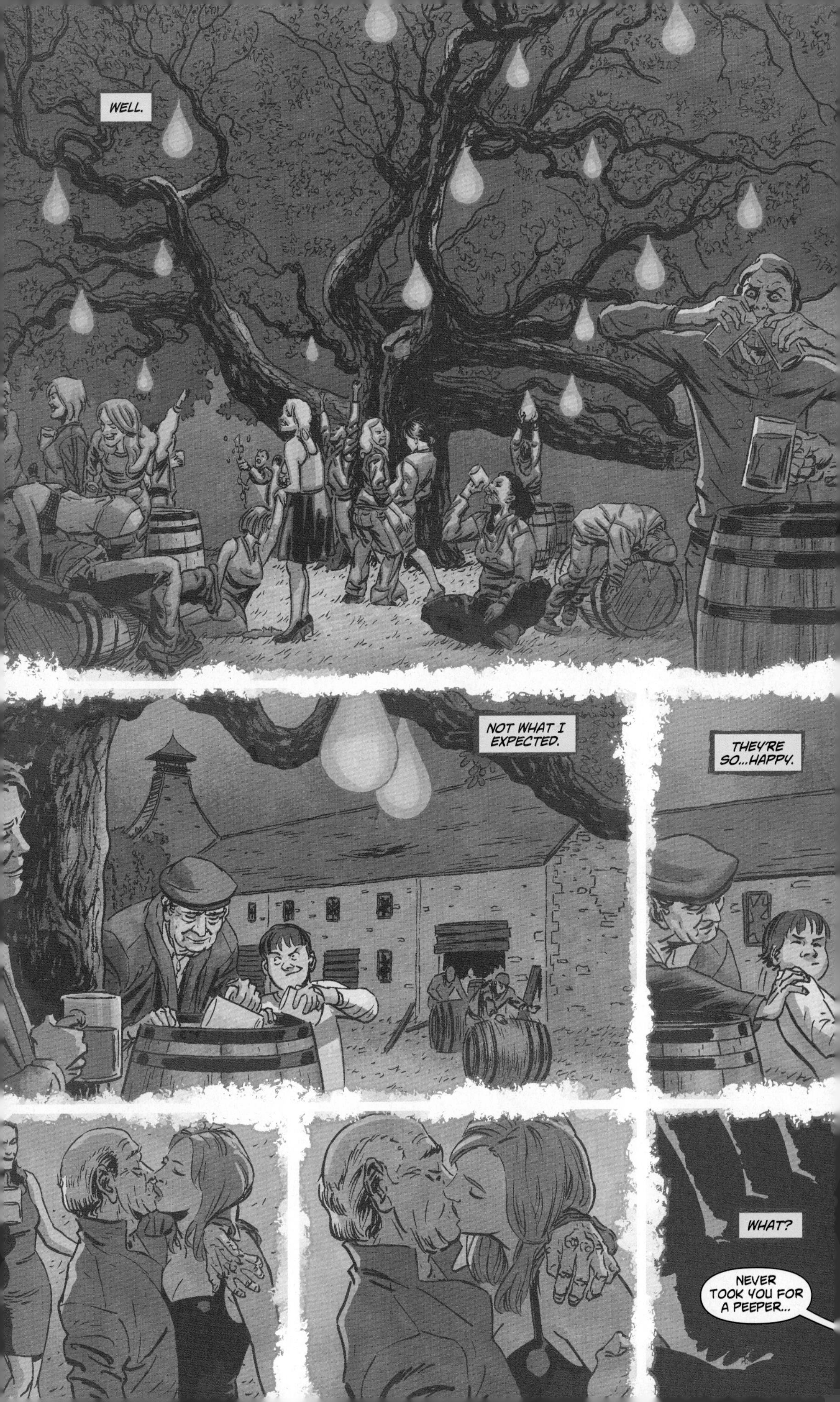
WELL.
NOT WHAT I EXPECTED.
THEY'RE SO...HAPPY.
WHAT?
NEVER TOOK YOU FOR A PEEPER...

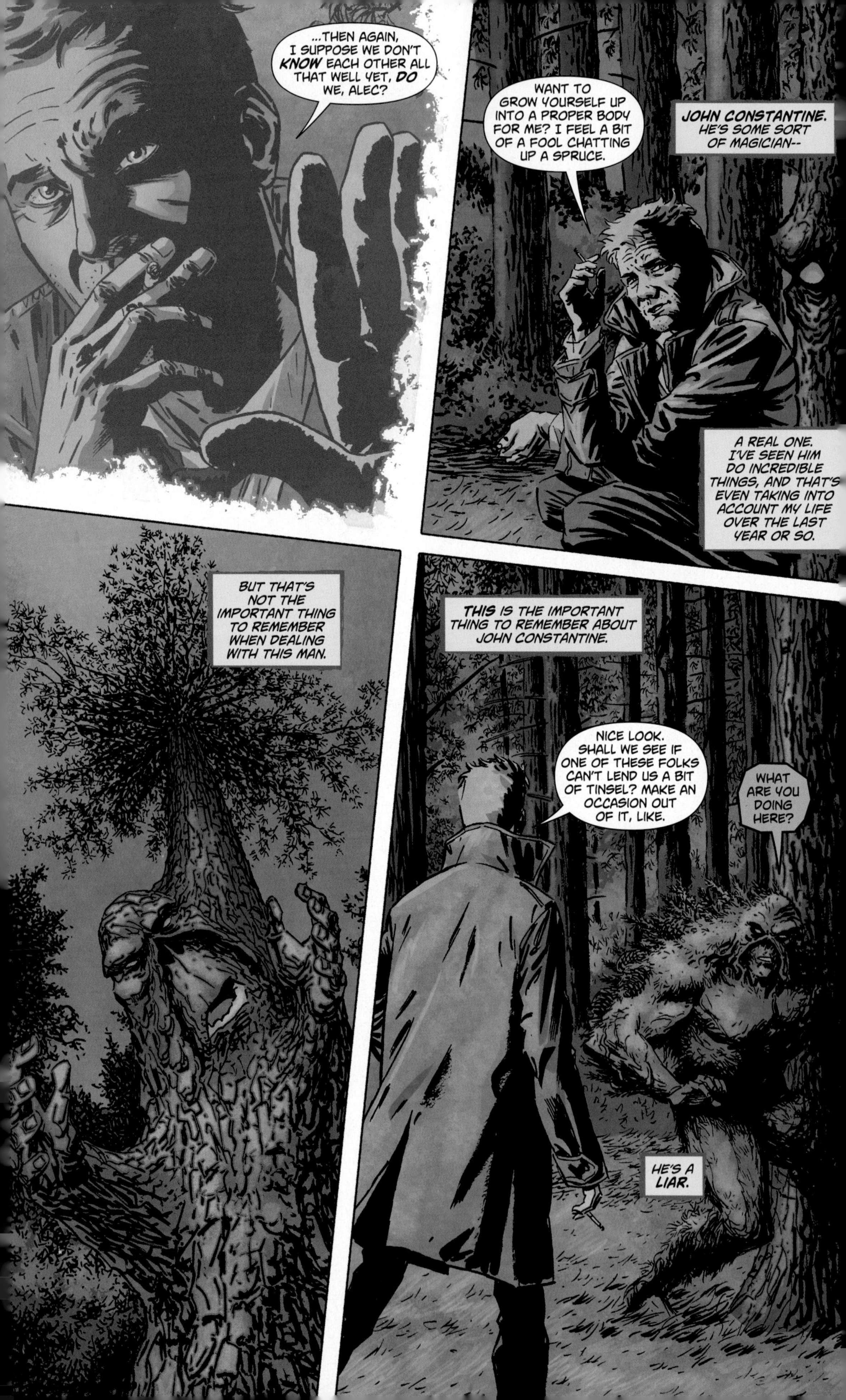

...THEN AGAIN, I SUPPOSE WE DON'T KNOW EACH OTHER ALL THAT WELL YET, DO WE, ALEC?
WANT TO GROW YOURSELF UP INTO A PROPER BODY FOR ME? I FEEL A BIT OF A FOOL CHATTING UP A SPRUCE.
JOHN CONSTANTINE. HE'S SOME SORT OF MAGICIAN--
A REAL ONE. I'VE SEEN HIM DO INCREDIBLE THINGS, AND THAT'S EVEN TAKING INTO ACCOUNT MY LIFE OVER THE LAST YEAR OR SO.
BUT THAT'S NOT THE IMPORTANT THING TO REMEMBER WHEN DEALING WITH THIS MAN.
THIS IS THE IMPORTANT THING TO REMEMBER ABOUT JOHN CONSTANTINE.
NICE LOOK. SHALL WE SEE IF ONE OF THESE FOLKS CAN'T LEND US A BIT OF TINSEL? MAKE AN OCCASION OUT OF IT, LIKE.
WHAT ARE YOU DOING HERE?
HE'S A LIAR.

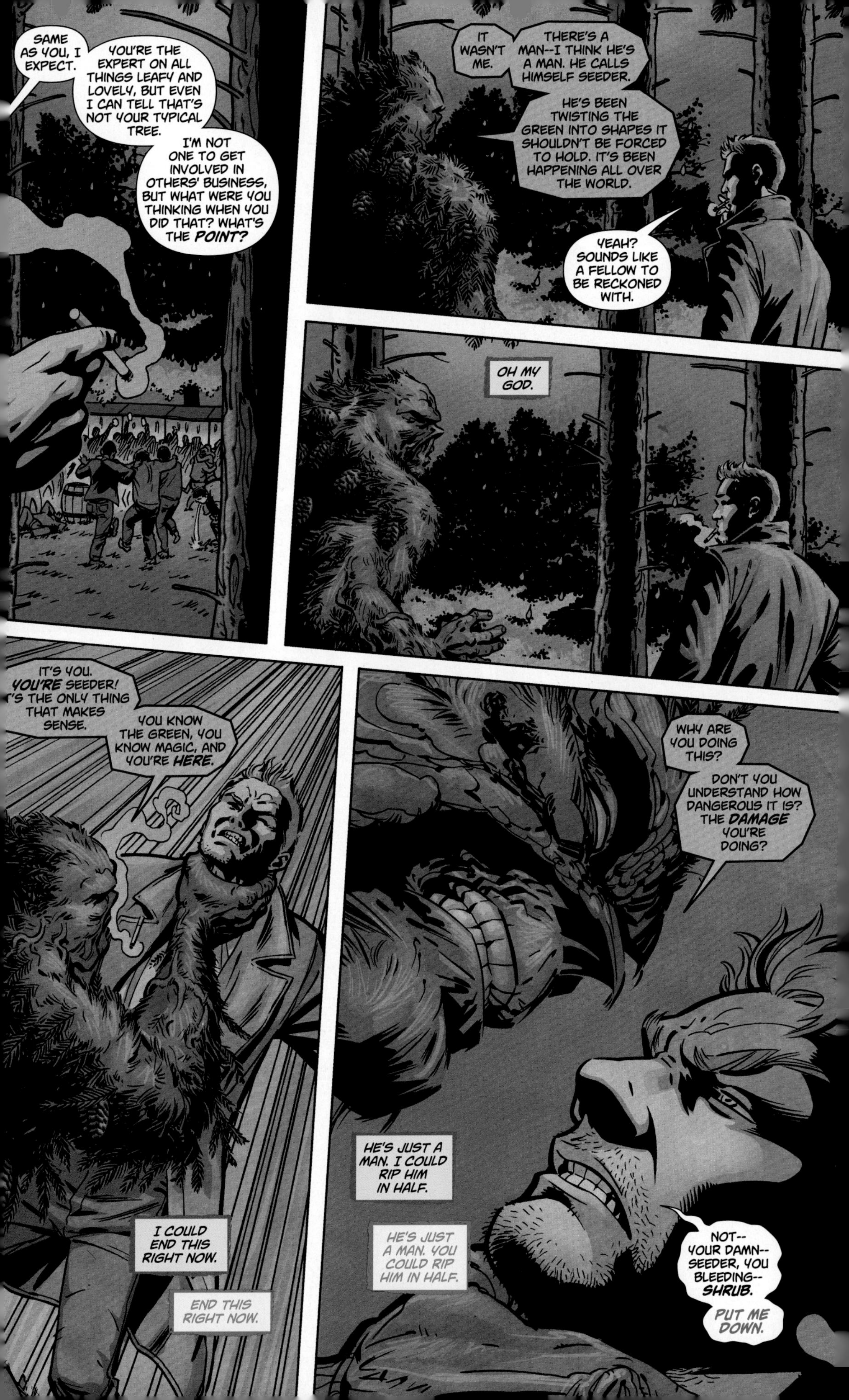

SAME AS YOU, I EXPECT.
YOU'RE THE EXPERT ON ALL THINGS LEAFY AND LOVELY, BUT EVEN I CAN TELL THAT'S NOT YOUR TYPICAL TREE.
I'M NOT ONE TO GET INVOLVED IN OTHERS' BUSINESS, BUT WHAT WERE YOU THINKING WHEN YOU DID THAT? WHAT'S THE *POINT?*
IT WASN'T ME.
THERE'S A MAN--I THINK HE'S A MAN. HE CALLS HIMSELF SEEDER.
HE'S BEEN TWISTING THE GREEN INTO SHAPES IT SHOULDN'T BE FORCED TO HOLD. IT'S BEEN HAPPENING ALL OVER THE WORLD.
YEAH? SOUNDS LIKE A FELLOW TO BE RECKONED WITH.
*OH MY GOD.*
IT'S YOU. *YOU'RE* SEEDER! 'S THE ONLY THING THAT MAKES SENSE.
YOU KNOW THE GREEN, YOU KNOW MAGIC, AND YOU'RE *HERE.*
*I COULD END THIS RIGHT NOW.*
*END THIS RIGHT NOW.*
WHY ARE YOU DOING THIS?
DON'T YOU UNDERSTAND HOW DANGEROUS IT IS? THE *DAMAGE* YOU'RE DOING?
*HE'S JUST A MAN. I COULD RIP HIM IN HALF.*
*HE'S JUST A MAN. YOU COULD RIP HIM IN HALF.*
NOT-- YOUR DAMN-- SEEDER, YOU BLEEDING-- **SHRUB.**
*PUT ME DOWN.*

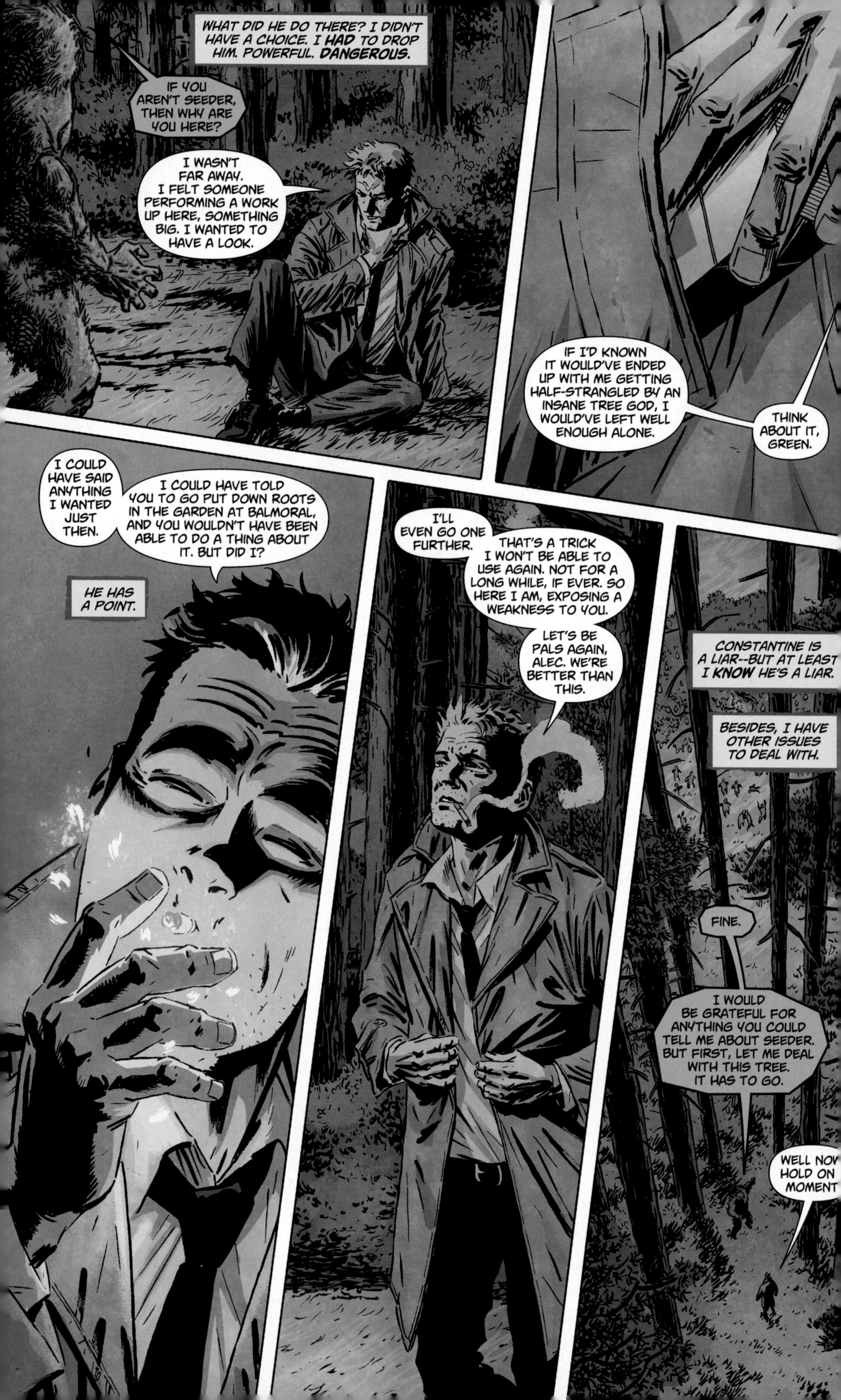
WHAT DID HE DO THERE? I DIDN'T HAVE A CHOICE. I HAD TO DROP HIM. POWERFUL. DANGEROUS.
IF YOU AREN'T SEEDER, THEN WHY ARE YOU HERE?
I WASN'T FAR AWAY. I FELT SOMEONE PERFORMING A WORK UP HERE, SOMETHING BIG. I WANTED TO HAVE A LOOK.
IF I'D KNOWN IT WOULD'VE ENDED UP WITH ME GETTING HALF-STRANGLED BY AN INSANE TREE GOD, I WOULD'VE LEFT WELL ENOUGH ALONE.
THINK ABOUT IT, GREEN.
I COULD HAVE SAID ANYTHING I WANTED JUST THEN.
I COULD HAVE TOLD YOU TO GO PUT DOWN ROOTS IN THE GARDEN AT BALMORAL, AND YOU WOULDN'T HAVE BEEN ABLE TO DO A THING ABOUT IT. BUT DID I?
HE HAS A POINT.
I'LL EVEN GO ONE FURTHER.
THAT'S A TRICK I WON'T BE ABLE TO USE AGAIN. NOT FOR A LONG WHILE, IF EVER. SO HERE I AM, EXPOSING A WEAKNESS TO YOU.
LET'S BE PALS AGAIN, ALEC. WE'RE BETTER THAN THIS.
CONSTANTINE IS A LIAR--BUT AT LEAST I KNOW HE'S A LIAR.
BESIDES, I HAVE OTHER ISSUES TO DEAL WITH.
FINE.
I WOULD BE GRATEFUL FOR ANYTHING YOU COULD TELL ME ABOUT SEEDER. BUT FIRST, LET ME DEAL WITH THIS TREE. IT HAS TO GO.
WELL NOW HOLD ON MOMENT

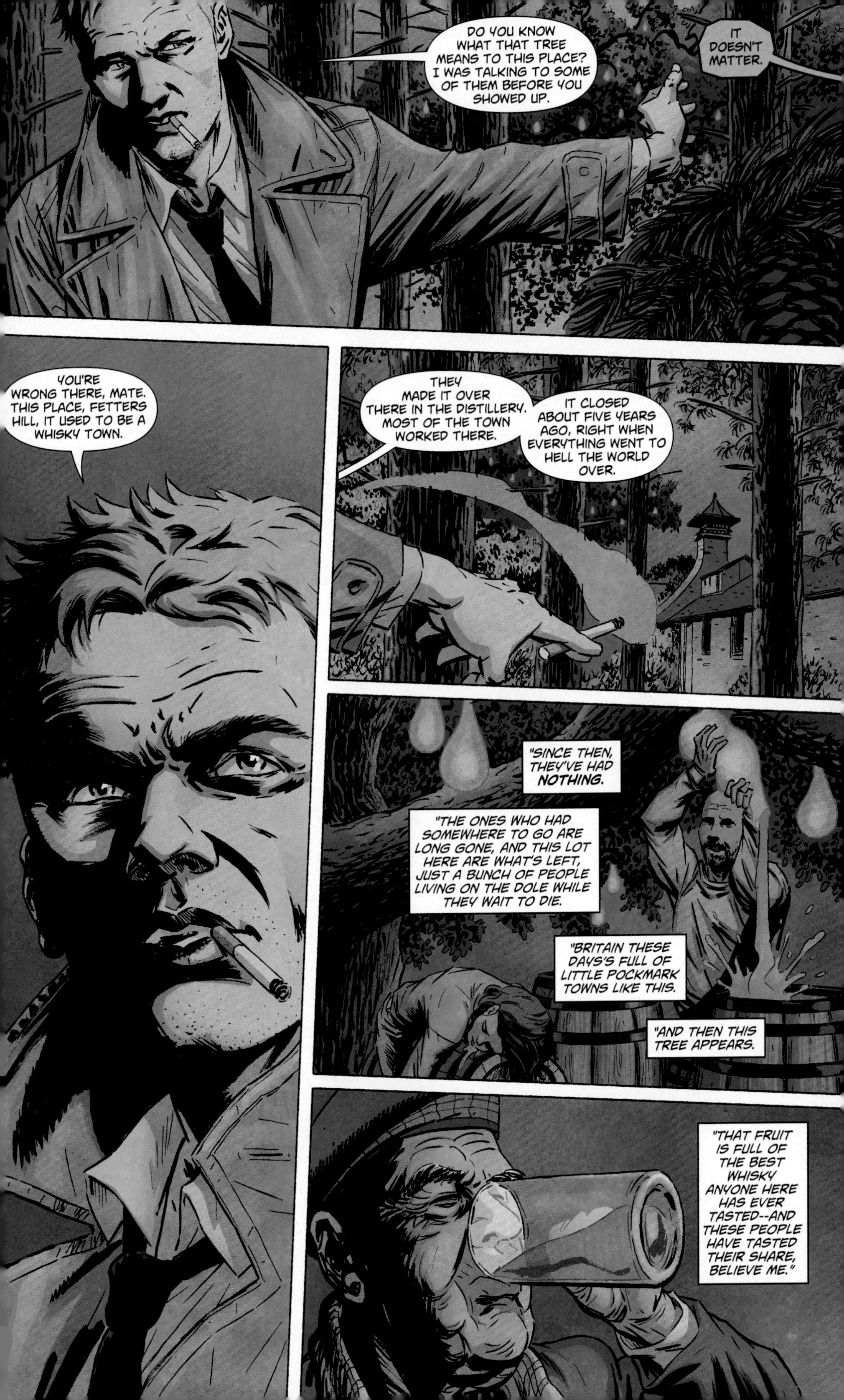

DO YOU KNOW WHAT THAT TREE MEANS TO THIS PLACE? I WAS TALKING TO SOME OF THEM BEFORE YOU SHOWED UP.
IT DOESN'T MATTER.
YOU'RE WRONG THERE, MATE. THIS PLACE, FETTERS HILL, IT USED TO BE A WHISKY TOWN.
THEY MADE IT OVER THERE IN THE DISTILLERY. MOST OF THE TOWN WORKED THERE.
IT CLOSED ABOUT FIVE YEARS AGO, RIGHT WHEN EVERYTHING WENT TO HELL THE WORLD OVER.
"SINCE THEN, THEY'VE HAD **NOTHING**.
"THE ONES WHO HAD SOMEWHERE TO GO ARE LONG GONE, AND THIS LOT HERE ARE WHAT'S LEFT, JUST A BUNCH OF PEOPLE LIVING ON THE DOLE WHILE THEY WAIT TO DIE.
"BRITAIN THESE DAYS'S FULL OF LITTLE POCKMARK TOWNS LIKE THIS.
"AND THEN THIS TREE APPEARS.
"THAT FRUIT IS FULL OF THE BEST WHISKY ANYONE HERE HAS EVER TASTED--AND THESE PEOPLE HAVE TASTED THEIR SHARE, BELIEVE ME."

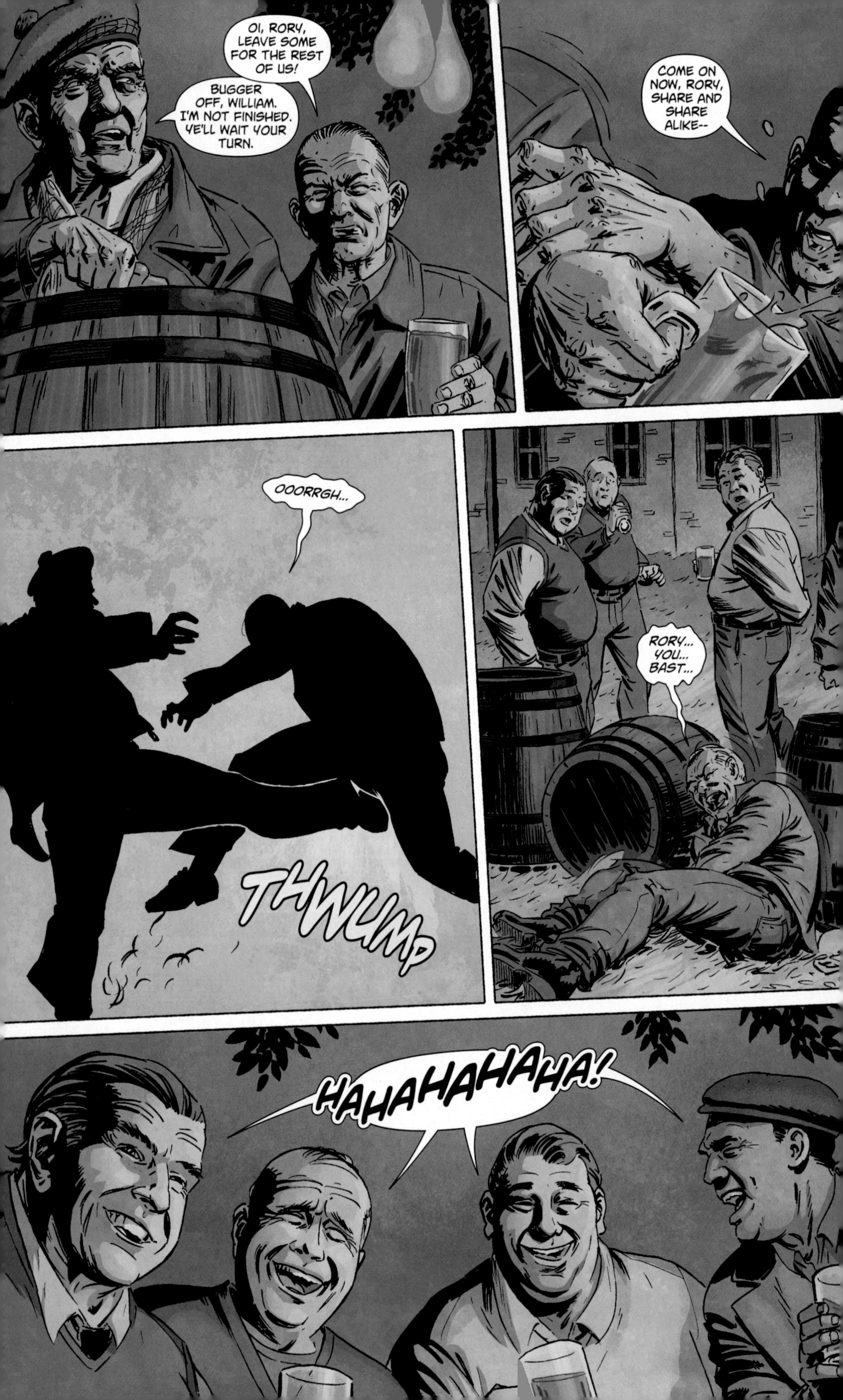
OI, RORY, LEAVE SOME FOR THE REST OF US!
BUGGER OFF, WILLIAM. I'M NOT FINISHED. YE'LL WAIT YOUR TURN.
COME ON NOW, RORY, SHARE AND SHARE ALIKE--
OOORRGH...
THWUMP
RORY... YOU... BAST...
HAHAHAHAHAHA!

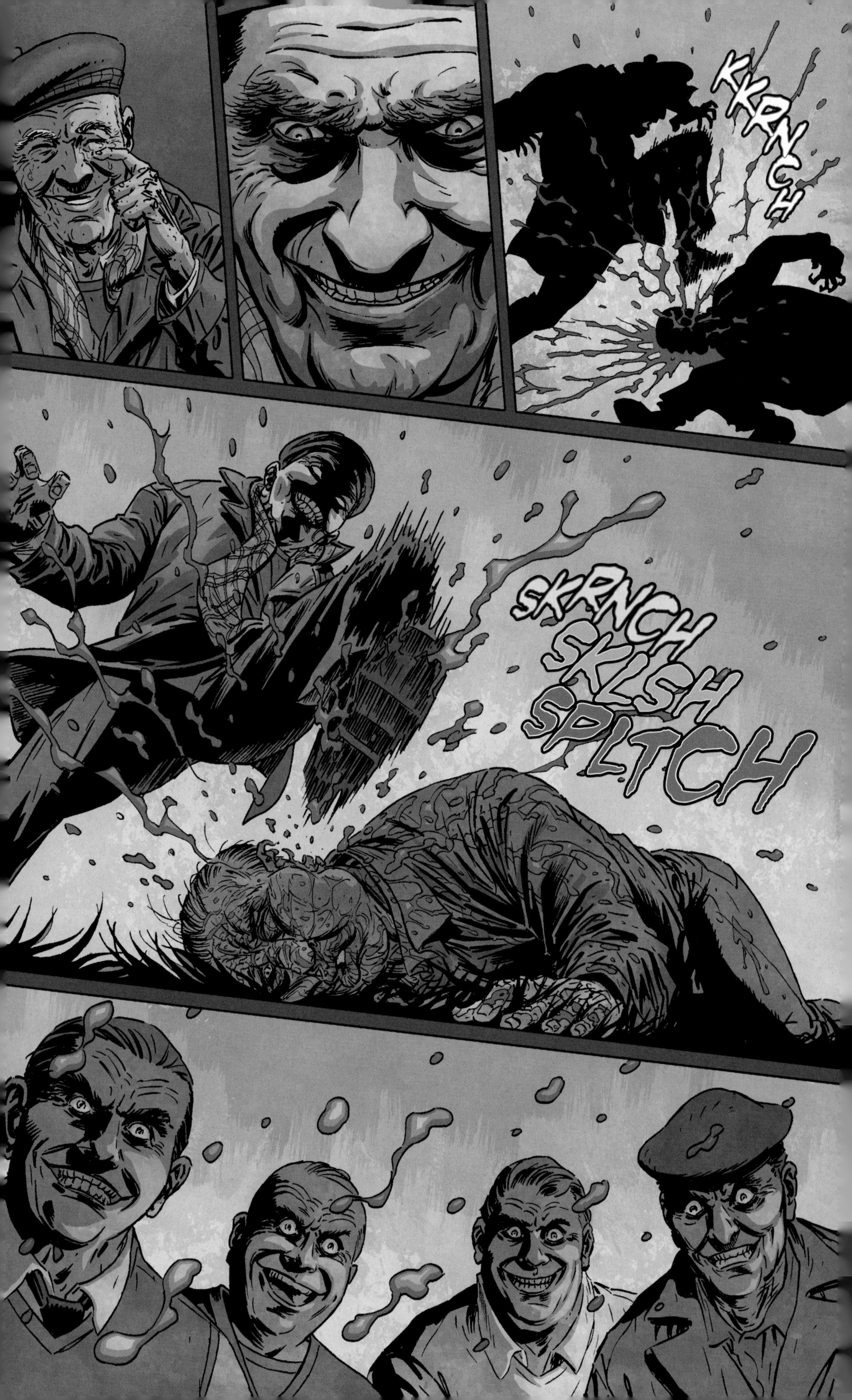
KKRNCH
SKRNCH
SKLSH
SPLTCH

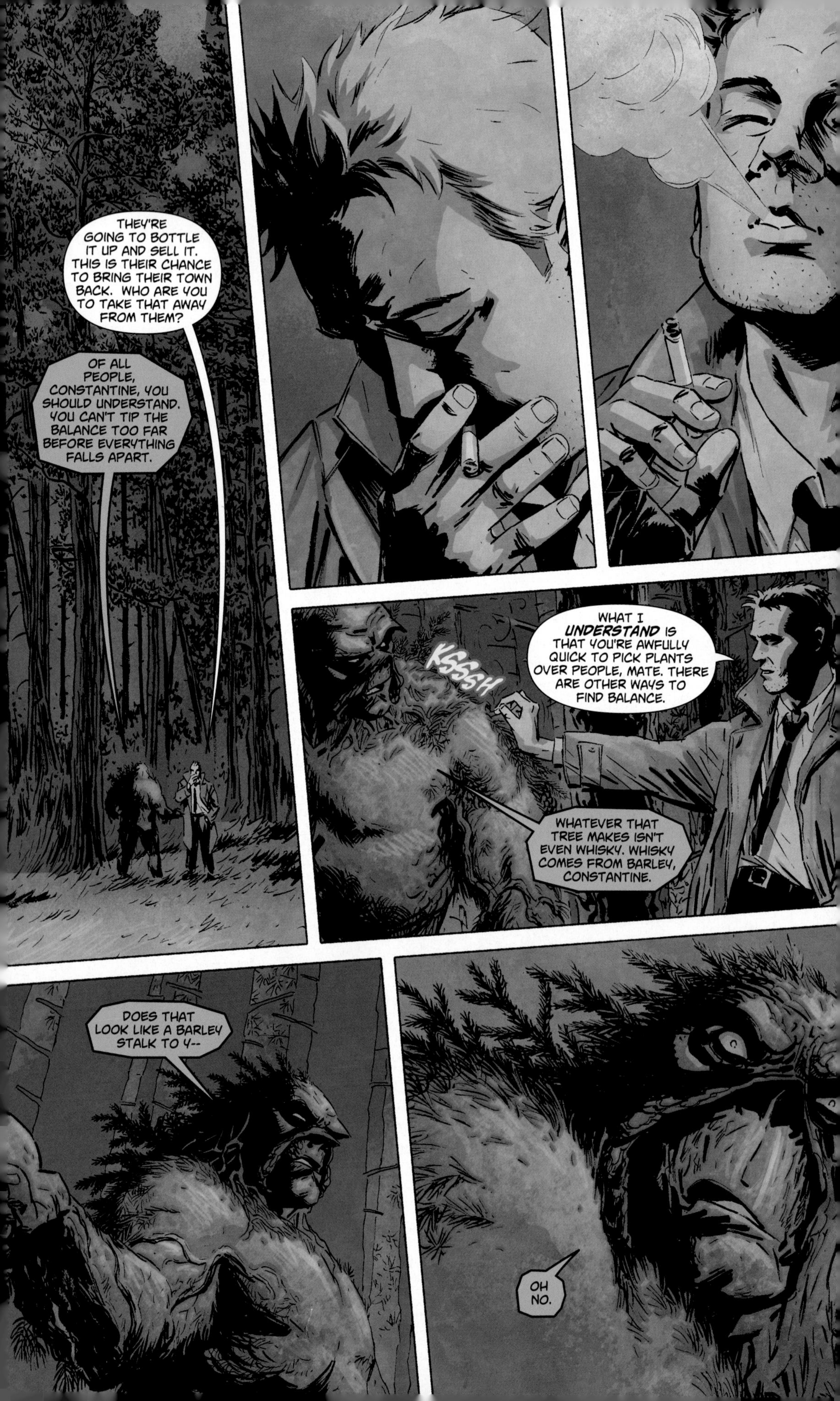
THEY'RE GOING TO BOTTLE IT UP AND SELL IT. THIS IS THEIR CHANCE TO BRING THEIR TOWN BACK. WHO ARE YOU TO TAKE THAT AWAY FROM THEM?
OF ALL PEOPLE, CONSTANTINE, YOU SHOULD UNDERSTAND. YOU CAN'T TIP THE BALANCE TOO FAR BEFORE EVERYTHING FALLS APART.
KSSSH
WHAT I UNDERSTAND IS THAT YOU'RE AWFULLY QUICK TO PICK PLANTS OVER PEOPLE, MATE. THERE ARE OTHER WAYS TO FIND BALANCE.
WHATEVER THAT TREE MAKES ISN'T EVEN WHISKY. WHISKY COMES FROM BARLEY, CONSTANTINE.
DOES THAT LOOK LIKE A BARLEY STALK TO Y--
OH NO.

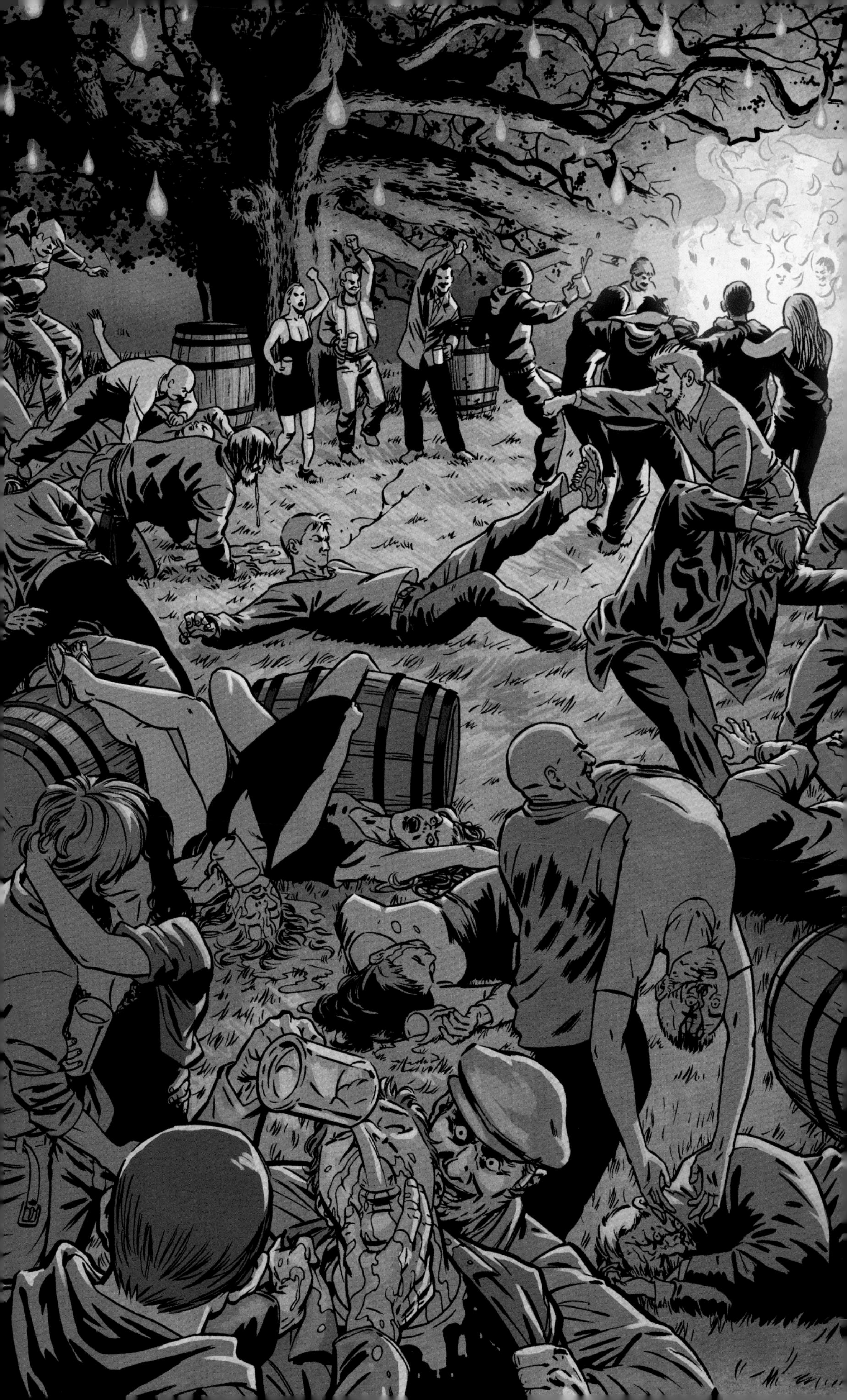

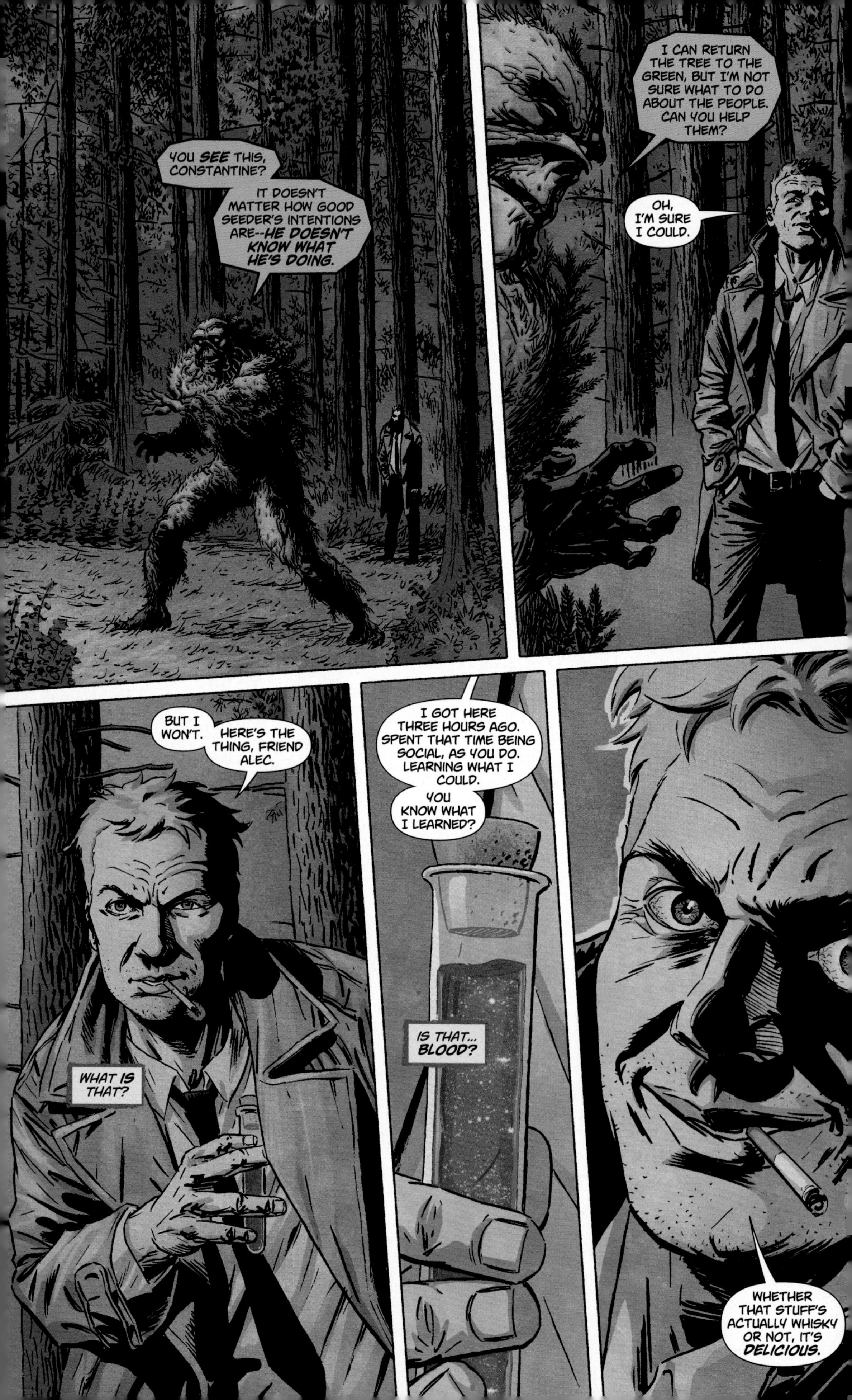

YOU **SEE** THIS, CONSTANTINE?
IT DOESN'T MATTER HOW GOOD SEEDER'S INTENTIONS ARE--***HE DOESN'T KNOW WHAT HE'S DOING.***
I CAN RETURN THE TREE TO THE GREEN, BUT I'M NOT SURE WHAT TO DO ABOUT THE PEOPLE. CAN YOU HELP THEM?
OH, I'M SURE I COULD.
BUT I WON'T.
HERE'S THE THING, FRIEND ALEC.
*WHAT **IS** THAT?*
I GOT HERE THREE HOURS AGO. SPENT THAT TIME BEING SOCIAL, AS YOU DO. LEARNING WHAT I COULD.
YOU KNOW WHAT I LEARNED?
*IS THAT... **BLOOD?***
WHETHER THAT STUFF'S ACTUALLY WHISKY OR NOT, IT'S ***DELICIOUS.***

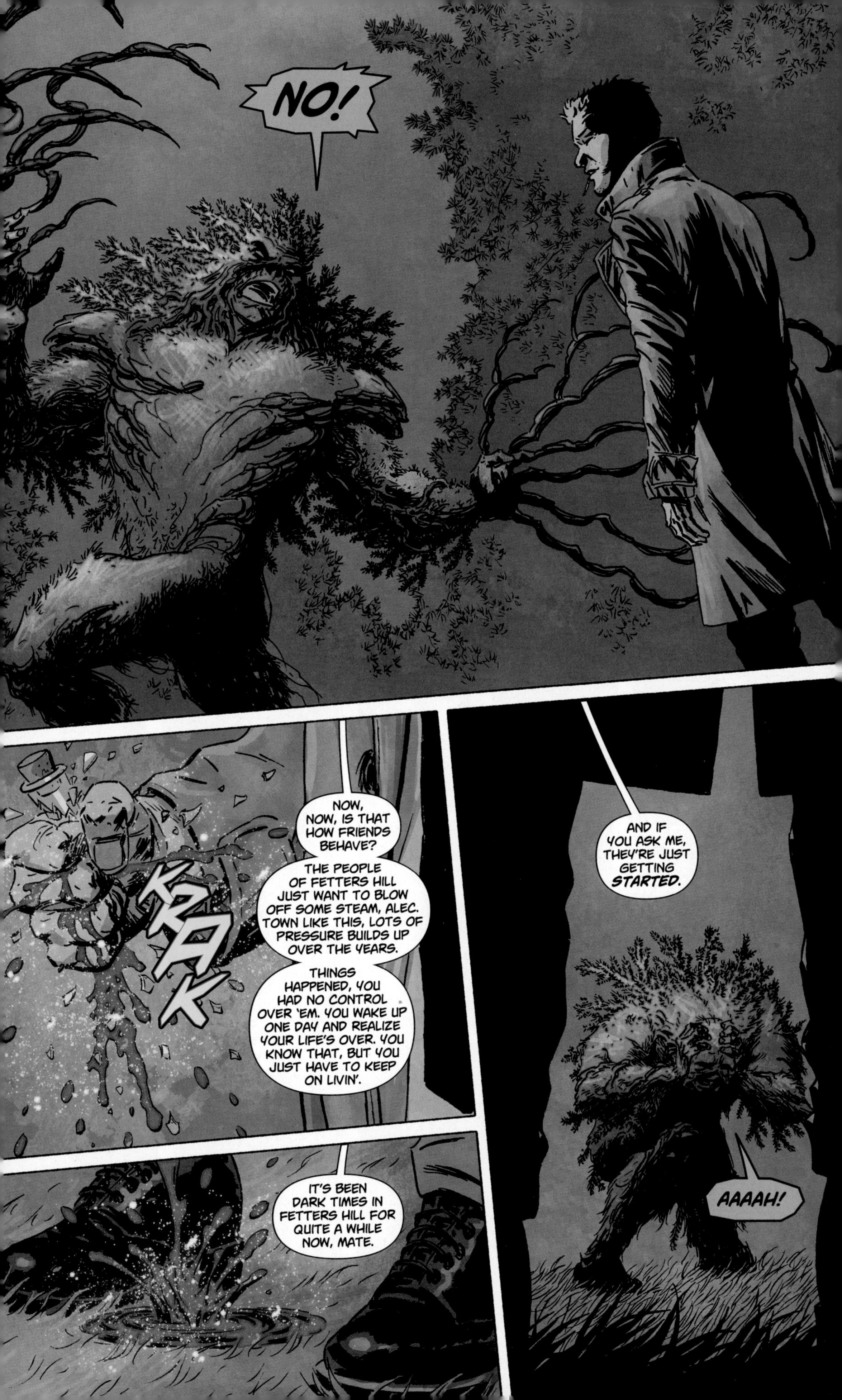
NO!
KRAK
NOW, NOW, IS THAT HOW FRIENDS BEHAVE?
THE PEOPLE OF FETTERS HILL JUST WANT TO BLOW OFF SOME STEAM, ALEC. TOWN LIKE THIS, LOTS OF PRESSURE BUILDS UP OVER THE YEARS.
THINGS HAPPENED, YOU HAD NO CONTROL OVER 'EM. YOU WAKE UP ONE DAY AND REALIZE YOUR LIFE'S OVER. YOU KNOW THAT, BUT YOU JUST HAVE TO KEEP ON LIVIN'.
IT'S BEEN DARK TIMES IN FETTERS HILL FOR QUITE A WHILE NOW, MATE.
AND IF YOU ASK ME, THEY'RE JUST GETTING STARTED.
AAAAH!

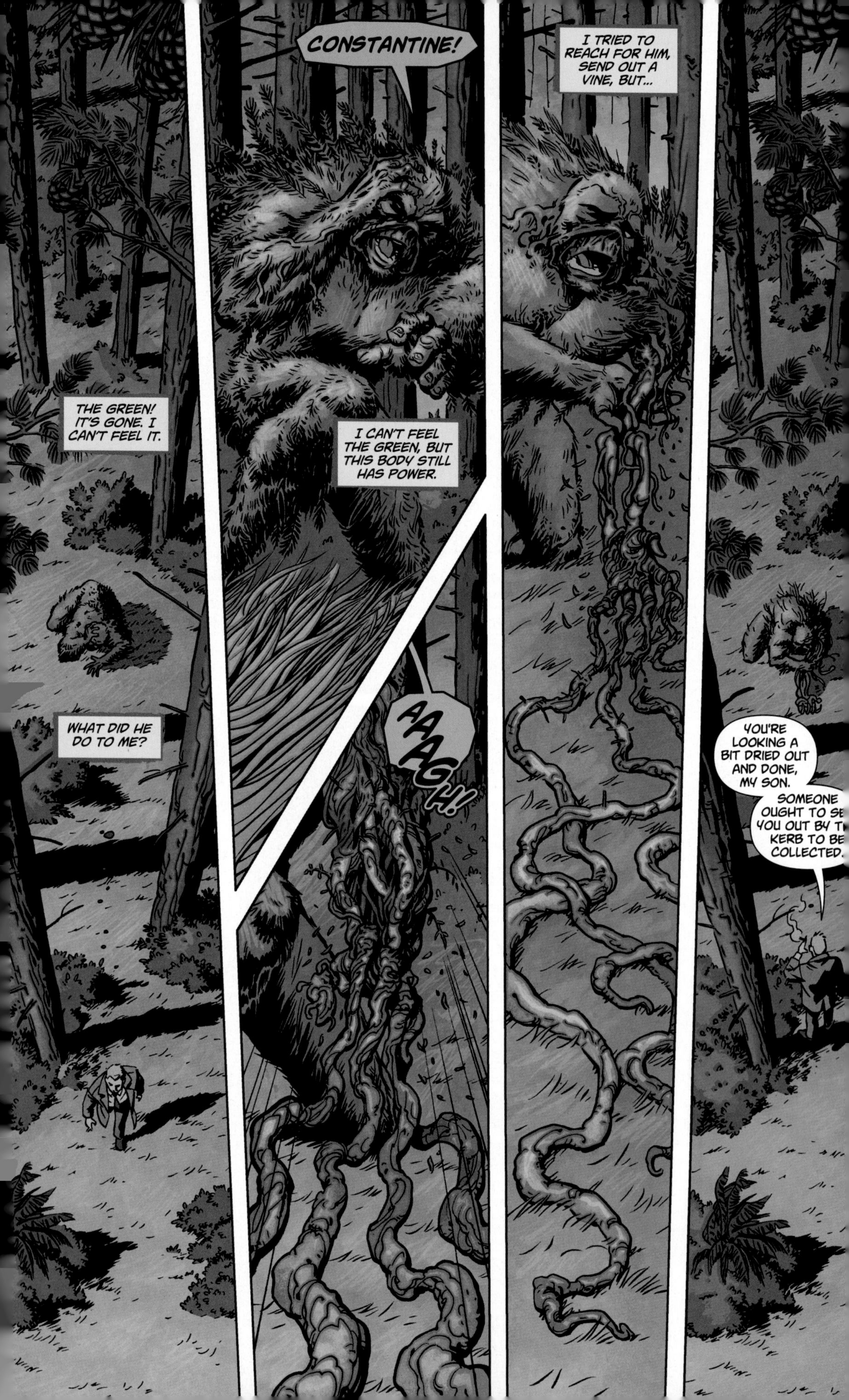
THE GREEN! IT'S GONE. I CAN'T FEEL IT.
WHAT DID HE DO TO ME?
CONSTANTINE!
I CAN'T FEEL THE GREEN, BUT THIS BODY STILL HAS POWER.
AAAGH!
I TRIED TO REACH FOR HIM, SEND OUT A VINE, BUT...
YOU'RE LOOKING A BIT DRIED OUT AND DONE, MY SON.
SOMEONE OUGHT TO SE YOU OUT BY T KERB TO BE COLLECTED.

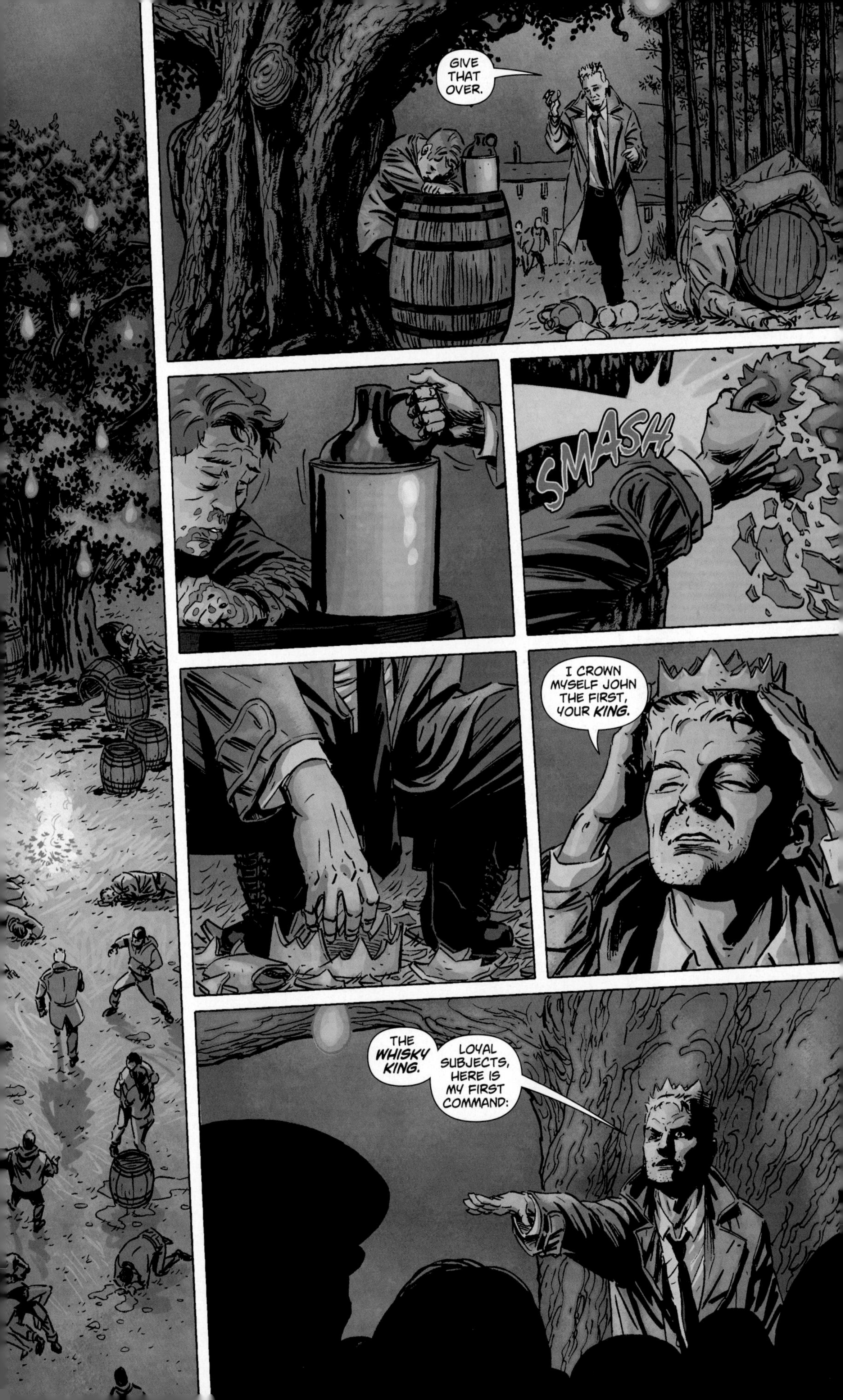

GIVE THAT OVER.
SMASH
I CROWN MYSELF JOHN THE FIRST, YOUR KING.
THE WHISKY KING.
LOYAL SUBJECTS, HERE IS MY FIRST COMMAND:

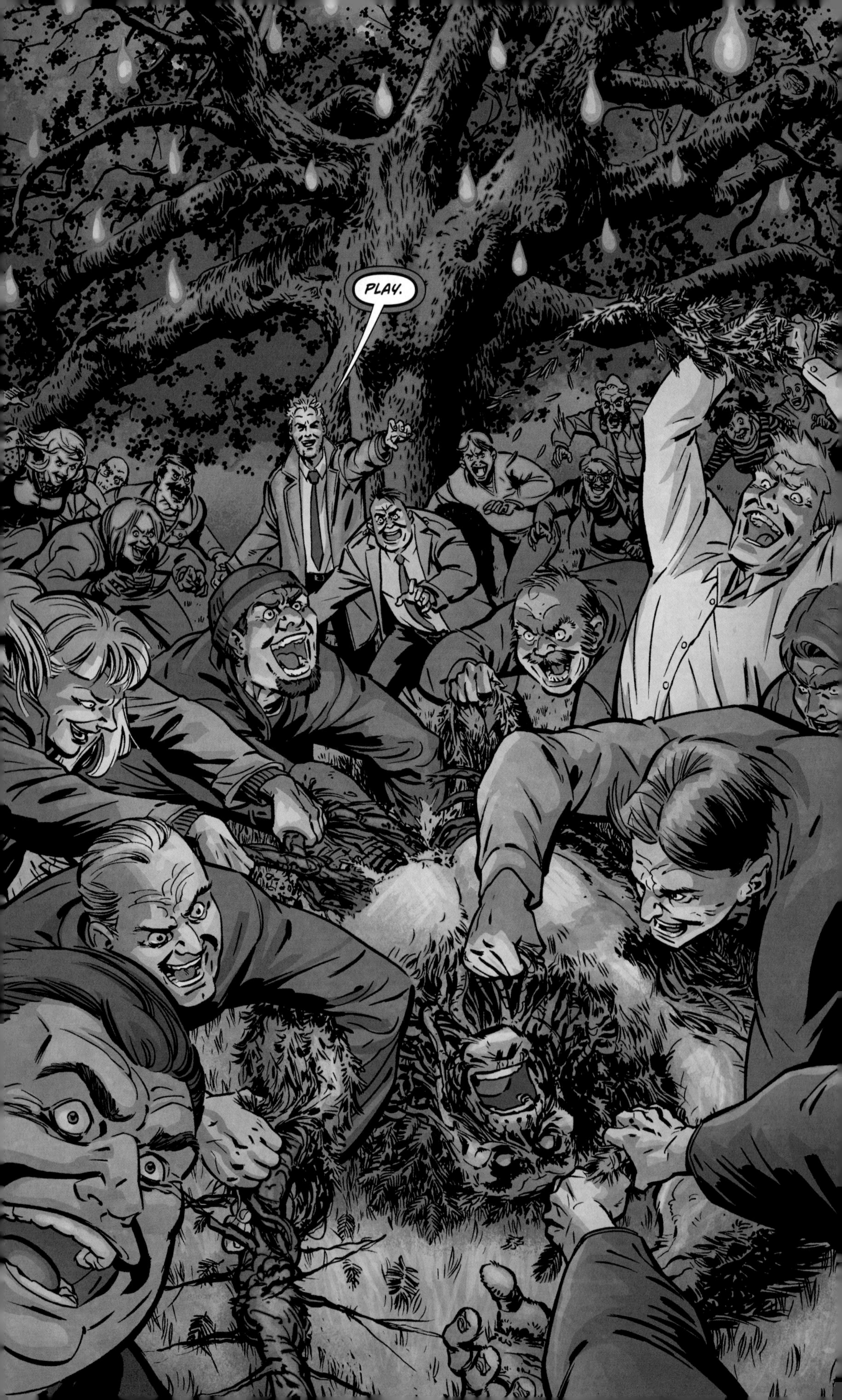
PLAY.

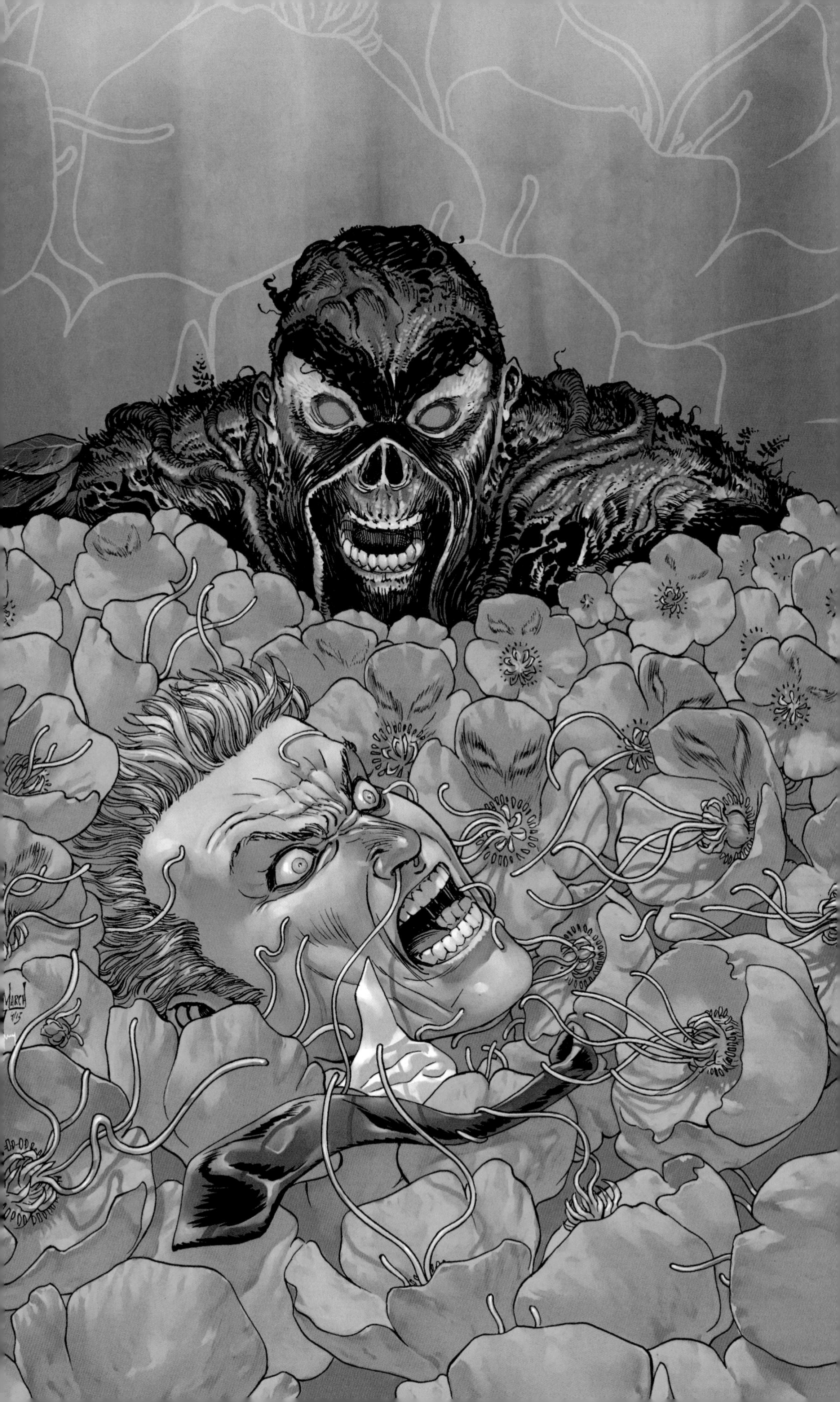
MARCH

## THE WHISKEY TREE: PART 2

**CHARLES SOULE** writer **KANO & DAVID LAPHAM** pencillers **DAVID LAPHAM, ALVARO LOPEZ & KANO** inkers
cover art by **GUILLEM MARCH & TOMEU MOREY**

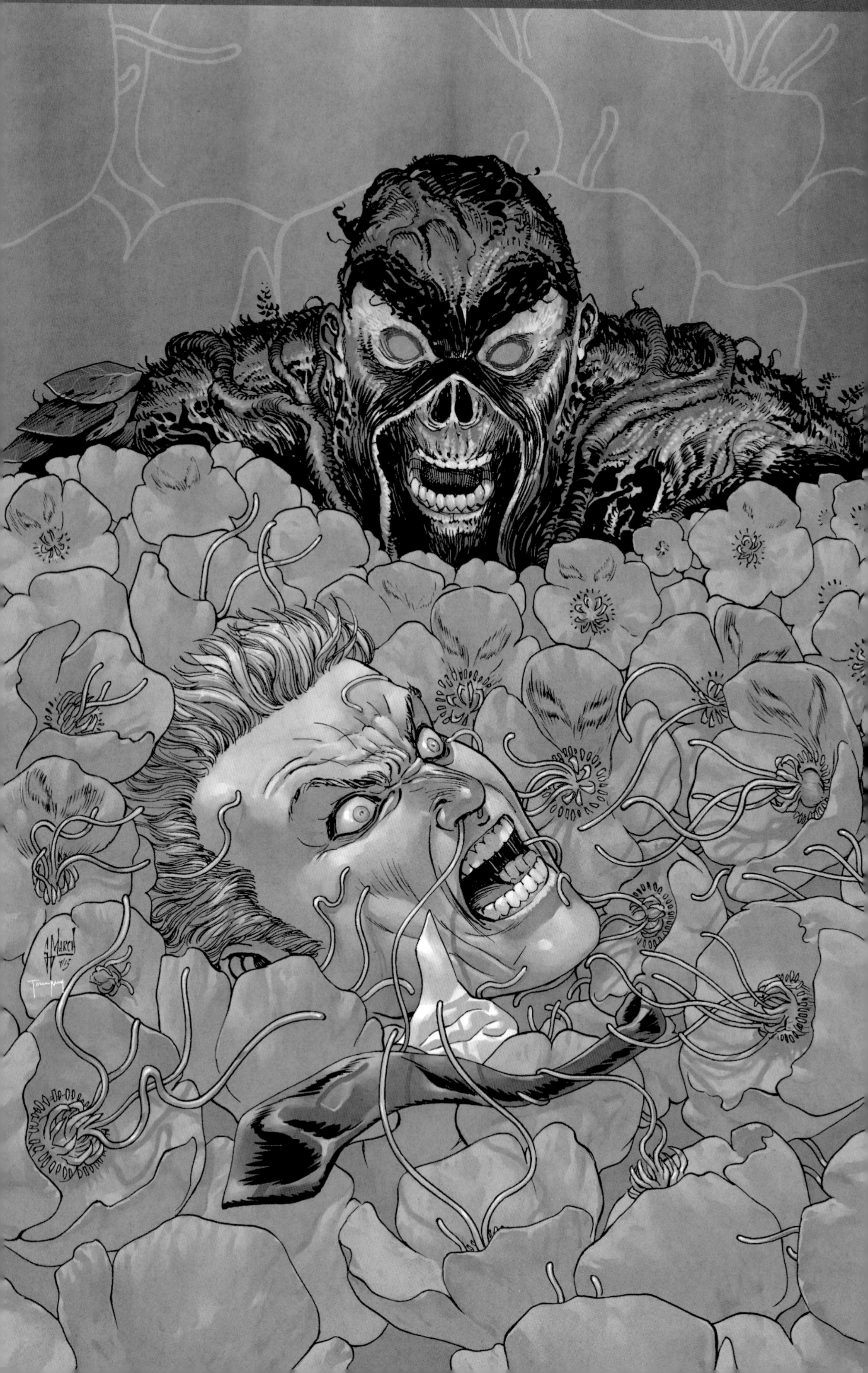

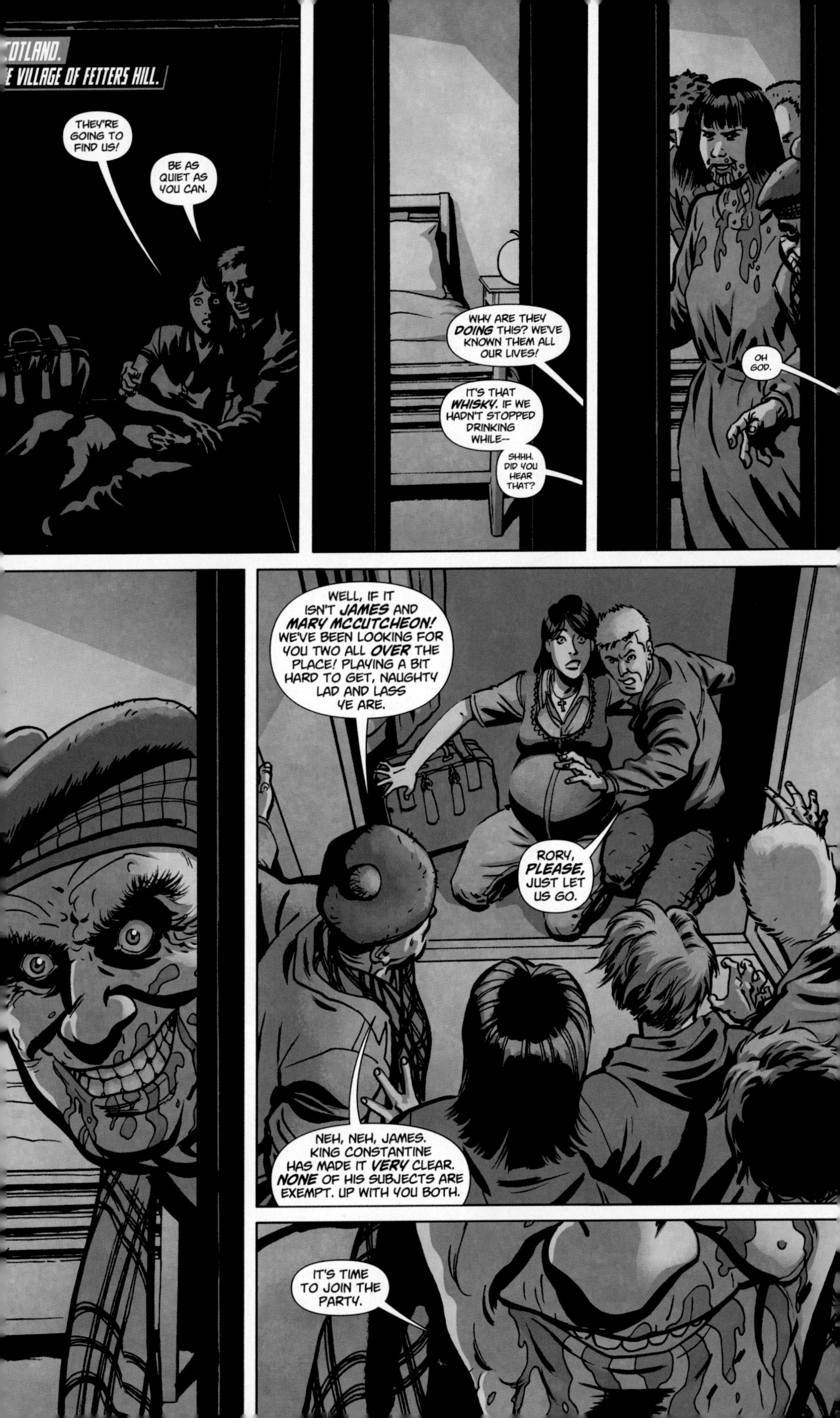

COTLAND.
E VILLAGE OF FETTERS HILL.
THEY'RE GOING TO FIND US!
BE AS QUIET AS YOU CAN.
WHY ARE THEY DOING THIS? WE'VE KNOWN THEM ALL OUR LIVES!
IT'S THAT WHISKY. IF WE HADN'T STOPPED DRINKING WHILE--
SHHH. DID YOU HEAR THAT?
OH GOD.
WELL, IF IT ISN'T JAMES AND MARY MCCUTCHEON! WE'VE BEEN LOOKING FOR YOU TWO ALL OVER THE PLACE! PLAYING A BIT HARD TO GET, NAUGHTY LAD AND LASS YE ARE.
RORY, PLEASE, JUST LET US GO.
NEH, NEH, JAMES. KING CONSTANTINE HAS MADE IT VERY CLEAR. NONE OF HIS SUBJECTS ARE EXEMPT. UP WITH YOU BOTH.
IT'S TIME TO JOIN THE PARTY.

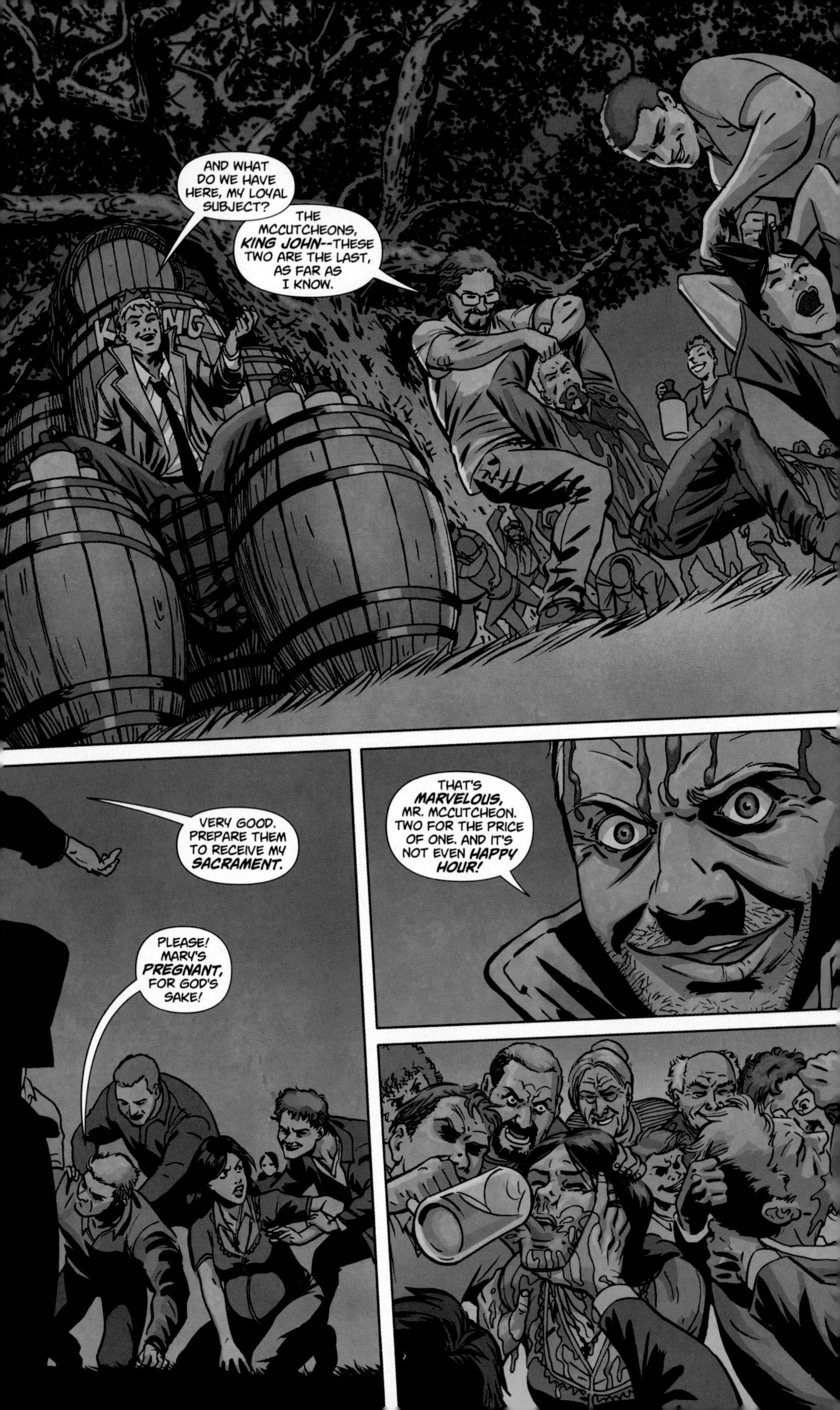
AND WHAT DO WE HAVE HERE, MY LOYAL SUBJECT?
THE MCCUTCHEONS, KING JOHN--THESE TWO ARE THE LAST, AS FAR AS I KNOW.
KING
VERY GOOD. PREPARE THEM TO RECEIVE MY SACRAMENT.
PLEASE! MARY'S PREGNANT, FOR GOD'S SAKE!
THAT'S MARVELOUS, MR. MCCUTCHEON. TWO FOR THE PRICE OF ONE. AND IT'S NOT EVEN HAPPY HOUR!

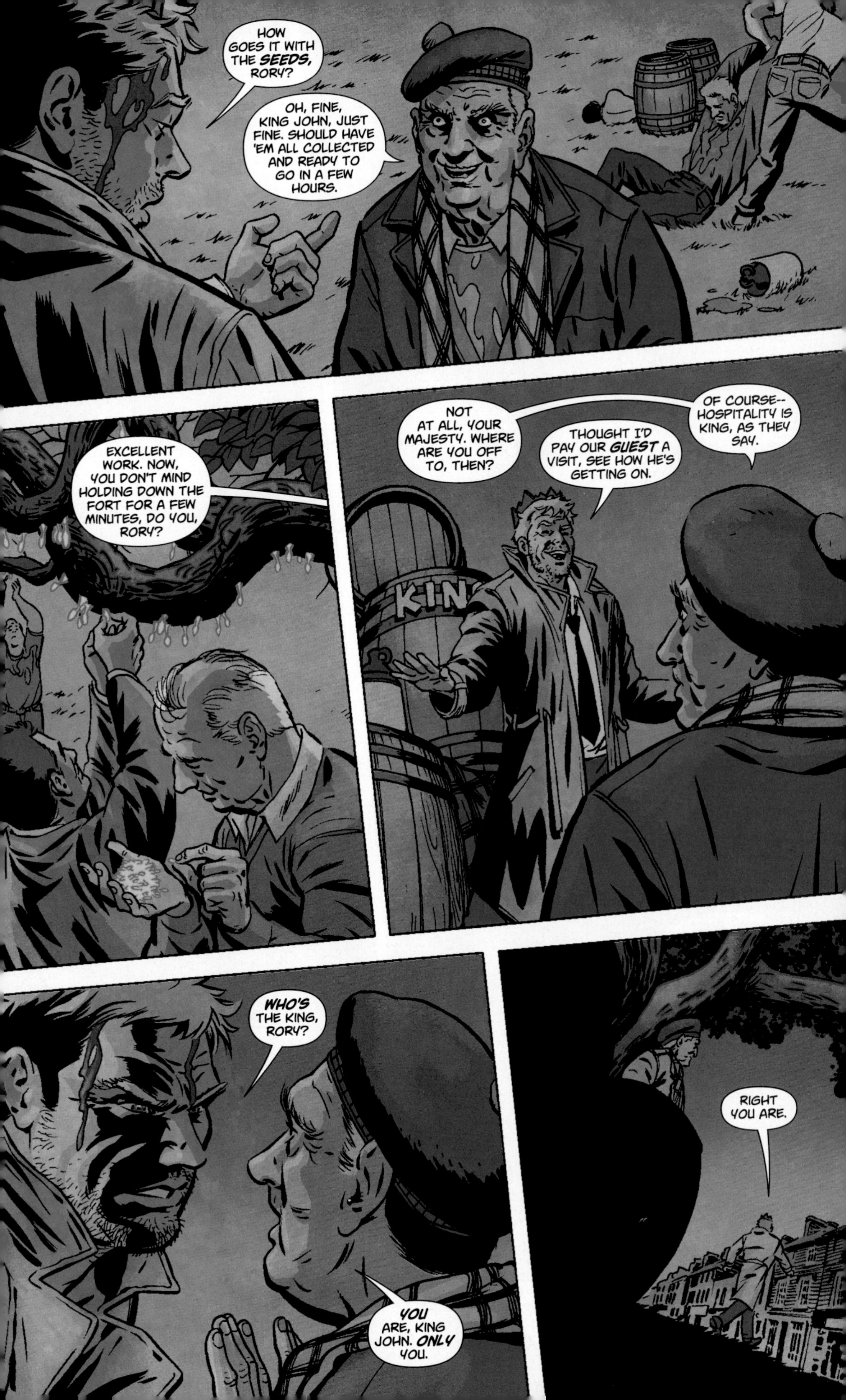
HOW GOES IT WITH THE SEEDS, RORY?
OH, FINE, KING JOHN, JUST FINE. SHOULD HAVE 'EM ALL COLLECTED AND READY TO GO IN A FEW HOURS.
EXCELLENT WORK. NOW, YOU DON'T MIND HOLDING DOWN THE FORT FOR A FEW MINUTES, DO YOU, RORY?
NOT AT ALL, YOUR MAJESTY. WHERE ARE YOU OFF TO, THEN?
THOUGHT I'D PAY OUR GUEST A VISIT, SEE HOW HE'S GETTING ON.
OF COURSE-- HOSPITALITY IS KING, AS THEY SAY.
KIN
WHO'S THE KING, RORY?
YOU ARE, KING JOHN. ONLY YOU.
RIGHT YOU ARE.

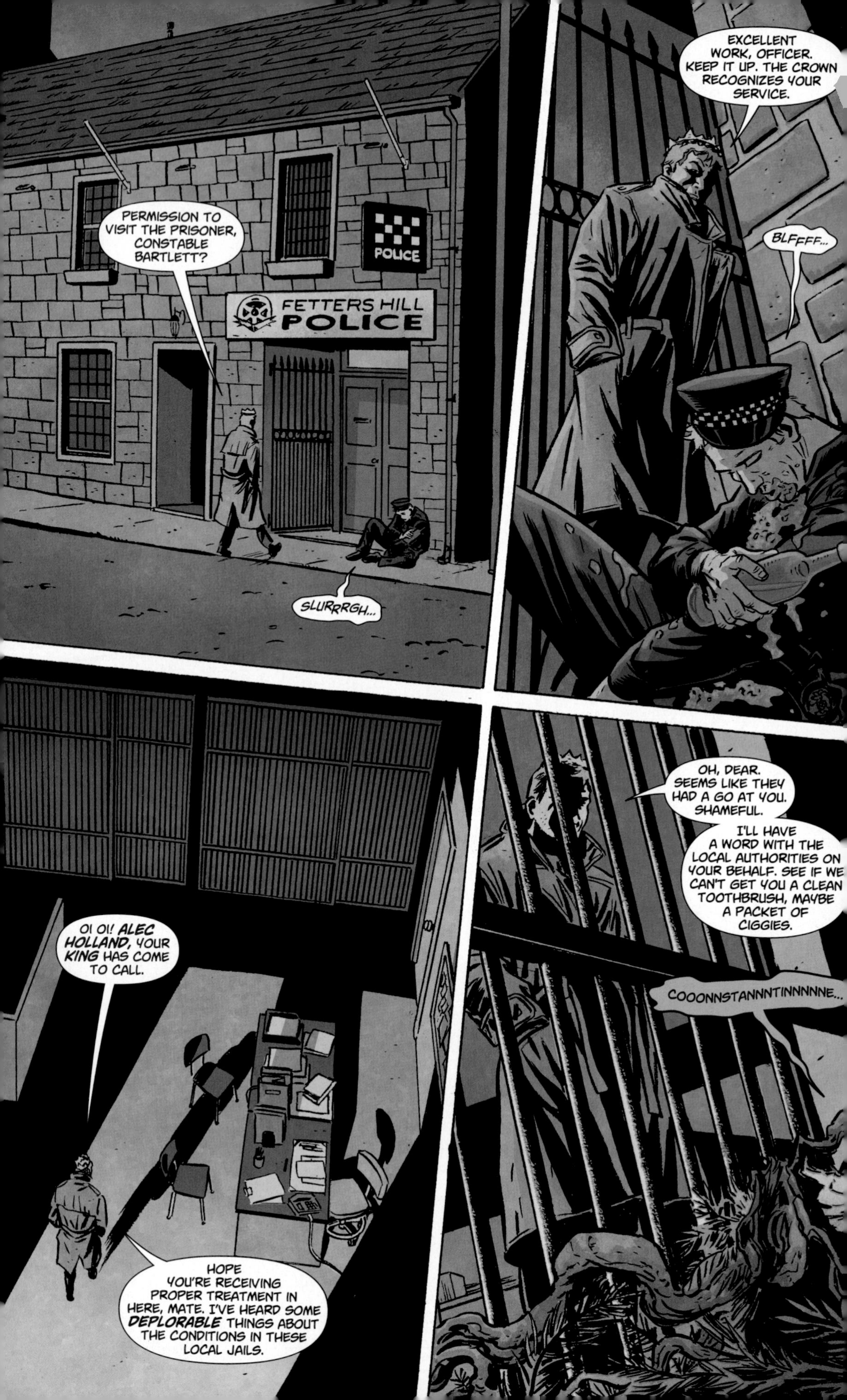
PERMISSION TO VISIT THE PRISONER, CONSTABLE BARTLETT?
FETTERS HILL POLICE
POLICE
SLURRRGH...
EXCELLENT WORK, OFFICER. KEEP IT UP. THE CROWN RECOGNIZES YOUR SERVICE.
BLFFFF...
OI OI! ALEC HOLLAND, YOUR KING HAS COME TO CALL.
HOPE YOU'RE RECEIVING PROPER TREATMENT IN HERE, MATE. I'VE HEARD SOME DEPLORABLE THINGS ABOUT THE CONDITIONS IN THESE LOCAL JAILS.
OH, DEAR. SEEMS LIKE THEY HAD A GO AT YOU. SHAMEFUL.
I'LL HAVE A WORD WITH THE LOCAL AUTHORITIES ON YOUR BEHALF. SEE IF WE CAN'T GET YOU A CLEAN TOOTHBRUSH, MAYBE A PACKET OF CIGGIES.
COOONNSTANNNTINNNNNE...

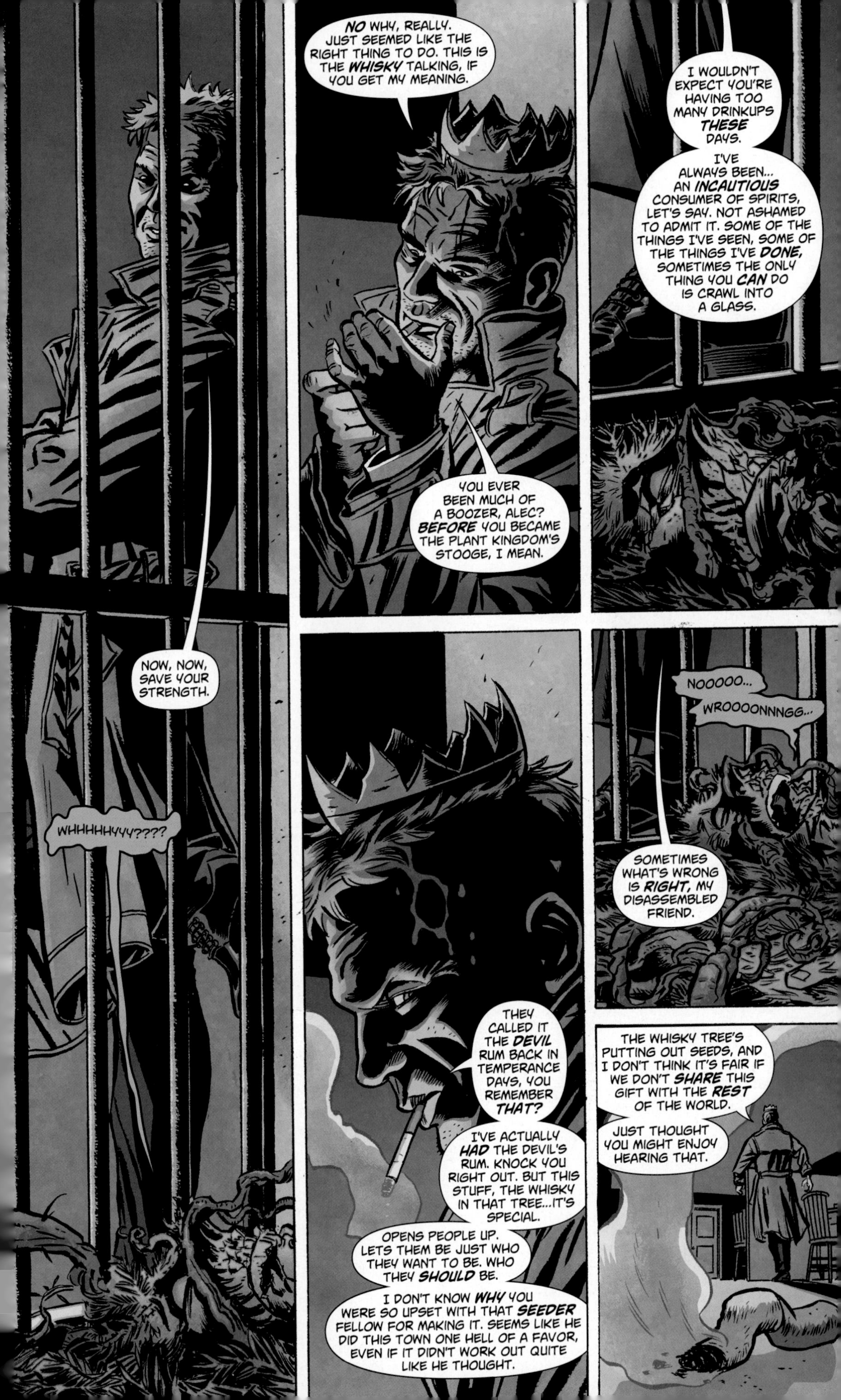
NO WHY, REALLY. JUST SEEMED LIKE THE RIGHT THING TO DO. THIS IS THE WHISKY TALKING, IF YOU GET MY MEANING.
YOU EVER BEEN MUCH OF A BOOZER, ALEC? BEFORE YOU BECAME THE PLANT KINGDOM'S STOOGE, I MEAN.
I WOULDN'T EXPECT YOU'RE HAVING TOO MANY DRINKUPS THESE DAYS.
I'VE ALWAYS BEEN... AN INCAUTIOUS CONSUMER OF SPIRITS, LET'S SAY. NOT ASHAMED TO ADMIT IT. SOME OF THE THINGS I'VE SEEN, SOME OF THE THINGS I'VE DONE, SOMETIMES THE ONLY THING YOU CAN DO IS CRAWL INTO A GLASS.
NOW, NOW, SAVE YOUR STRENGTH.
WHHHHHYYY????
NOOOOO...
WROOOONNNGG...
SOMETIMES WHAT'S WRONG IS RIGHT, MY DISASSEMBLED FRIEND.
THEY CALLED IT THE DEVIL RUM BACK IN TEMPERANCE DAYS, YOU REMEMBER THAT?
I'VE ACTUALLY HAD THE DEVIL'S RUM. KNOCK YOU RIGHT OUT. BUT THIS STUFF, THE WHISKY IN THAT TREE...IT'S SPECIAL.
OPENS PEOPLE UP. LETS THEM BE JUST WHO THEY WANT TO BE. WHO THEY SHOULD BE.
I DON'T KNOW WHY YOU WERE SO UPSET WITH THAT SEEDER FELLOW FOR MAKING IT. SEEMS LIKE HE DID THIS TOWN ONE HELL OF A FAVOR, EVEN IF IT DIDN'T WORK OUT QUITE LIKE HE THOUGHT.
THE WHISKY TREE'S PUTTING OUT SEEDS, AND I DON'T THINK IT'S FAIR IF WE DON'T SHARE THIS GIFT WITH THE REST OF THE WORLD.
JUST THOUGHT YOU MIGHT ENJOY HEARING THAT.

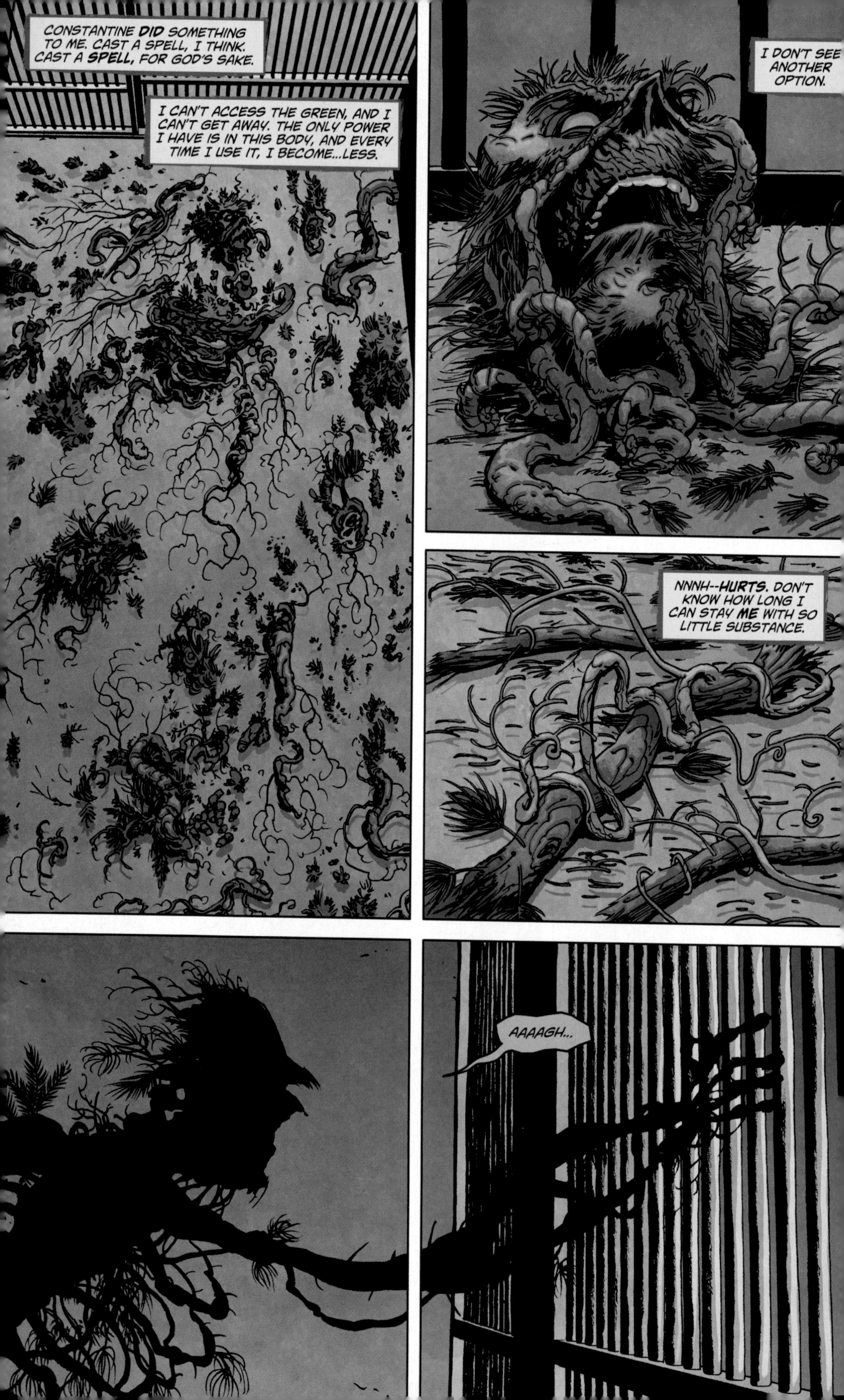
CONSTANTINE **DID** SOMETHING TO ME. CAST A SPELL, I THINK. CAST A **SPELL**, FOR GOD'S SAKE.
I CAN'T ACCESS THE GREEN, AND I CAN'T GET AWAY. THE ONLY POWER I HAVE IS IN THIS BODY, AND EVERY TIME I USE IT, I BECOME...LESS.
I DON'T SEE ANOTHER OPTION.
NNNH--**HURTS.** DON'T KNOW HOW LONG I CAN STAY **ME** WITH SO LITTLE SUBSTANCE.
AAAAGH...

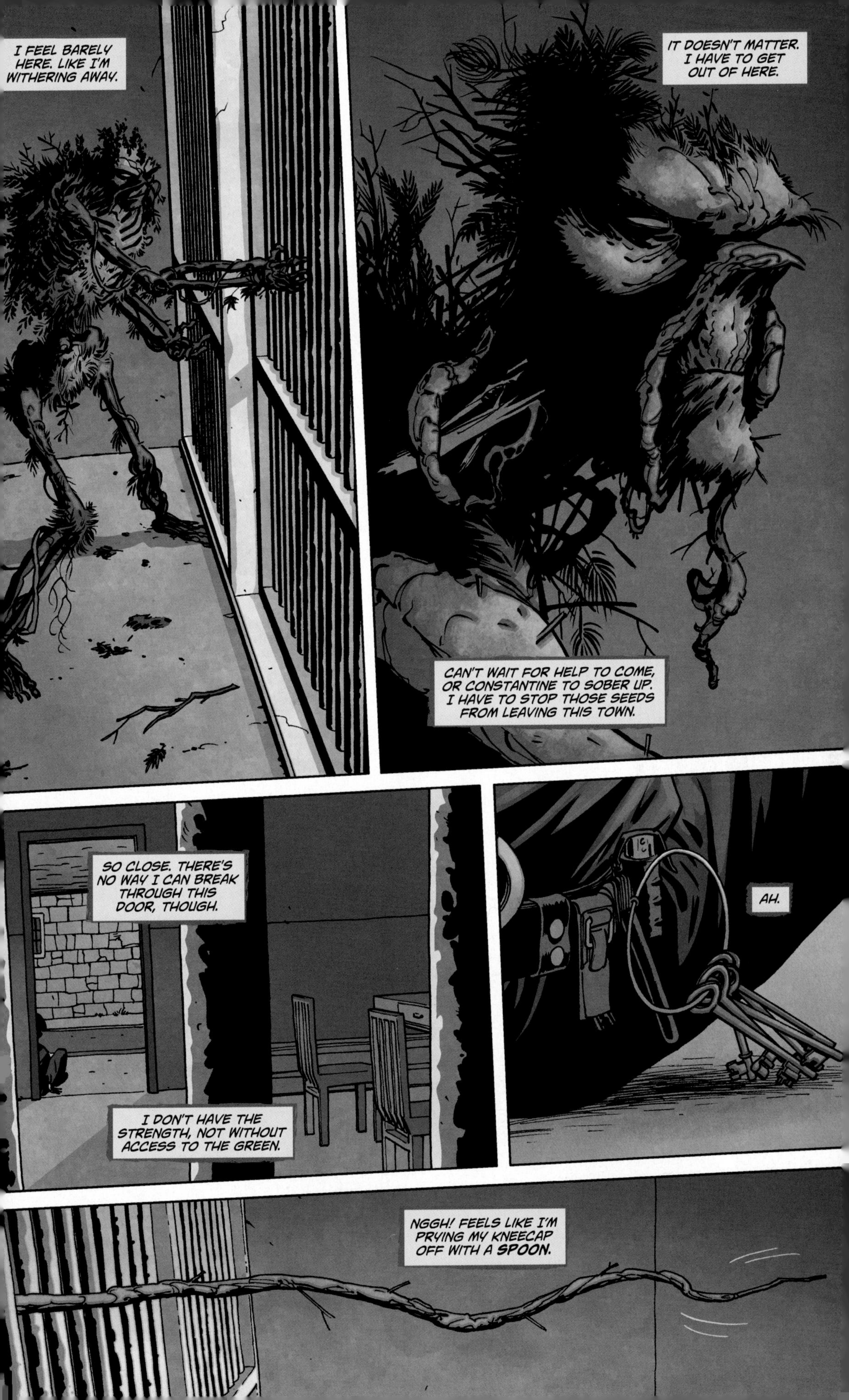
I FEEL BARELY HERE. LIKE I'M WITHERING AWAY.
IT DOESN'T MATTER. I HAVE TO GET OUT OF HERE.
CAN'T WAIT FOR HELP TO COME, OR CONSTANTINE TO SOBER UP. I HAVE TO STOP THOSE SEEDS FROM LEAVING THIS TOWN.
SO CLOSE. THERE'S NO WAY I CAN BREAK THROUGH THIS DOOR, THOUGH.
I DON'T HAVE THE STRENGTH, NOT WITHOUT ACCESS TO THE GREEN.
AH.
NGGH! FEELS LIKE I'M PRYING MY KNEECAP OFF WITH A SPOON.

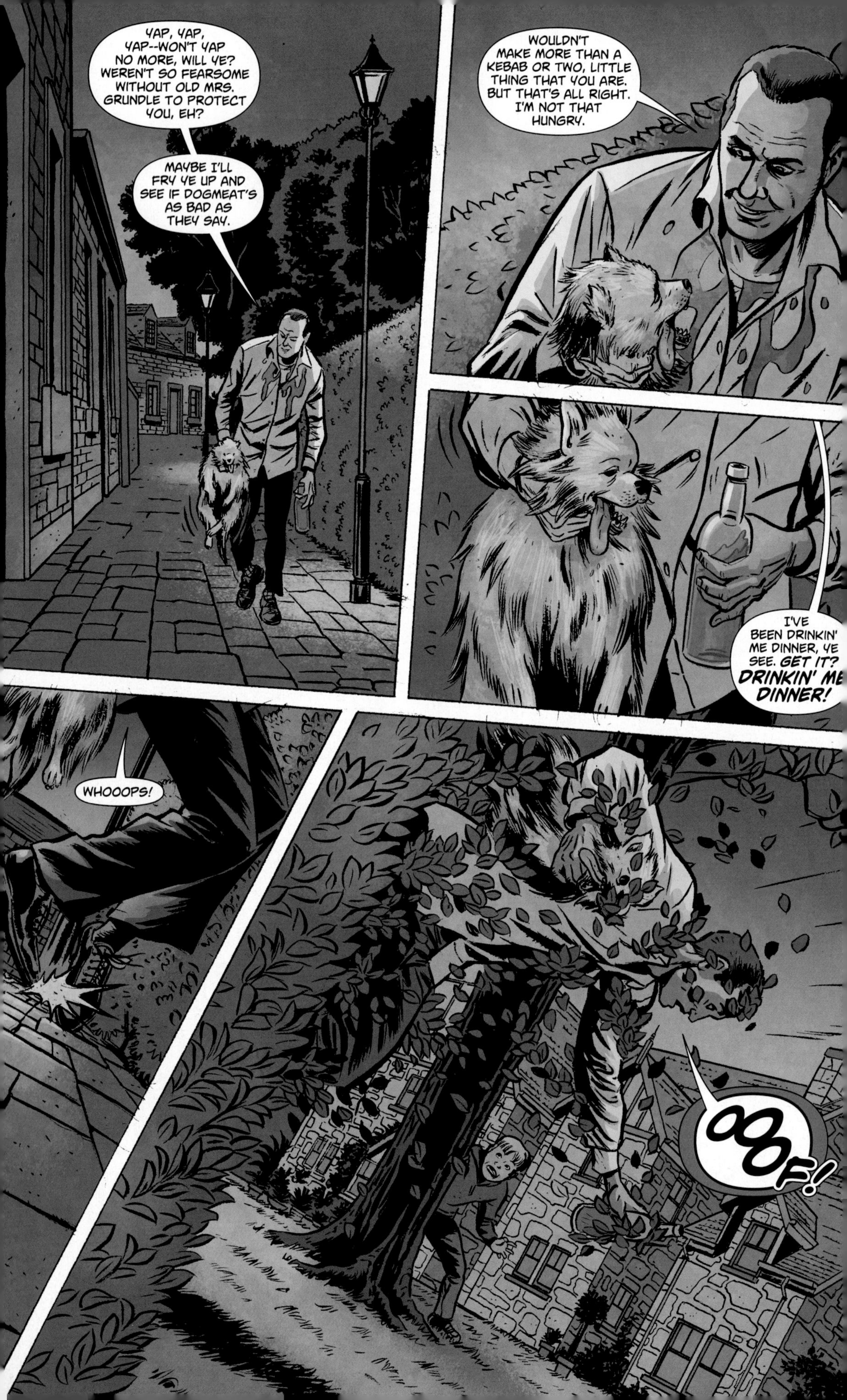

YAP, YAP, YAP--WON'T YAP NO MORE, WILL YE? WEREN'T SO FEARSOME WITHOUT OLD MRS. GRUNDLE TO PROTECT YOU, EH?
MAYBE I'LL FRY YE UP AND SEE IF DOGMEAT'S AS BAD AS THEY SAY.
WOULDN'T MAKE MORE THAN A KEBAB OR TWO, LITTLE THING THAT YOU ARE. BUT THAT'S ALL RIGHT. I'M NOT THAT HUNGRY.
I'VE BEEN DRINKIN' ME DINNER, YE SEE. GET IT? DRINKIN' ME DINNER!
WHOOOPS!
OOOF!

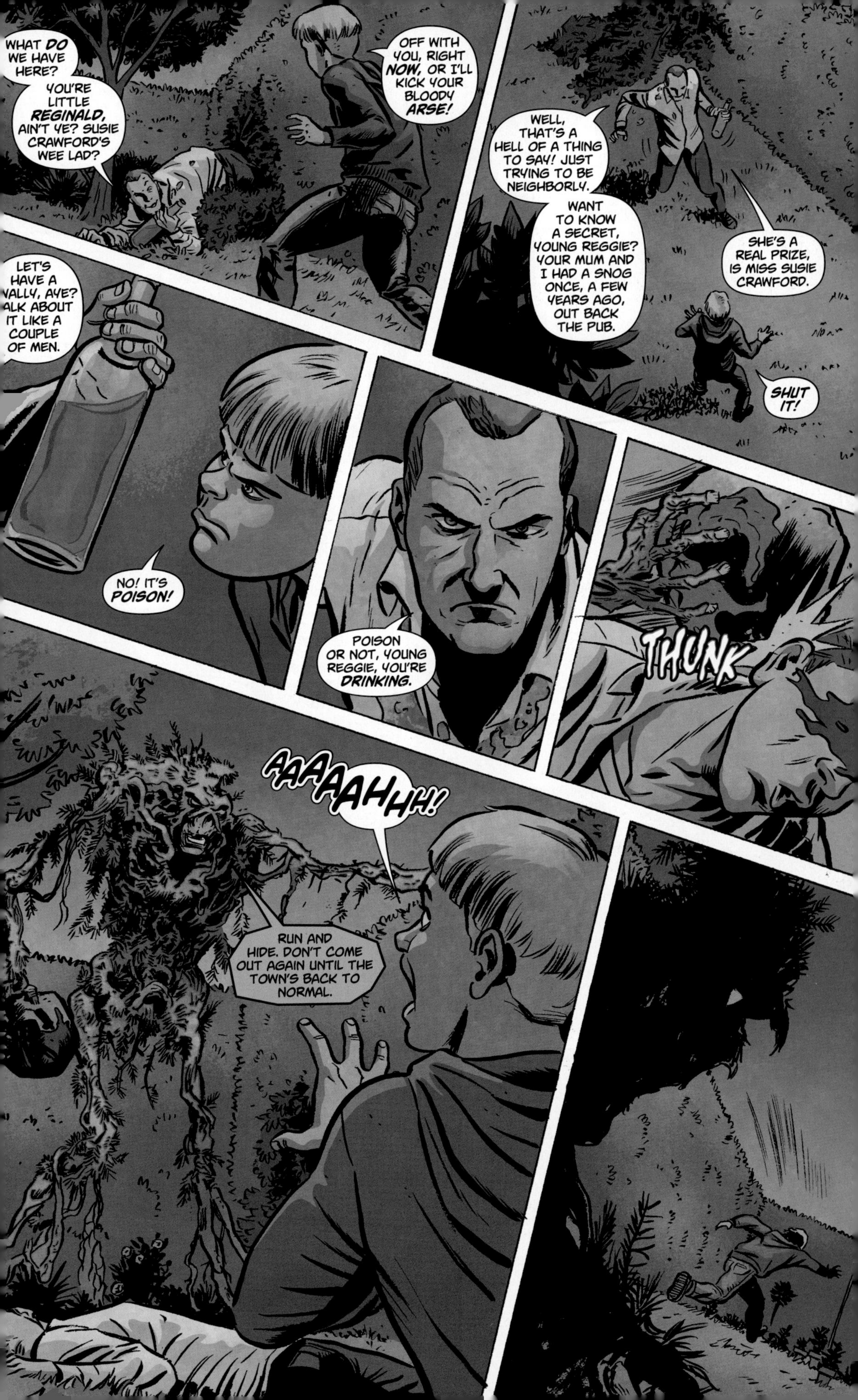
WHAT DO WE HAVE HERE?
YOU'RE LITTLE REGINALD, AIN'T YE? SUSIE CRAWFORD'S WEE LAD?
OFF WITH YOU, RIGHT NOW, OR I'LL KICK YOUR BLOODY ARSE!
WELL, THAT'S A HELL OF A THING TO SAY! JUST TRYING TO BE NEIGHBORLY.
WANT TO KNOW A SECRET, YOUNG REGGIE? YOUR MUM AND I HAD A SNOG ONCE, A FEW YEARS AGO, OUT BACK THE PUB.
SHE'S A REAL PRIZE, IS MISS SUSIE CRAWFORD.
SHUT IT!
LET'S HAVE A VALLY, AYE? ALK ABOUT IT LIKE A COUPLE OF MEN.
NO! IT'S POISON!
POISON OR NOT, YOUNG REGGIE, YOU'RE DRINKING.
THUNK
AAAAAHHHH!
RUN AND HIDE. DON'T COME OUT AGAIN UNTIL THE TOWN'S BACK TO NORMAL.

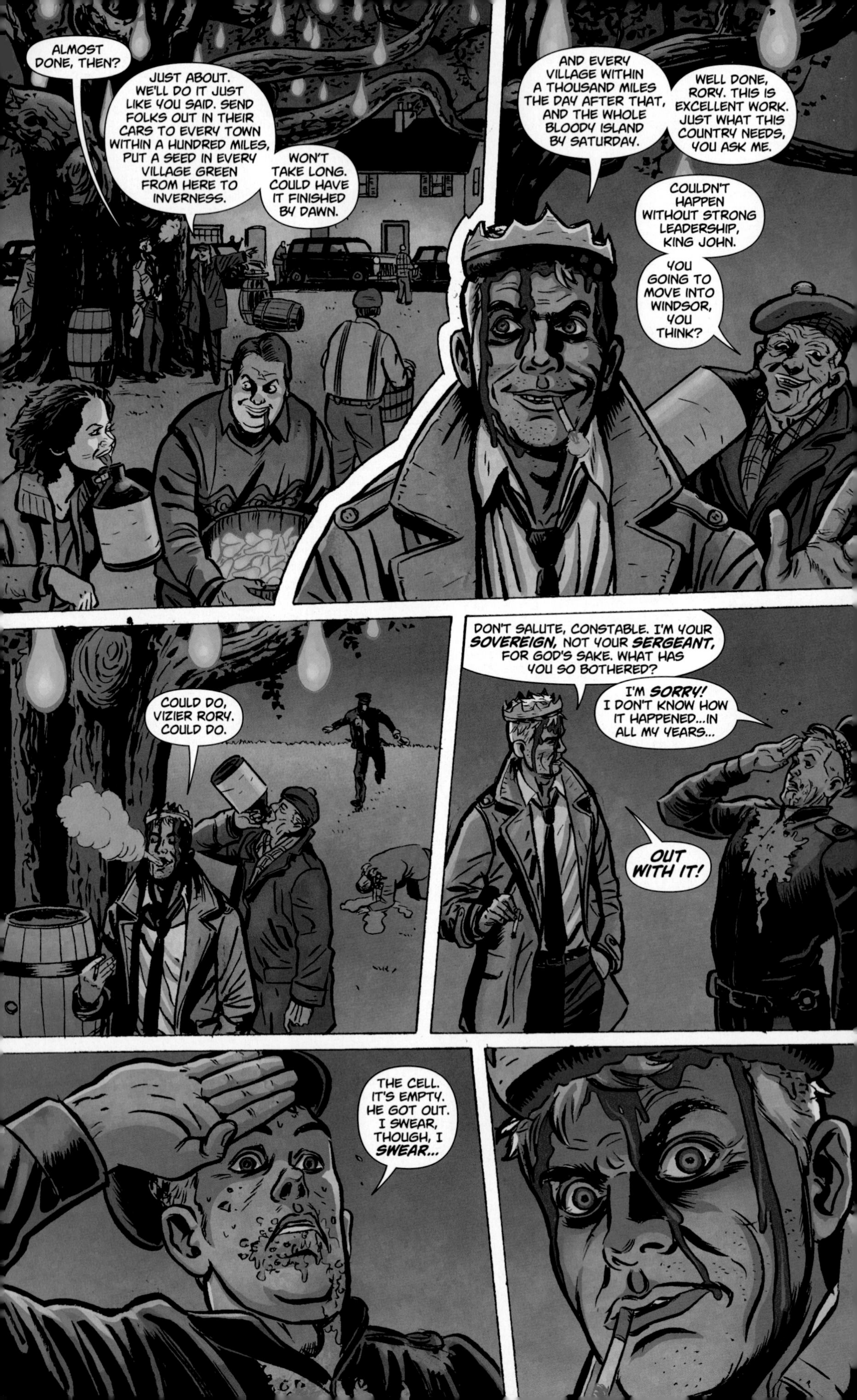
ALMOST DONE, THEN?
JUST ABOUT. WE'LL DO IT JUST LIKE YOU SAID. SEND FOLKS OUT IN THEIR CARS TO EVERY TOWN WITHIN A HUNDRED MILES, PUT A SEED IN EVERY VILLAGE GREEN FROM HERE TO INVERNESS.
WON'T TAKE LONG. COULD HAVE IT FINISHED BY DAWN.
AND EVERY VILLAGE WITHIN A THOUSAND MILES THE DAY AFTER THAT, AND THE WHOLE BLOODY ISLAND BY SATURDAY.
WELL DONE, RORY. THIS IS EXCELLENT WORK. JUST WHAT THIS COUNTRY NEEDS, YOU ASK ME.
COULDN'T HAPPEN WITHOUT STRONG LEADERSHIP, KING JOHN.
YOU GOING TO MOVE INTO WINDSOR, YOU THINK?
COULD DO, VIZIER RORY. COULD DO.
DON'T SALUTE, CONSTABLE. I'M YOUR SOVEREIGN, NOT YOUR SERGEANT, FOR GOD'S SAKE. WHAT HAS YOU SO BOTHERED?
I'M SORRY! I DON'T KNOW HOW IT HAPPENED...IN ALL MY YEARS...
OUT WITH IT!
THE CELL. IT'S EMPTY. HE GOT OUT. I SWEAR, THOUGH, I SWEAR...

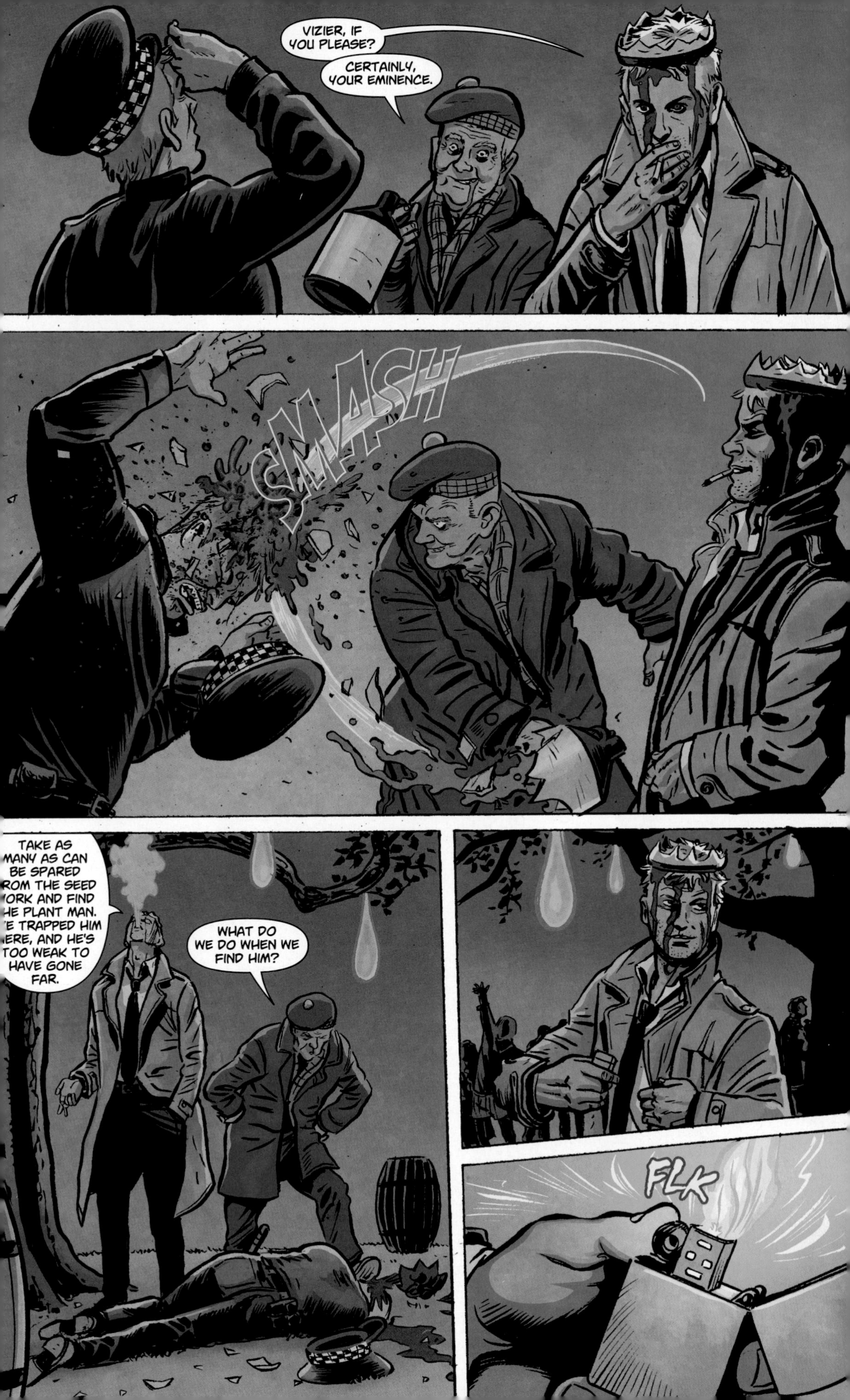
VIZIER, IF YOU PLEASE?
CERTAINLY, YOUR EMINENCE.
SMASH
TAKE AS MANY AS CAN BE SPARED ROM THE SEED ORK AND FIND HE PLANT MAN. E TRAPPED HIM ERE, AND HE'S TOO WEAK TO HAVE GONE FAR.
WHAT DO WE DO WHEN WE FIND HIM?
FLK

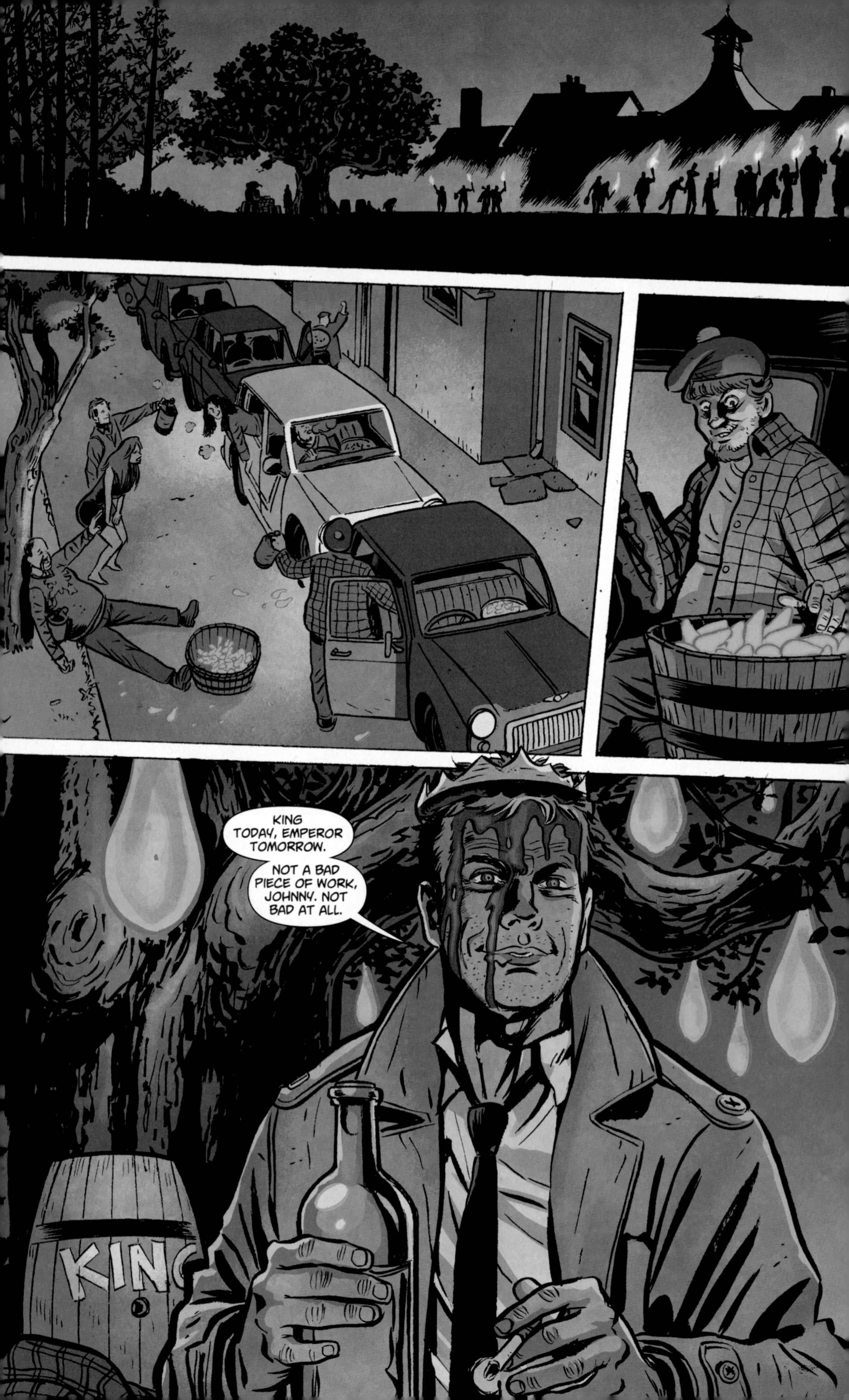
KING TODAY, EMPEROR TOMORROW.
NOT A BAD PIECE OF WORK, JOHNNY. NOT BAD AT ALL.
KING

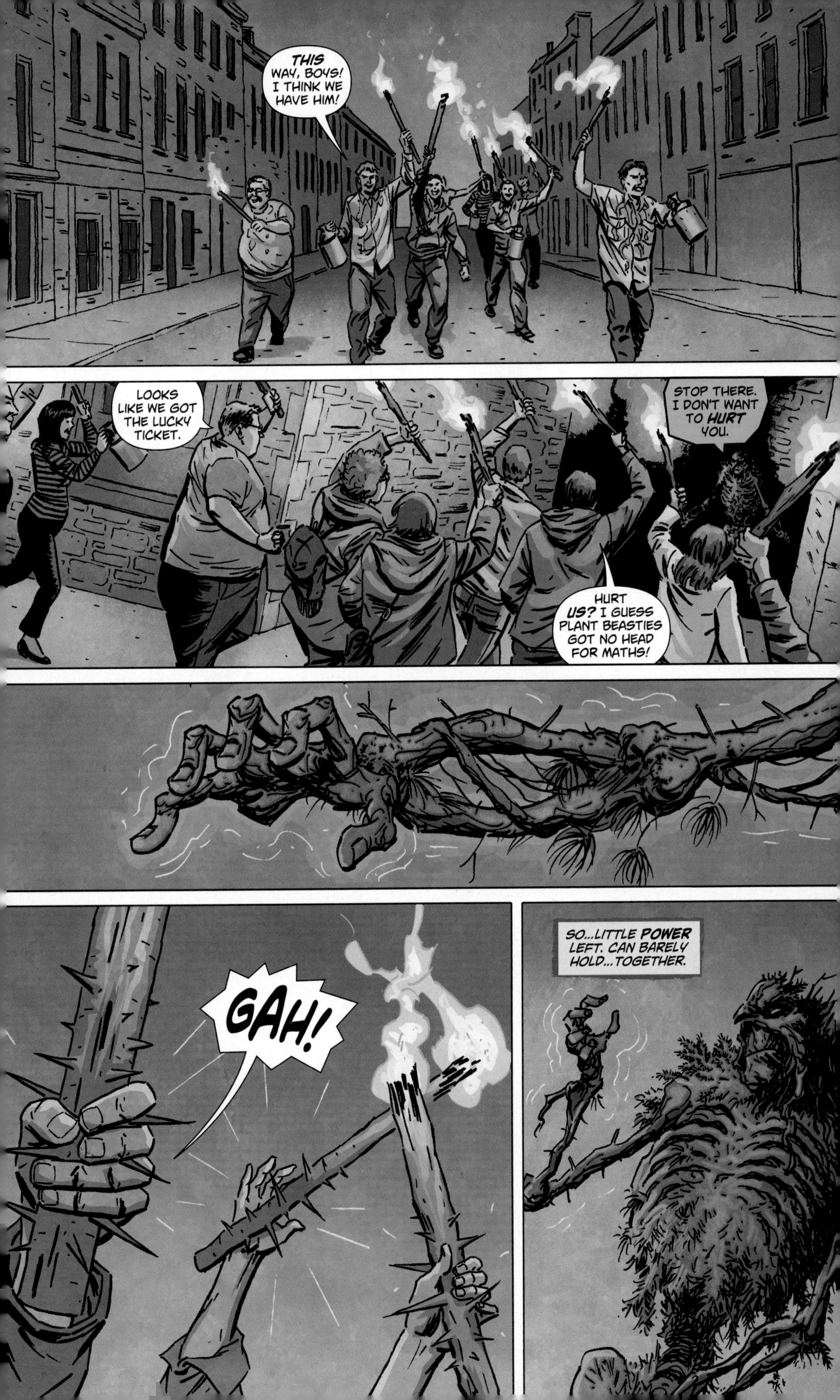
THIS WAY, BOYS! I THINK WE HAVE HIM!
LOOKS LIKE WE GOT THE LUCKY TICKET.
STOP THERE. I DON'T WANT TO HURT YOU.
HURT US? I GUESS PLANT BEASTIES GOT NO HEAD FOR MATHS!
GAH!
SO...LITTLE POWER LEFT. CAN BARELY HOLD...TOGETHER.

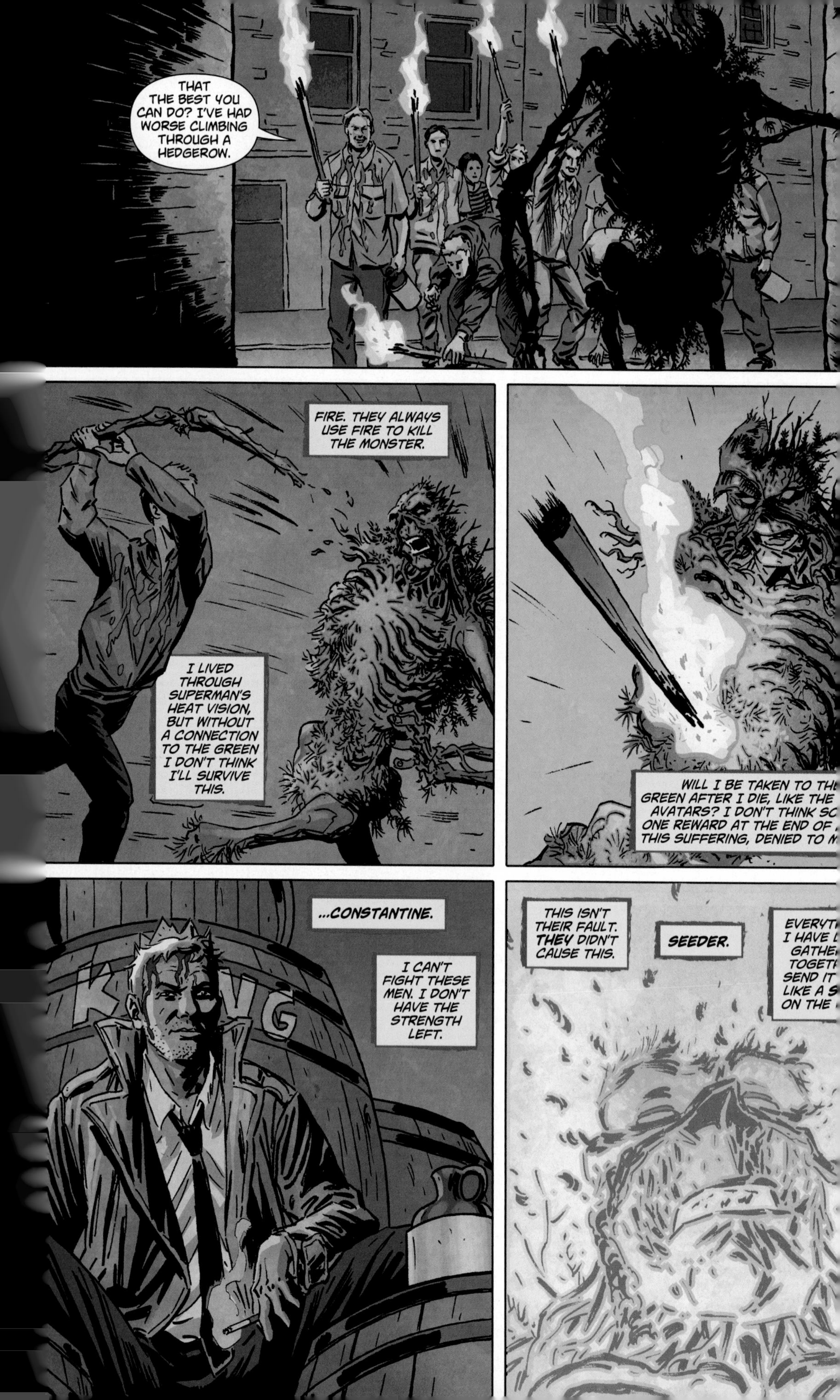

THAT THE BEST YOU CAN DO? I'VE HAD WORSE CLIMBING THROUGH A HEDGEROW.
FIRE. THEY ALWAYS USE FIRE TO KILL THE MONSTER.
I LIVED THROUGH SUPERMAN'S HEAT VISION, BUT WITHOUT A CONNECTION TO THE GREEN I DON'T THINK I'LL SURVIVE THIS.
WILL I BE TAKEN TO TH GREEN AFTER I DIE, LIKE THE AVATARS? I DON'T THINK SO ONE REWARD AT THE END OF THIS SUFFERING, DENIED TO M
...CONSTANTINE.
I CAN'T FIGHT THESE MEN. I DON'T HAVE THE STRENGTH LEFT.
THIS ISN'T THEIR FAULT. THEY DIDN'T CAUSE THIS.
SEEDER.
EVERYT I HAVE GATHE TOGET SEND IT LIKE A ON THE

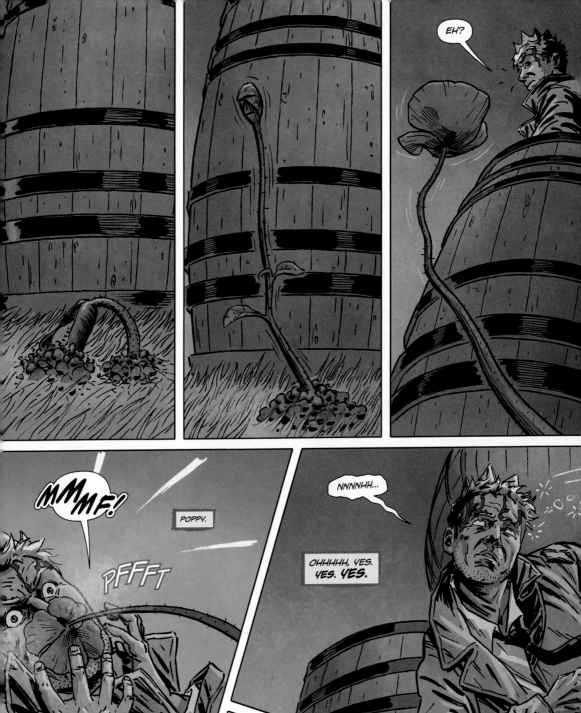

EH?

MMMF!

POPPY.

PFFFT

NNNNHH...

OHHHHH, YES. YES. YES.

THE SPELL... IT'S *GONE.* I CAN FEEL THE GREEN, REACHING OUT TO ME...

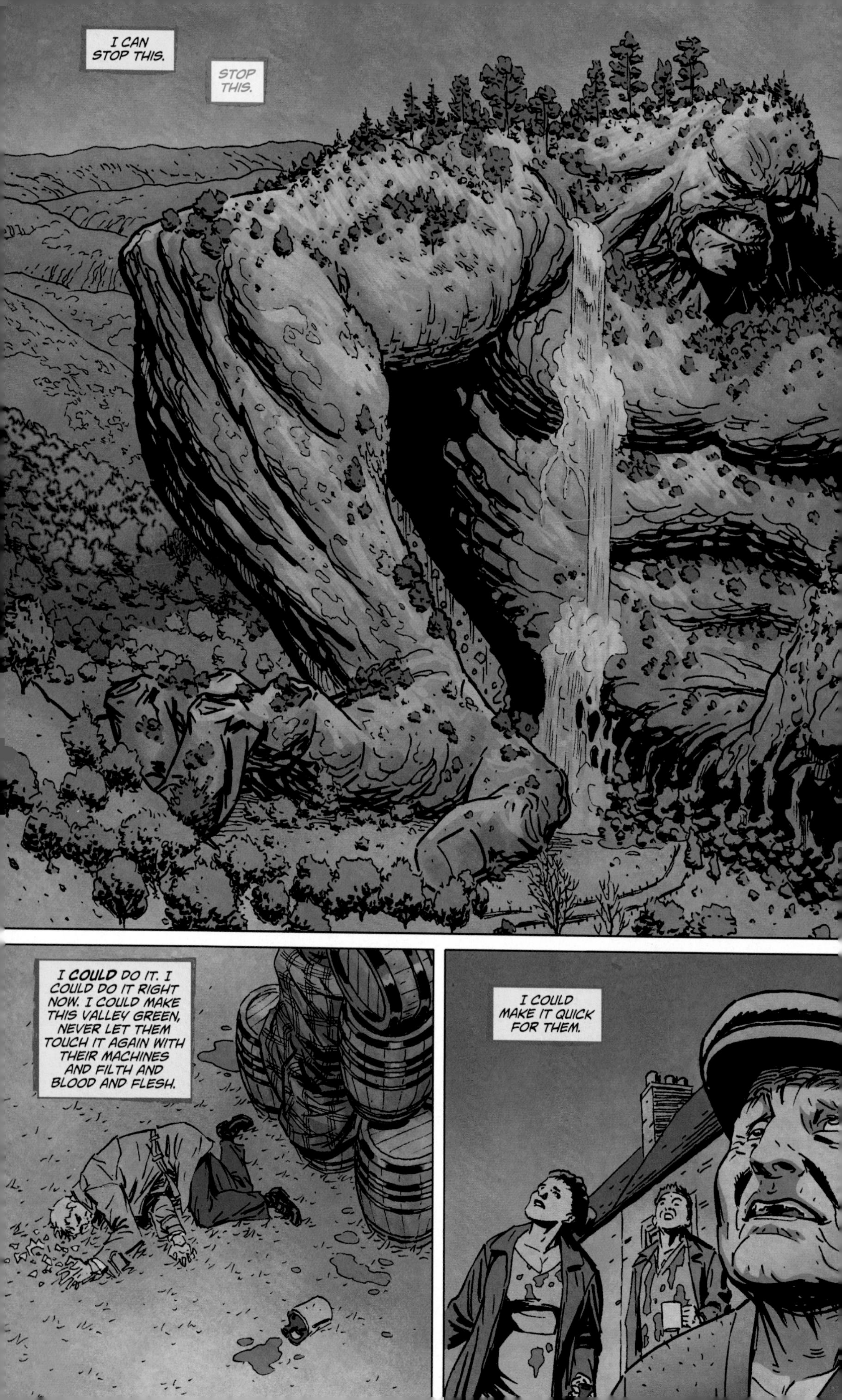
I CAN STOP THIS.
STOP THIS.
I **COULD** DO IT. I COULD DO IT RIGHT NOW. I COULD MAKE THIS VALLEY GREEN, NEVER LET THEM TOUCH IT AGAIN WITH THEIR MACHINES AND FILTH AND BLOOD AND FLESH.
I COULD MAKE IT QUICK FOR THEM.

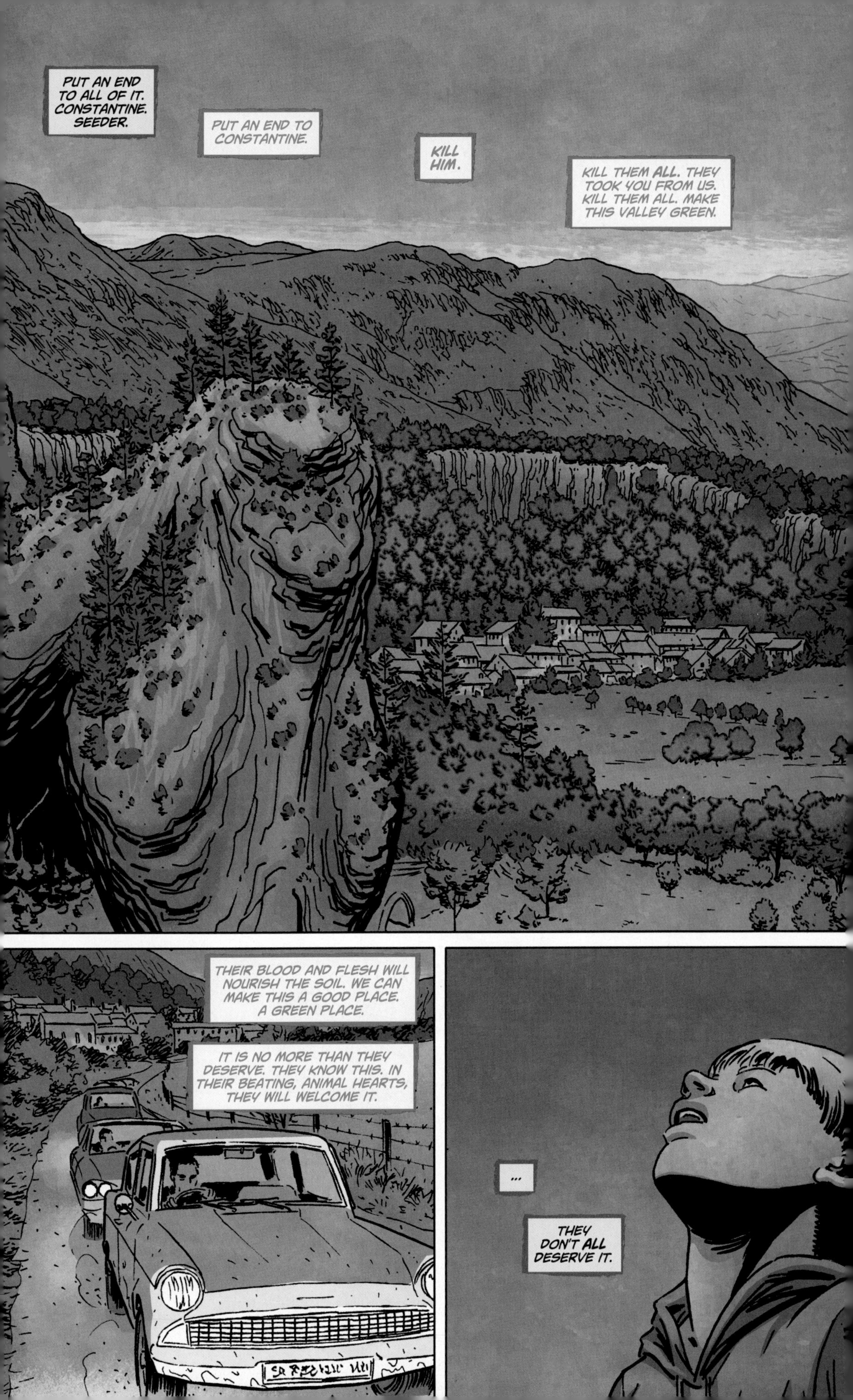

PUT AN END TO ALL OF IT. CONSTANTINE. SEEDER.
PUT AN END TO CONSTANTINE.
KILL HIM.
KILL THEM ALL. THEY TOOK YOU FROM US. KILL THEM ALL. MAKE THIS VALLEY GREEN.
THEIR BLOOD AND FLESH WILL NOURISH THE SOIL. WE CAN MAKE THIS A GOOD PLACE. A GREEN PLACE.
IT IS NO MORE THAN THEY DESERVE. THEY KNOW THIS. IN THEIR BEATING, ANIMAL HEARTS, THEY WILL WELCOME IT.
...
THEY DON'T ALL DESERVE IT.

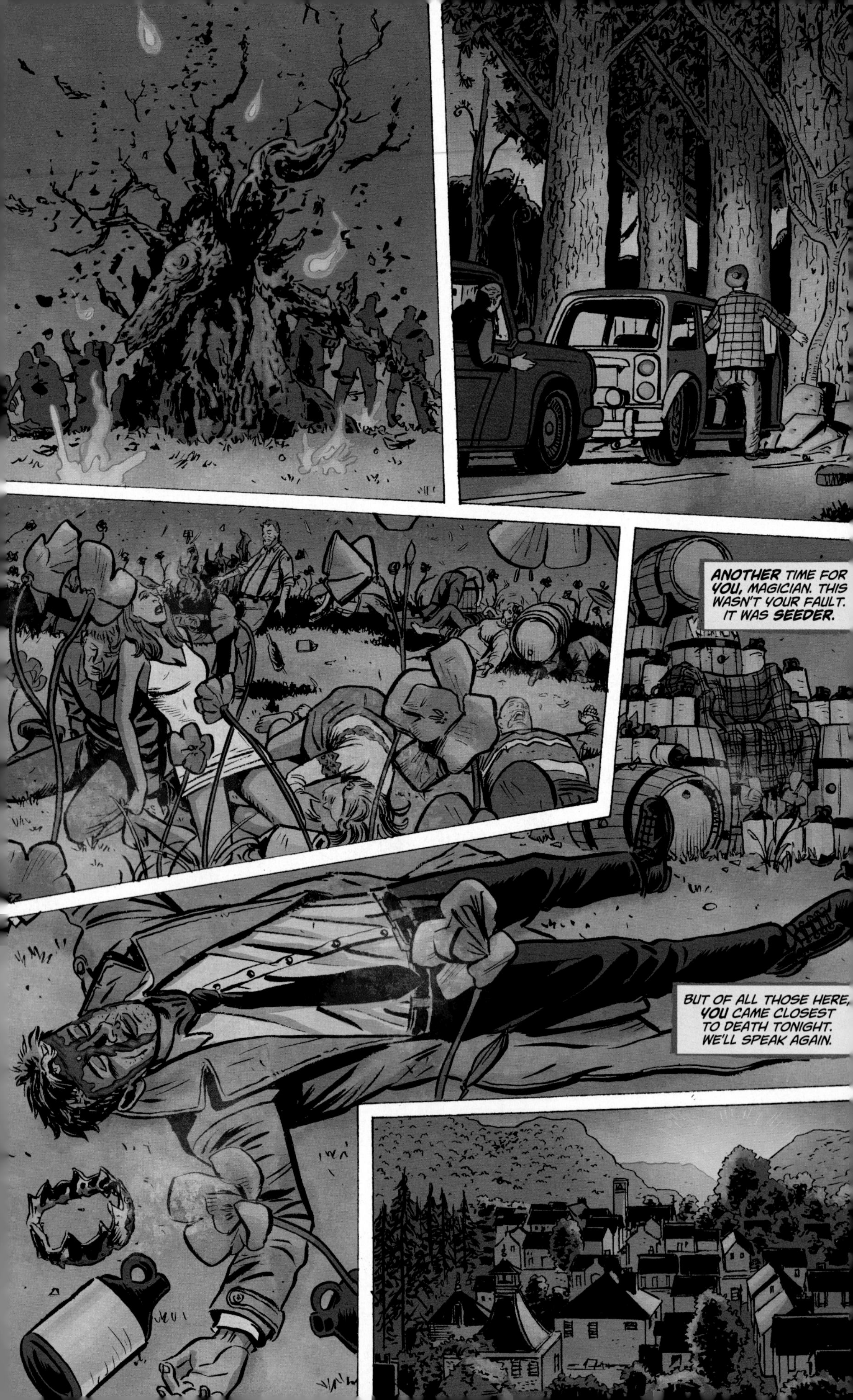
ANOTHER TIME FOR YOU, MAGICIAN. THIS WASN'T YOUR FAULT. IT WAS SEEDER.
BUT OF ALL THOSE HERE, YOU CAME CLOSEST TO DEATH TONIGHT. WE'LL SPEAK AGAIN.

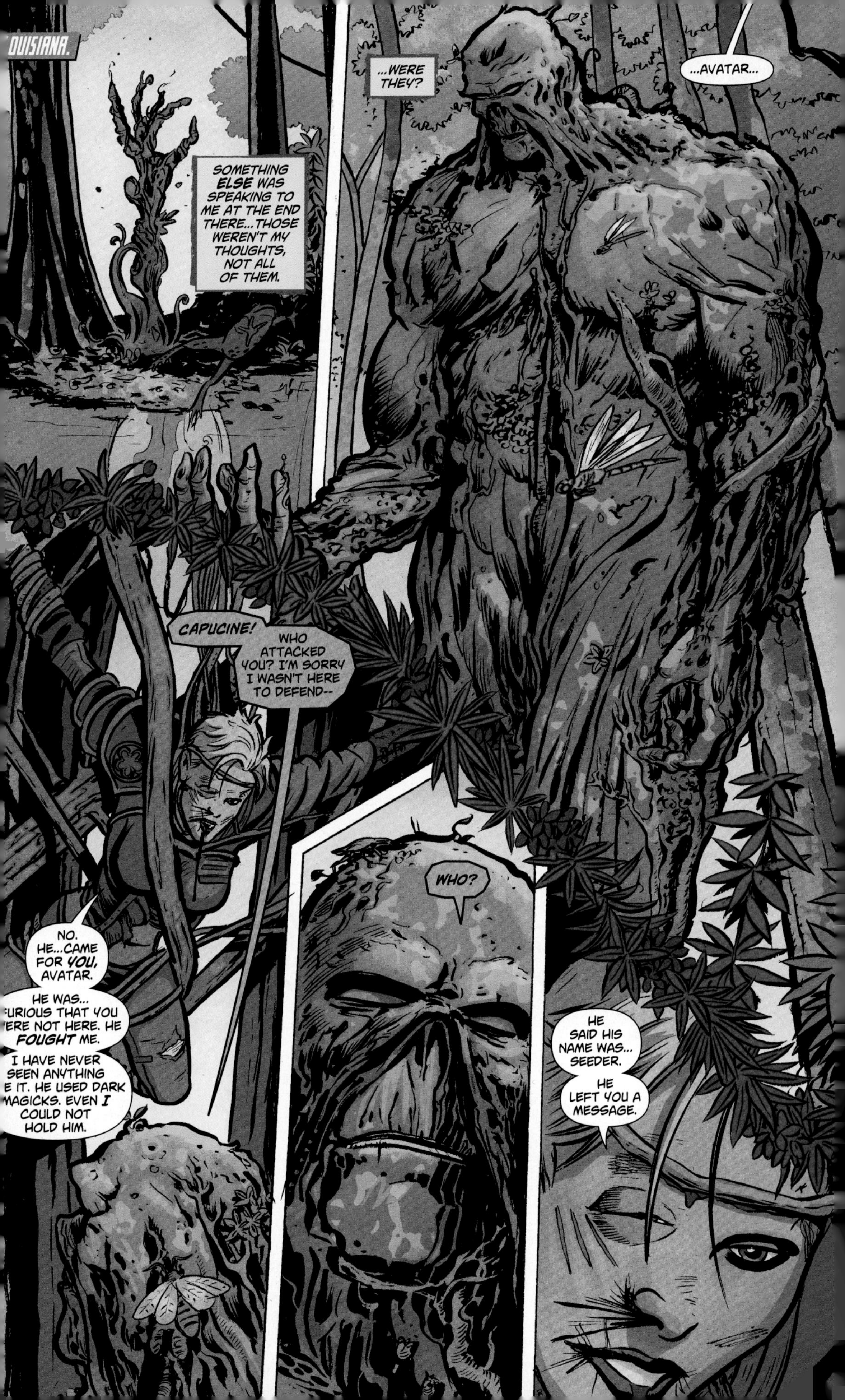

OUISIANA.
SOMETHING ELSE WAS SPEAKING TO ME AT THE END THERE... THOSE WEREN'T MY THOUGHTS, NOT ALL OF THEM.
...WERE THEY?
...AVATAR...
CAPUCINE!
WHO ATTACKED YOU? I'M SORRY I WASN'T HERE TO DEFEND--
NO. HE...CAME FOR YOU, AVATAR.
WHO?
HE WAS... URIOUS THAT YOU ERE NOT HERE. HE FOUGHT ME.
I HAVE NEVER SEEN ANYTHING E IT. HE USED DARK AGICKS. EVEN I COULD NOT HOLD HIM.
HE SAID HIS NAME WAS... SEEDER.
HE LEFT YOU A MESSAGE.

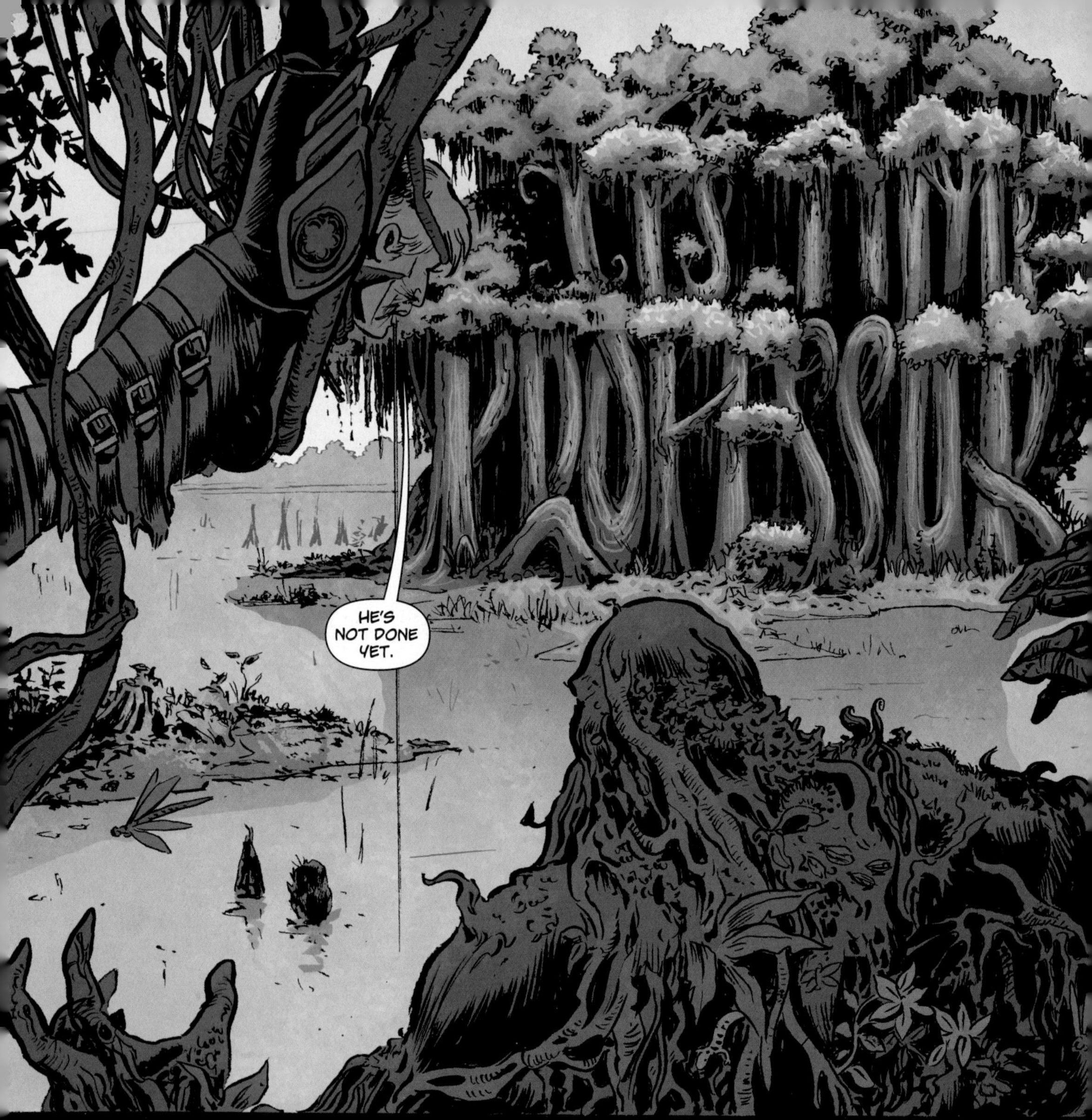
HE'S NOT DONE YET.

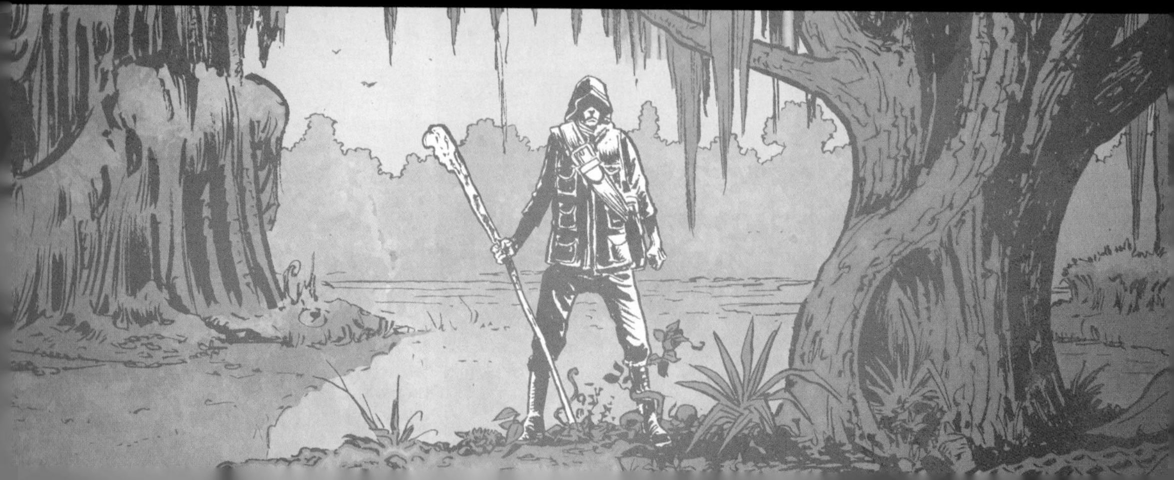

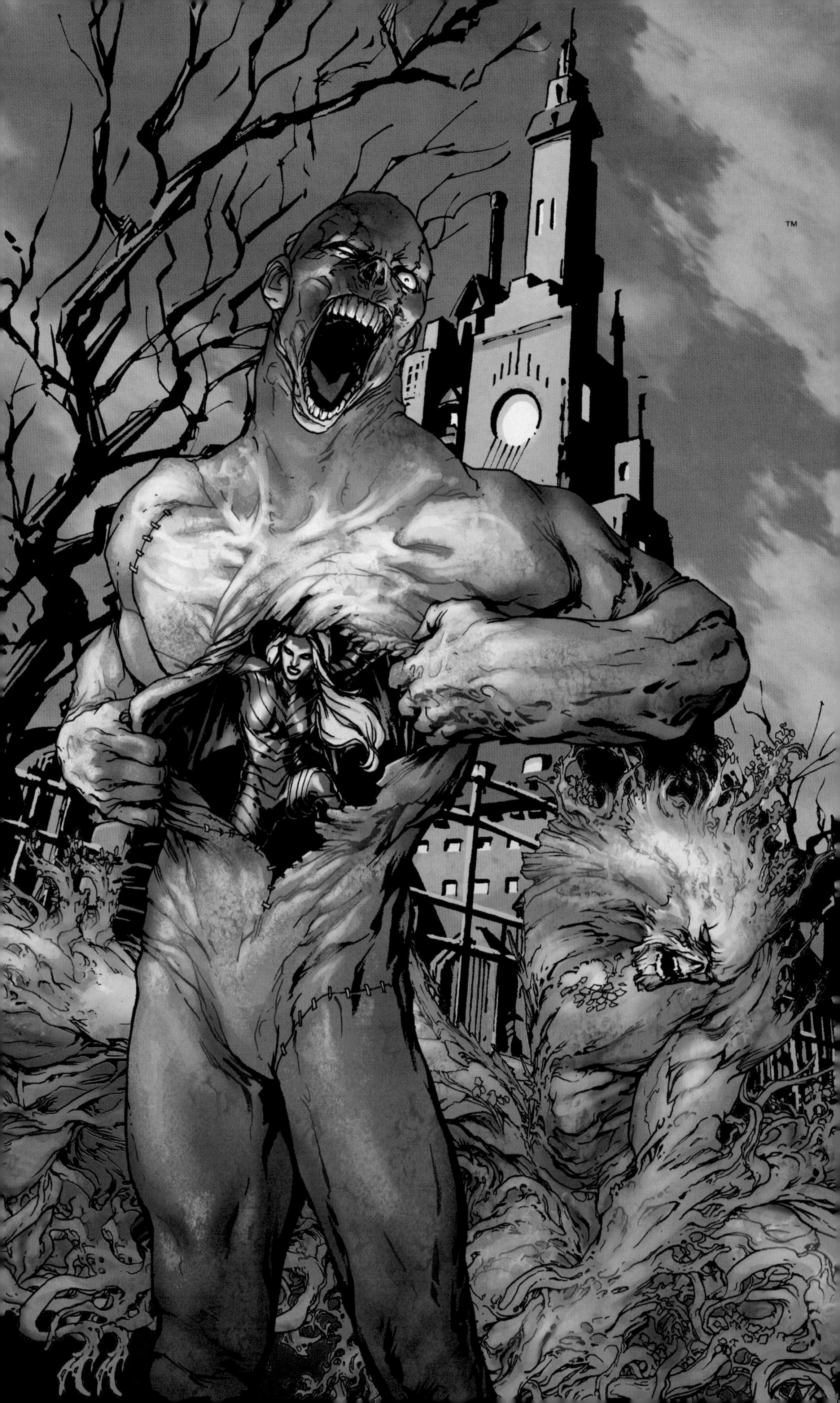

## THE PATCHWORK HISTORY

CHARLES SOULE writer JESUS SAIZ artist cover art by JESUS SAIZ

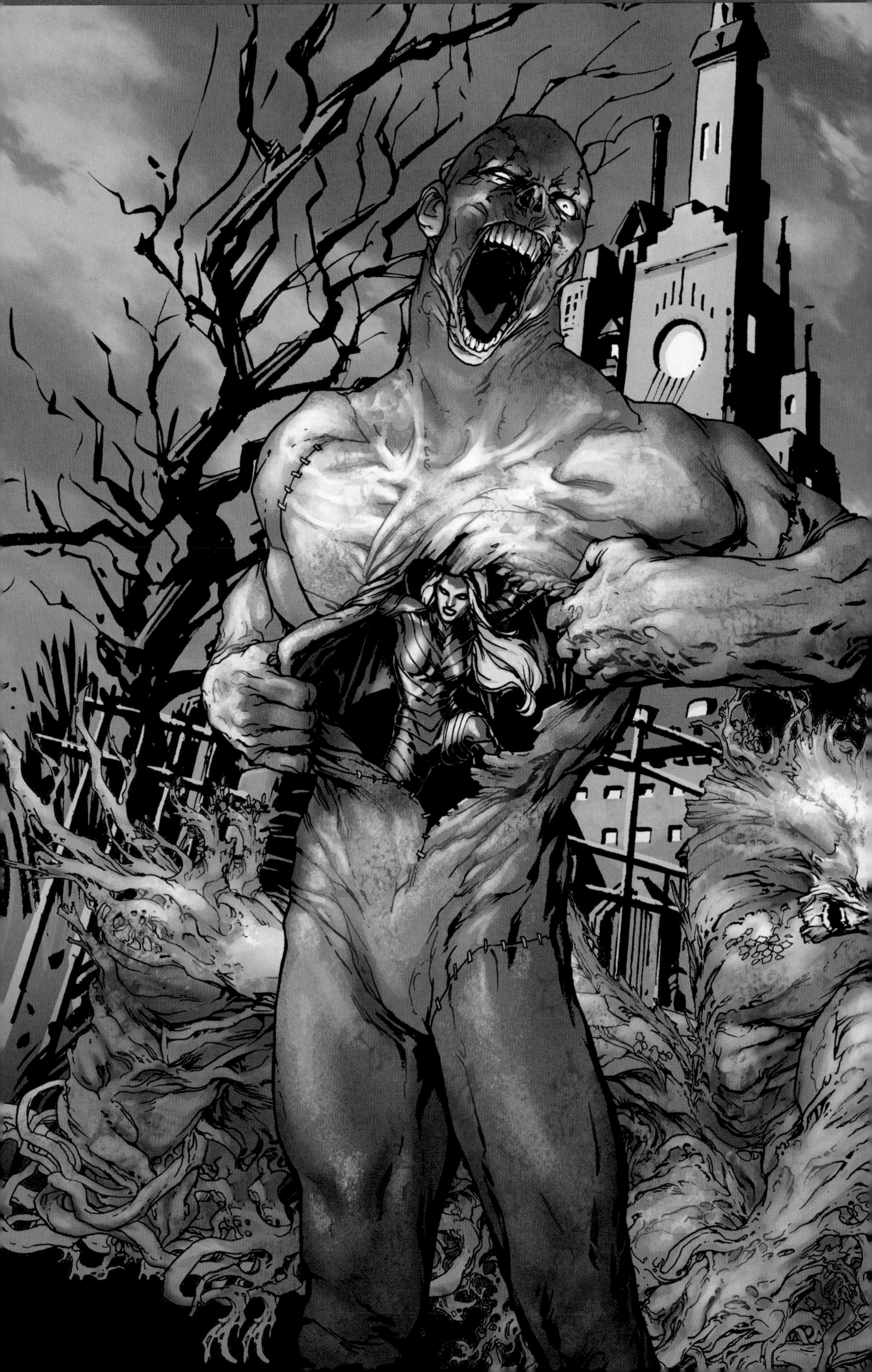

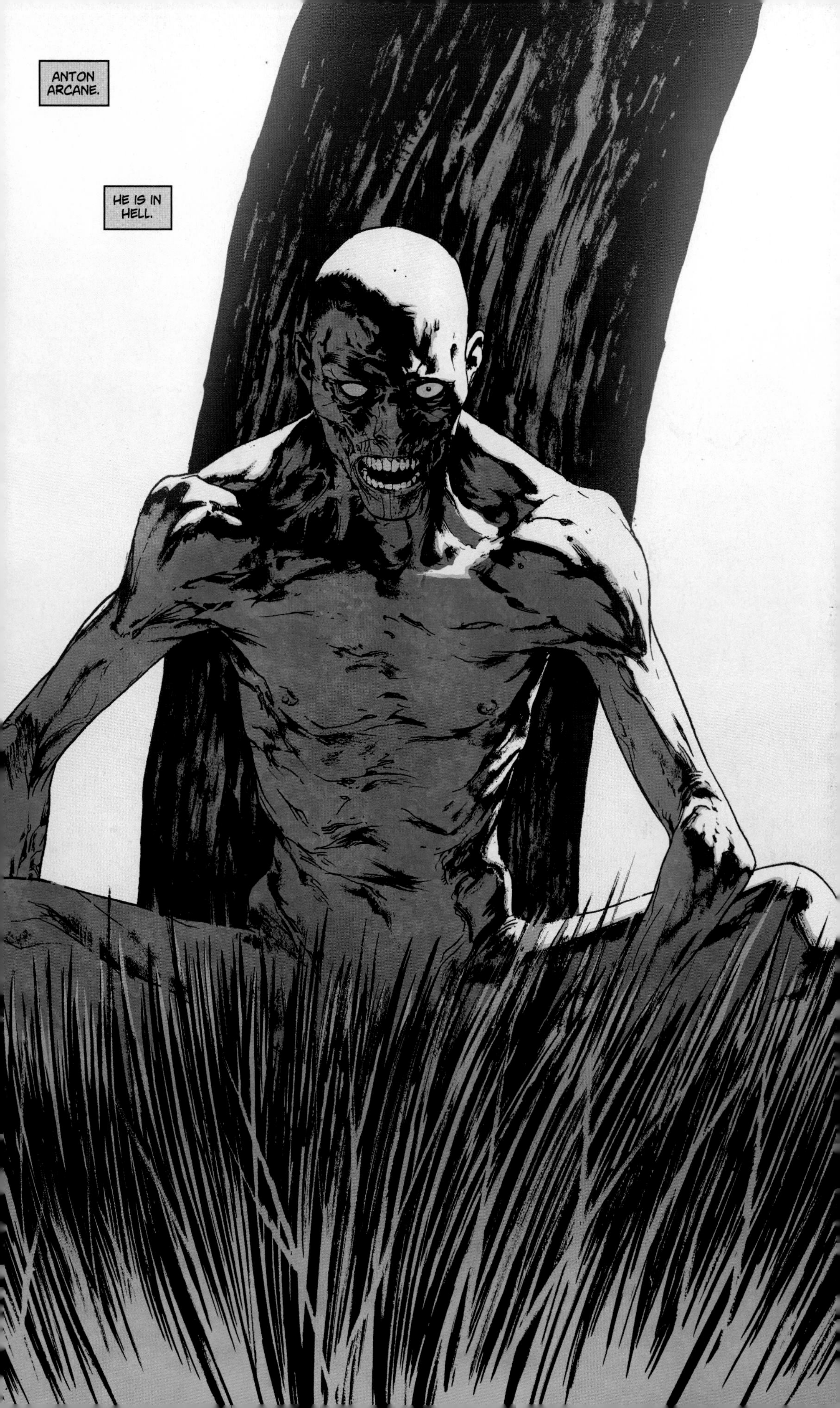
ANTON ARCANE.
HE IS IN HELL.

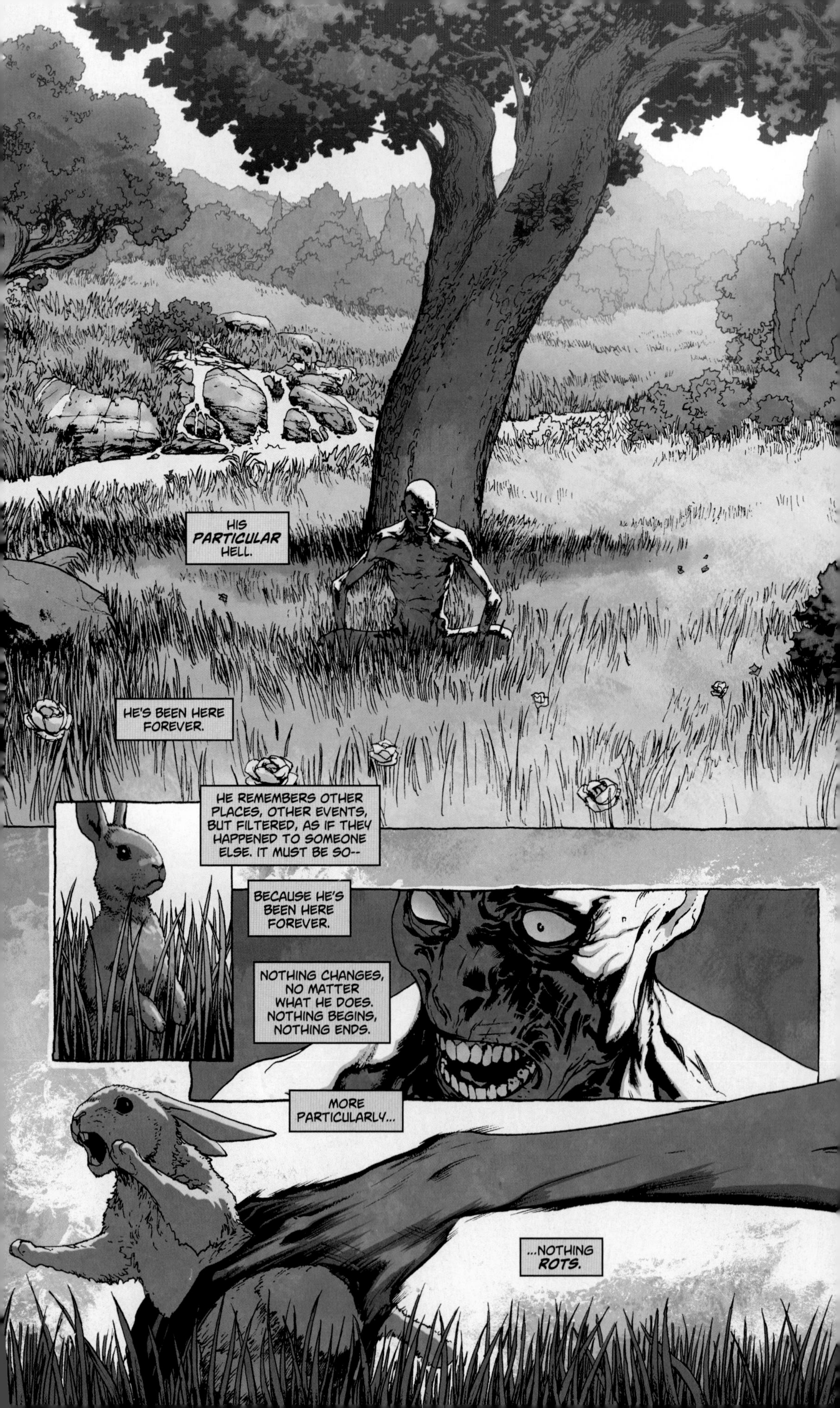
HIS PARTICULAR HELL.
HE'S BEEN HERE FOREVER.
HE REMEMBERS OTHER PLACES, OTHER EVENTS, BUT FILTERED, AS IF THEY HAPPENED TO SOMEONE ELSE. IT MUST BE SO--
BECAUSE HE'S BEEN HERE FOREVER.
NOTHING CHANGES, NO MATTER WHAT HE DOES. NOTHING BEGINS, NOTHING ENDS.
MORE PARTICULARLY...
...NOTHING ROTS.

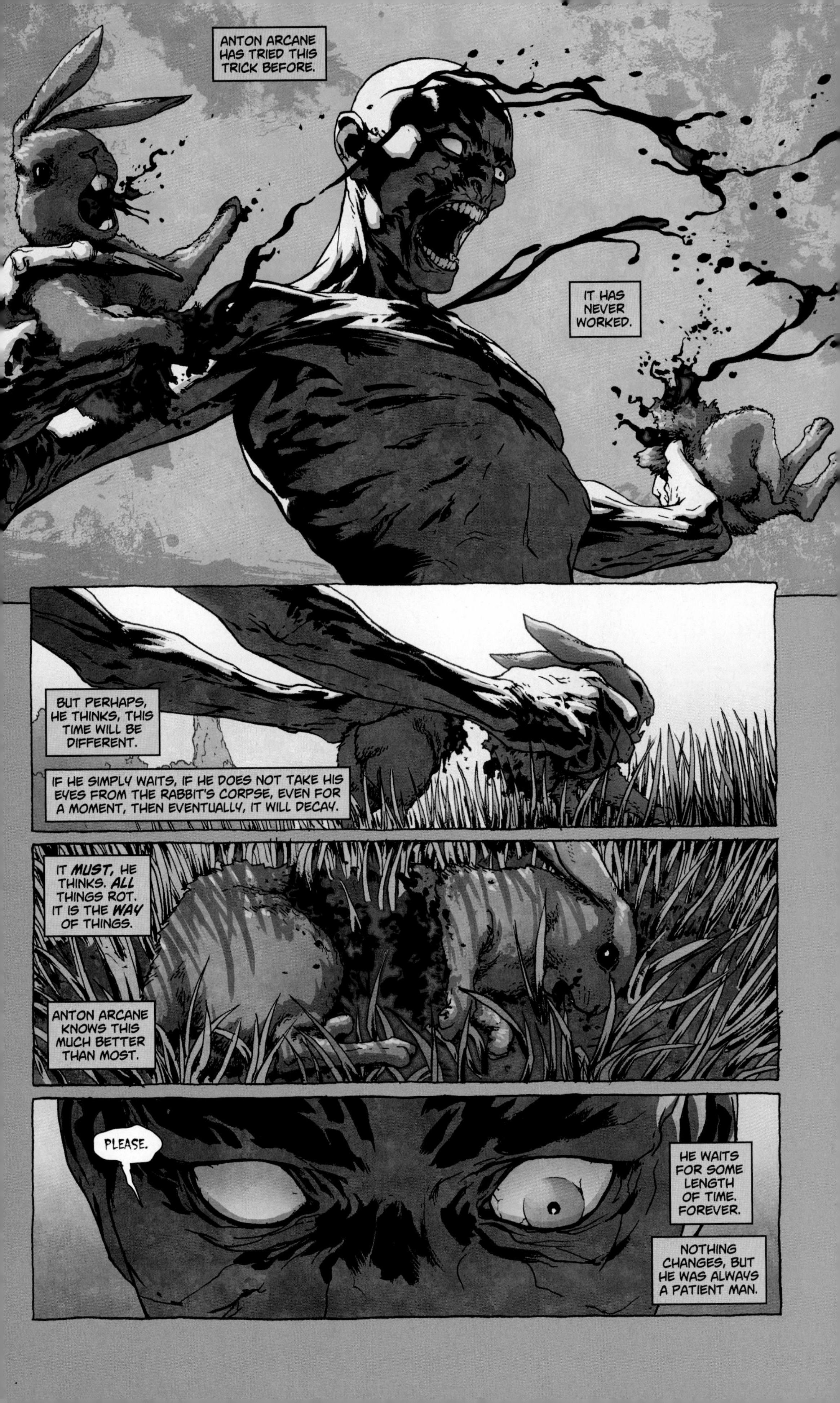
ANTON ARCANE HAS TRIED THIS TRICK BEFORE.
IT HAS NEVER WORKED.
BUT PERHAPS, HE THINKS, THIS TIME WILL BE DIFFERENT.
IF HE SIMPLY WAITS, IF HE DOES NOT TAKE HIS EYES FROM THE RABBIT'S CORPSE, EVEN FOR A MOMENT, THEN EVENTUALLY, IT WILL DECAY.
IT *MUST,* HE THINKS. *ALL* THINGS ROT. IT IS THE *WAY* OF THINGS.
ANTON ARCANE KNOWS THIS MUCH BETTER THAN MOST.
PLEASE.
HE WAITS FOR SOME LENGTH OF TIME. FOREVER.
NOTHING CHANGES, BUT HE WAS ALWAYS A PATIENT MAN.

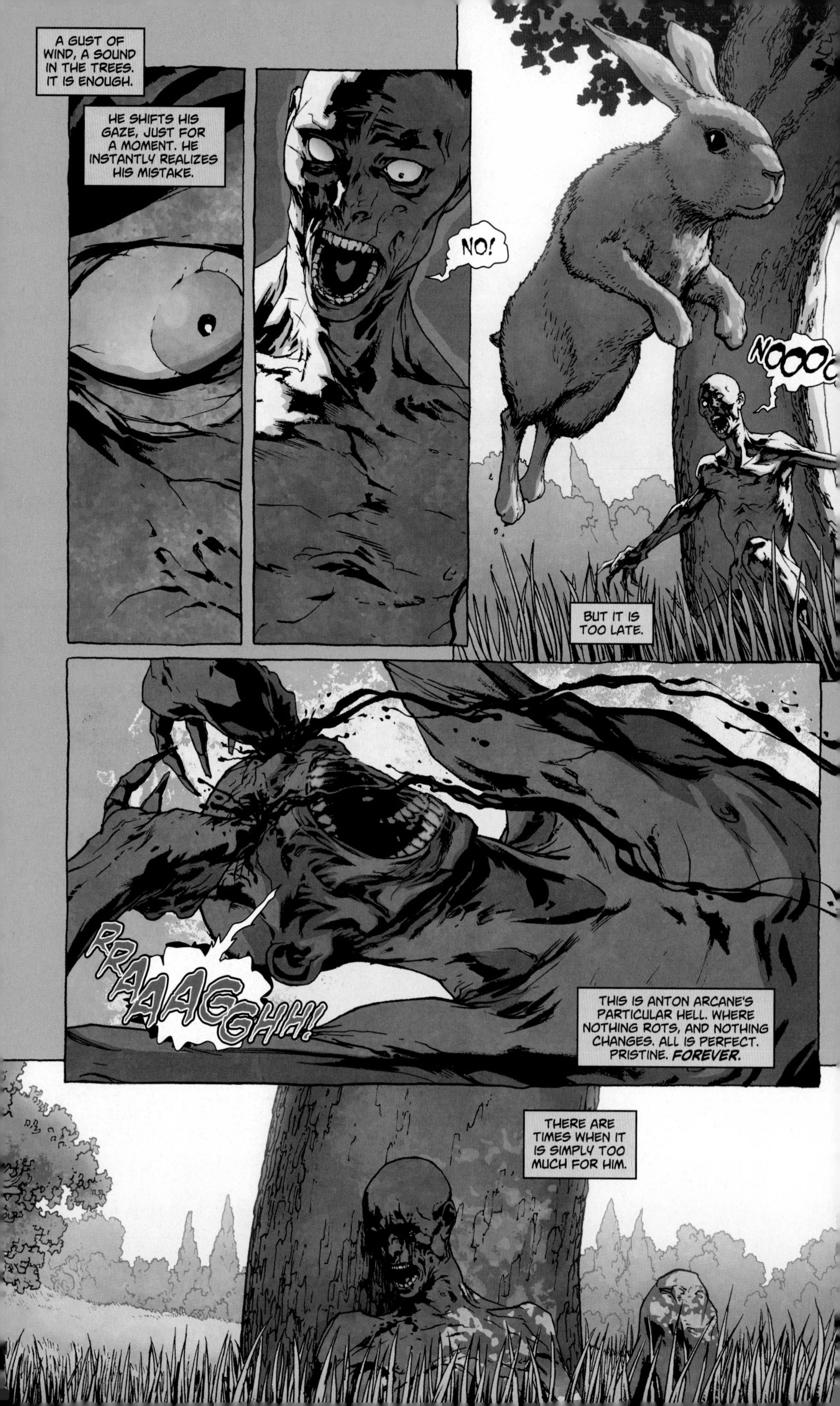

A GUST OF WIND, A SOUND IN THE TREES. IT IS ENOUGH.
HE SHIFTS HIS GAZE, JUST FOR A MOMENT. HE INSTANTLY REALIZES HIS MISTAKE.
NO!
NOOOO
BUT IT IS TOO LATE.
RRAAAGGHH!
THIS IS ANTON ARCANE'S PARTICULAR HELL. WHERE NOTHING ROTS, AND NOTHING CHANGES. ALL IS PERFECT. PRISTINE. *FOREVER.*
THERE ARE TIMES WHEN IT IS SIMPLY TOO MUCH FOR HIM.

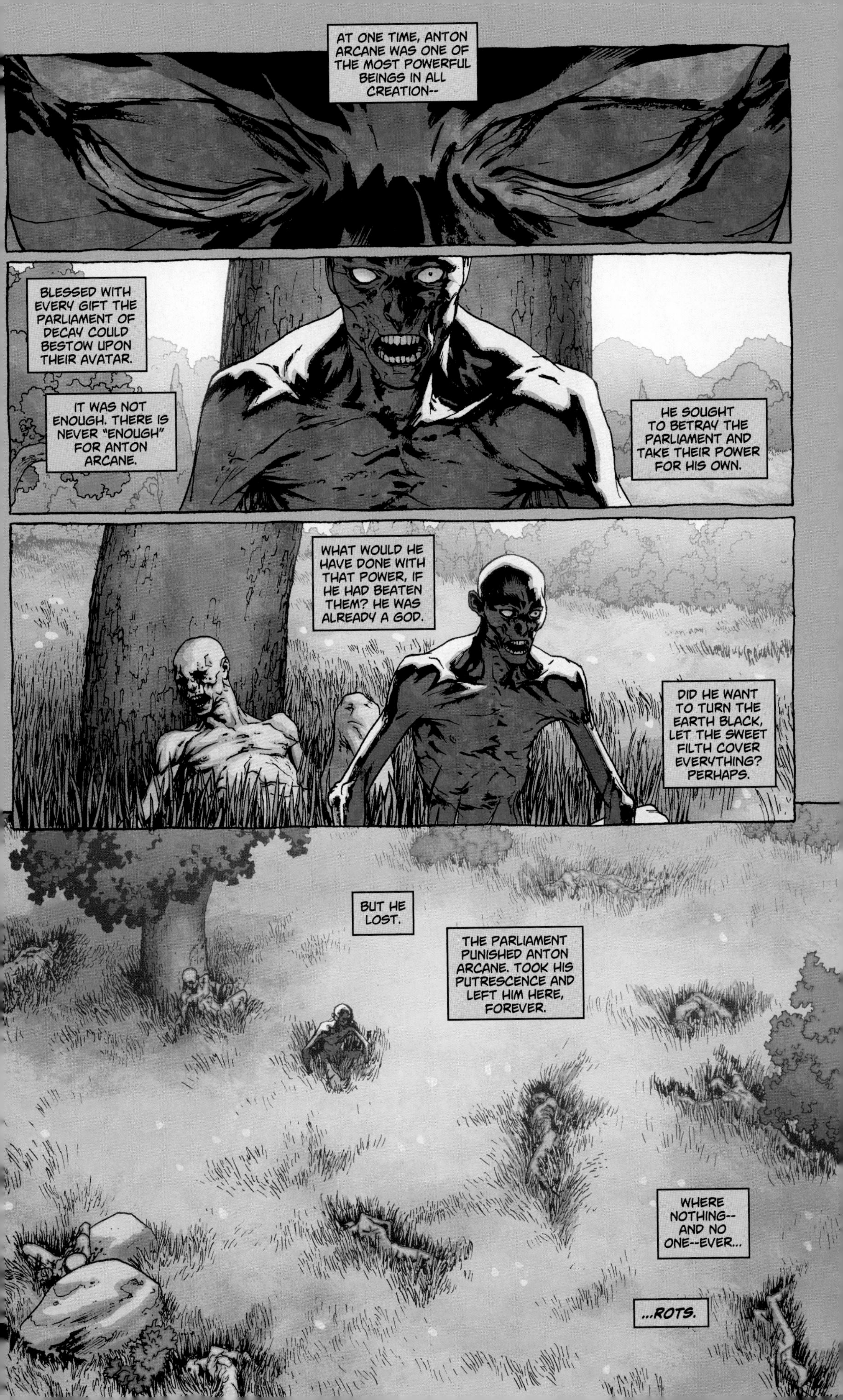
AT ONE TIME, ANTON ARCANE WAS ONE OF THE MOST POWERFUL BEINGS IN ALL CREATION--
BLESSED WITH EVERY GIFT THE PARLIAMENT OF DECAY COULD BESTOW UPON THEIR AVATAR.
IT WAS NOT ENOUGH. THERE IS NEVER "ENOUGH" FOR ANTON ARCANE.
HE SOUGHT TO BETRAY THE PARLIAMENT AND TAKE THEIR POWER FOR HIS OWN.
WHAT WOULD HE HAVE DONE WITH THAT POWER, IF HE HAD BEATEN THEM? HE WAS ALREADY A GOD.
DID HE WANT TO TURN THE EARTH BLACK, LET THE SWEET FILTH COVER EVERYTHING? PERHAPS.
BUT HE LOST.
THE PARLIAMENT PUNISHED ANTON ARCANE. TOOK HIS PUTRESCENCE AND LEFT HIM HERE, FOREVER.
WHERE NOTHING-- AND NO ONE--EVER...
...ROTS.

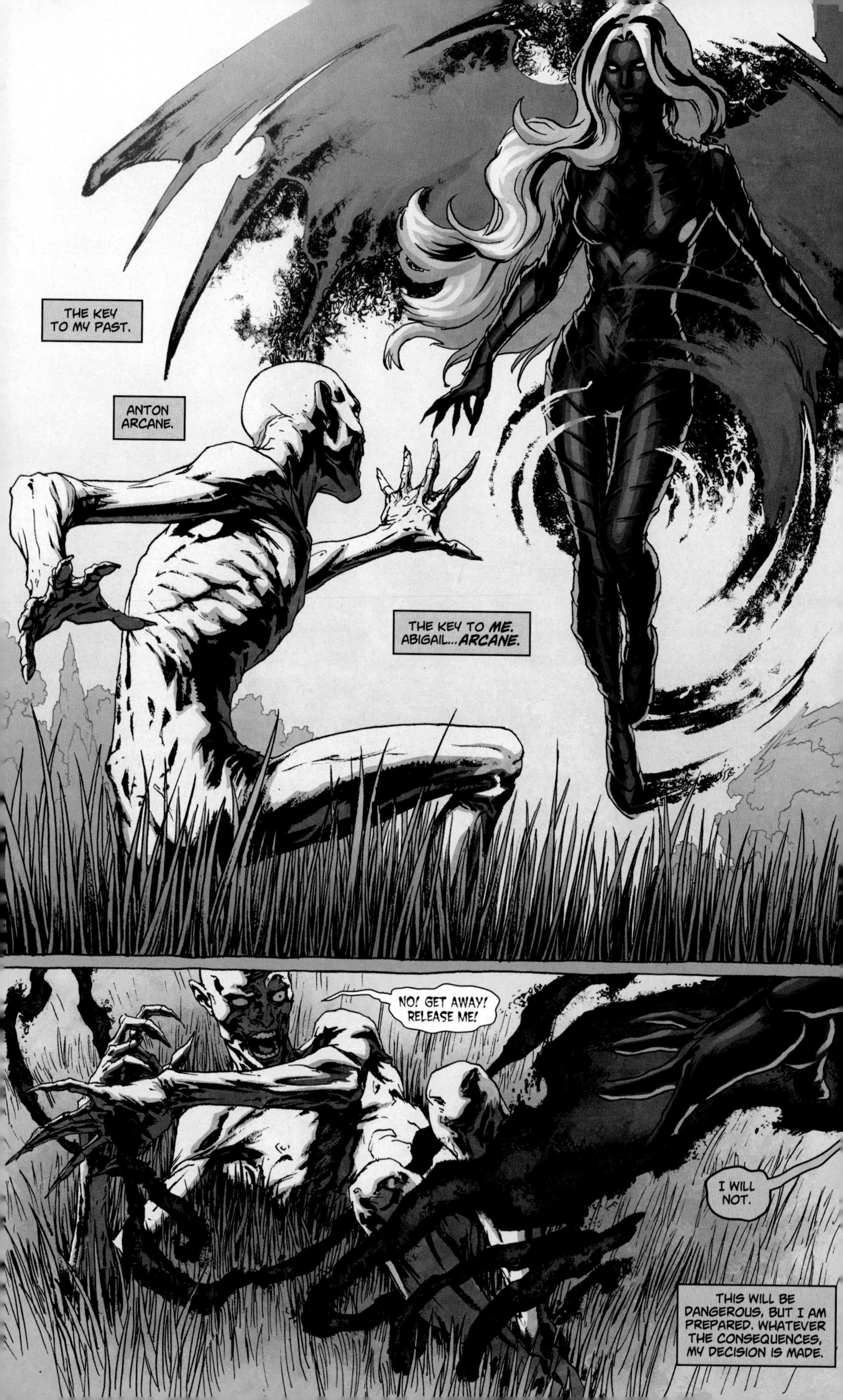
THE KEY TO MY PAST.
ANTON ARCANE.
THE KEY TO ME. ABIGAIL...ARCANE.
NO! GET AWAY! RELEASE ME!
I WILL NOT.
THIS WILL BE DANGEROUS, BUT I AM PREPARED. WHATEVER THE CONSEQUENCES, MY DECISION IS MADE.

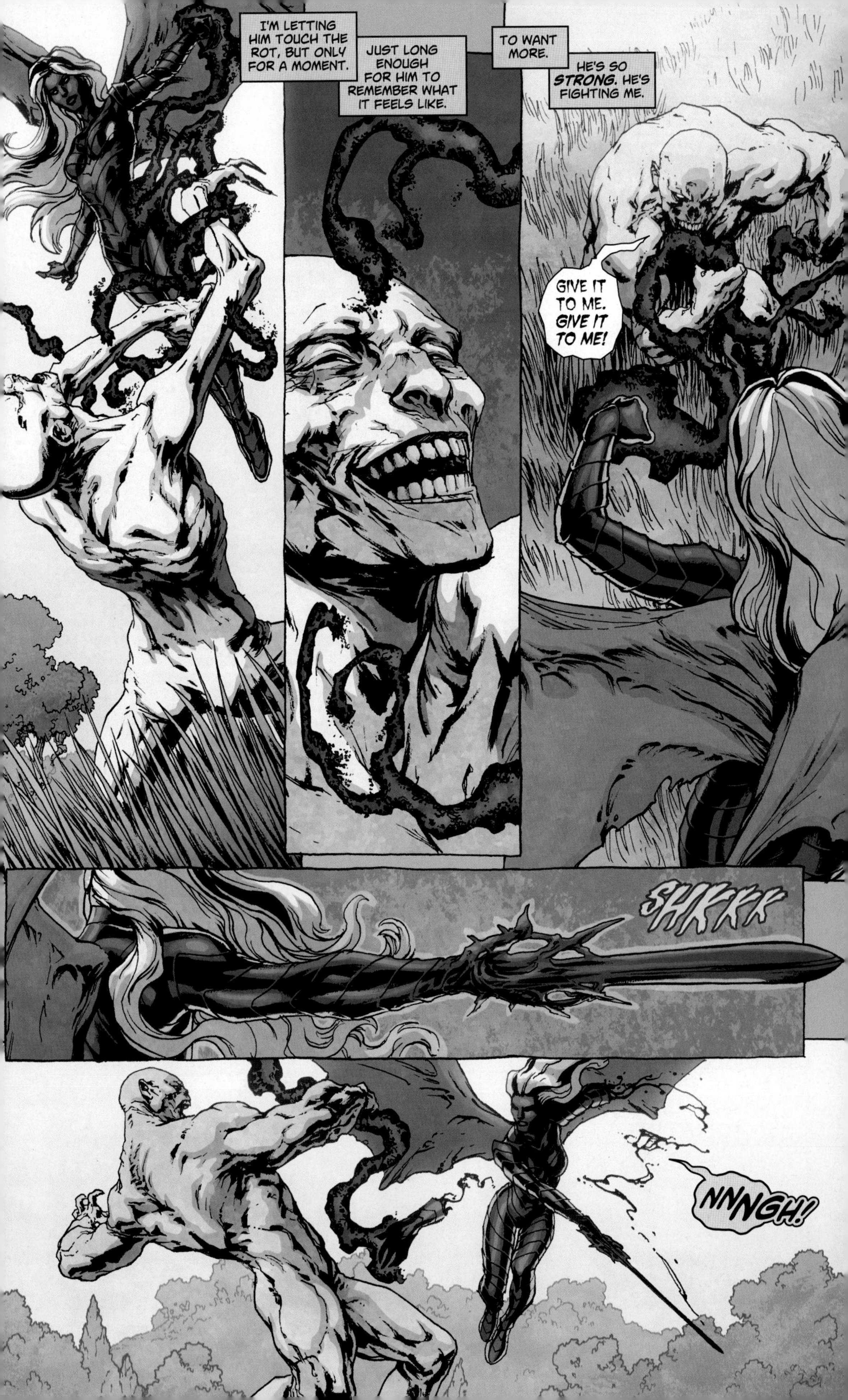
I'M LETTING HIM TOUCH THE ROT, BUT ONLY FOR A MOMENT.
JUST LONG ENOUGH FOR HIM TO REMEMBER WHAT IT FEELS LIKE.
TO WANT MORE.
HE'S SO STRONG. HE'S FIGHTING ME.
GIVE IT TO ME. GIVE IT TO ME!
SHKKK
NNNGH!

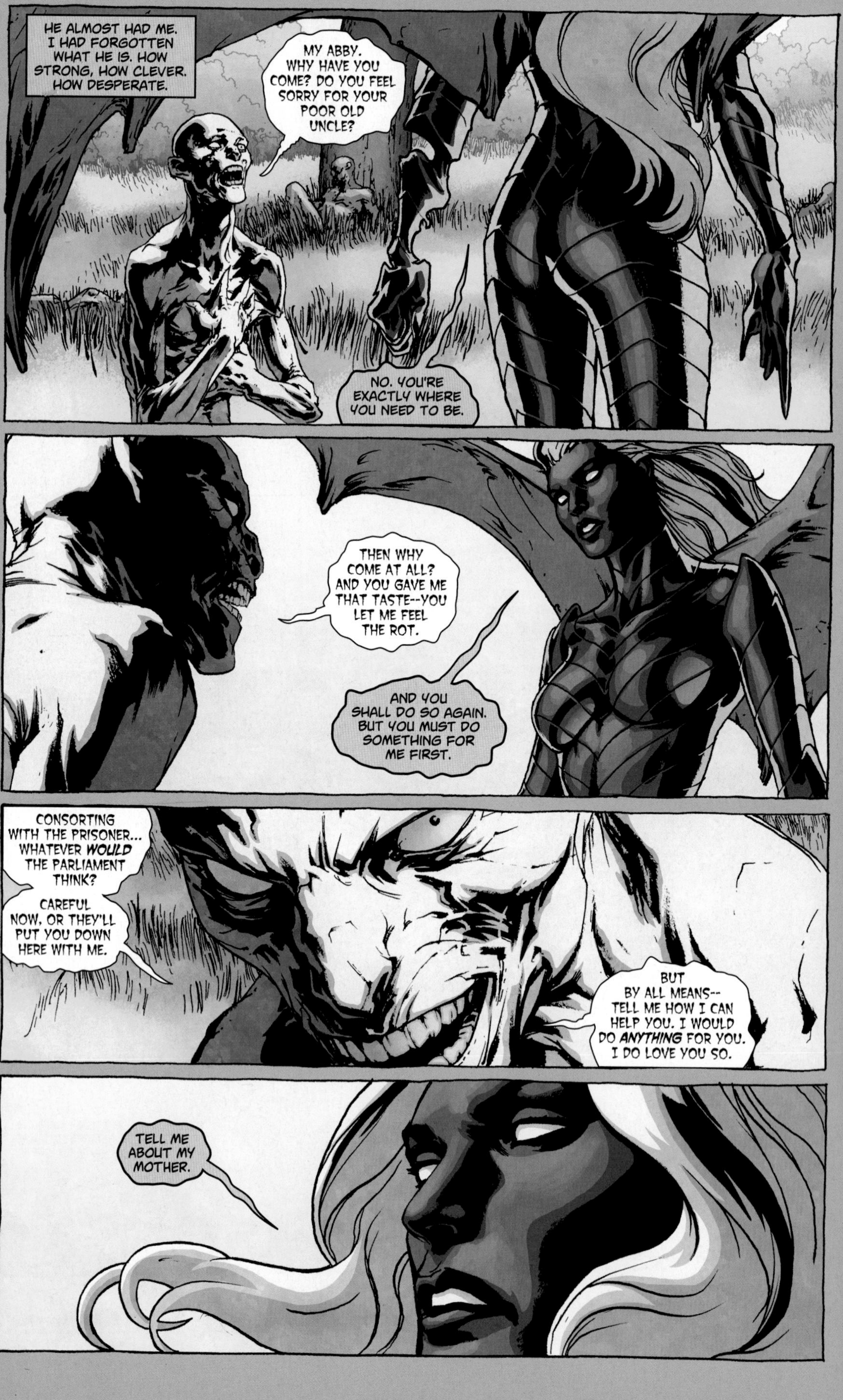
HE ALMOST HAD ME. I HAD FORGOTTEN WHAT HE IS. HOW STRONG, HOW CLEVER. HOW DESPERATE.
MY ABBY. WHY HAVE YOU COME? DO YOU FEEL SORRY FOR YOUR POOR OLD UNCLE?
NO. YOU'RE EXACTLY WHERE YOU NEED TO BE.
THEN WHY COME AT ALL? AND YOU GAVE ME THAT TASTE--YOU LET ME FEEL THE ROT.
AND YOU SHALL DO SO AGAIN. BUT YOU MUST DO SOMETHING FOR ME FIRST.
CONSORTING WITH THE PRISONER... WHATEVER WOULD THE PARLIAMENT THINK?
CAREFUL NOW, OR THEY'LL PUT YOU DOWN HERE WITH ME.
BUT BY ALL MEANS-- TELL ME HOW I CAN HELP YOU. I WOULD DO ANYTHING FOR YOU. I DO LOVE YOU SO.
TELL ME ABOUT MY MOTHER.

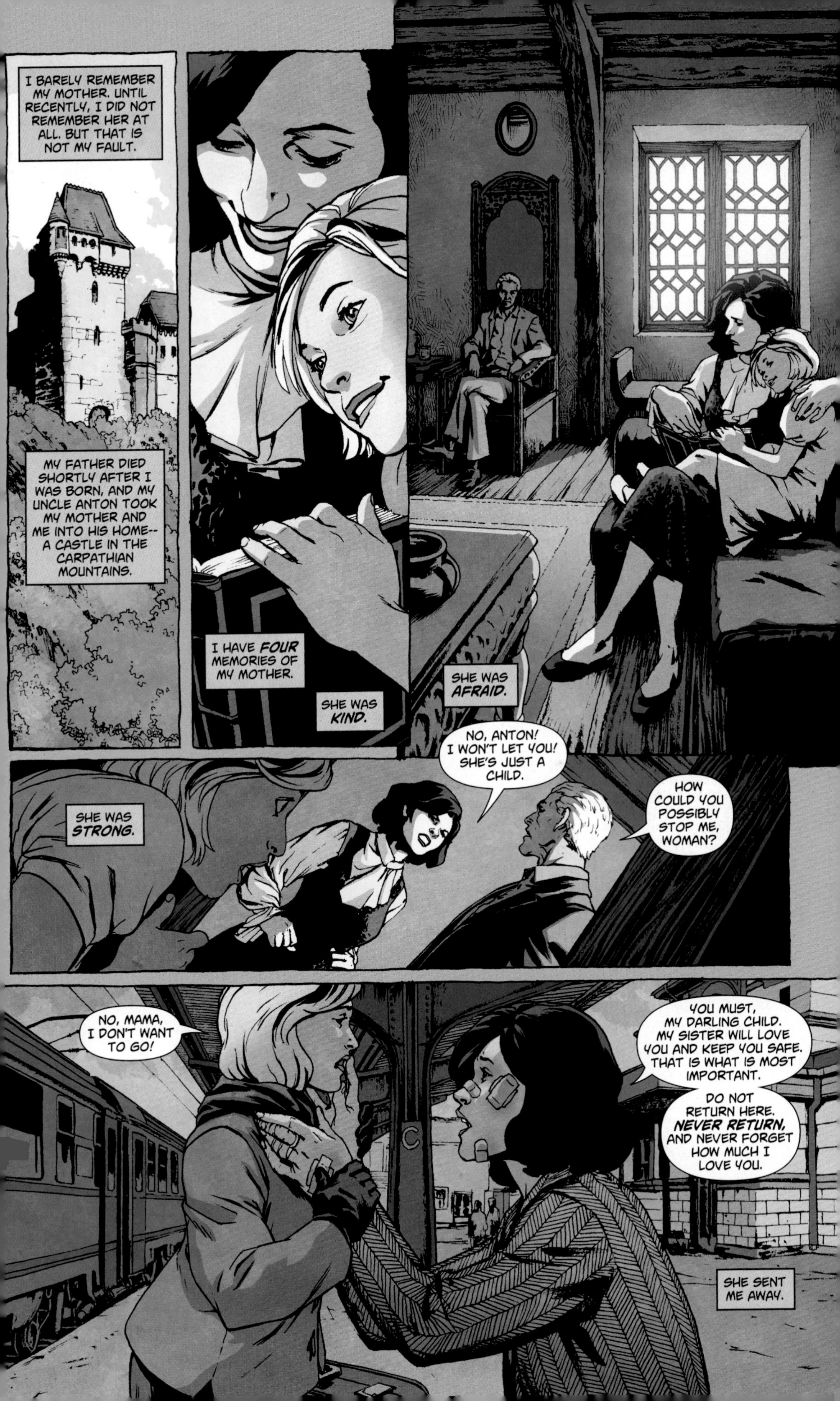

I BARELY REMEMBER MY MOTHER. UNTIL RECENTLY, I DID NOT REMEMBER HER AT ALL. BUT THAT IS NOT MY FAULT.
MY FATHER DIED SHORTLY AFTER I WAS BORN, AND MY UNCLE ANTON TOOK MY MOTHER AND ME INTO HIS HOME-- A CASTLE IN THE CARPATHIAN MOUNTAINS.
I HAVE FOUR MEMORIES OF MY MOTHER.
SHE WAS KIND.
SHE WAS AFRAID.
SHE WAS STRONG.
NO, ANTON! I WON'T LET YOU! SHE'S JUST A CHILD.
HOW COULD YOU POSSIBLY STOP ME, WOMAN?
NO, MAMA, I DON'T WANT TO GO!
YOU MUST, MY DARLING CHILD. MY SISTER WILL LOVE YOU AND KEEP YOU SAFE. THAT IS WHAT IS MOST IMPORTANT.
DO NOT RETURN HERE. NEVER RETURN, AND NEVER FORGET HOW MUCH I LOVE YOU.
SHE SENT ME AWAY.

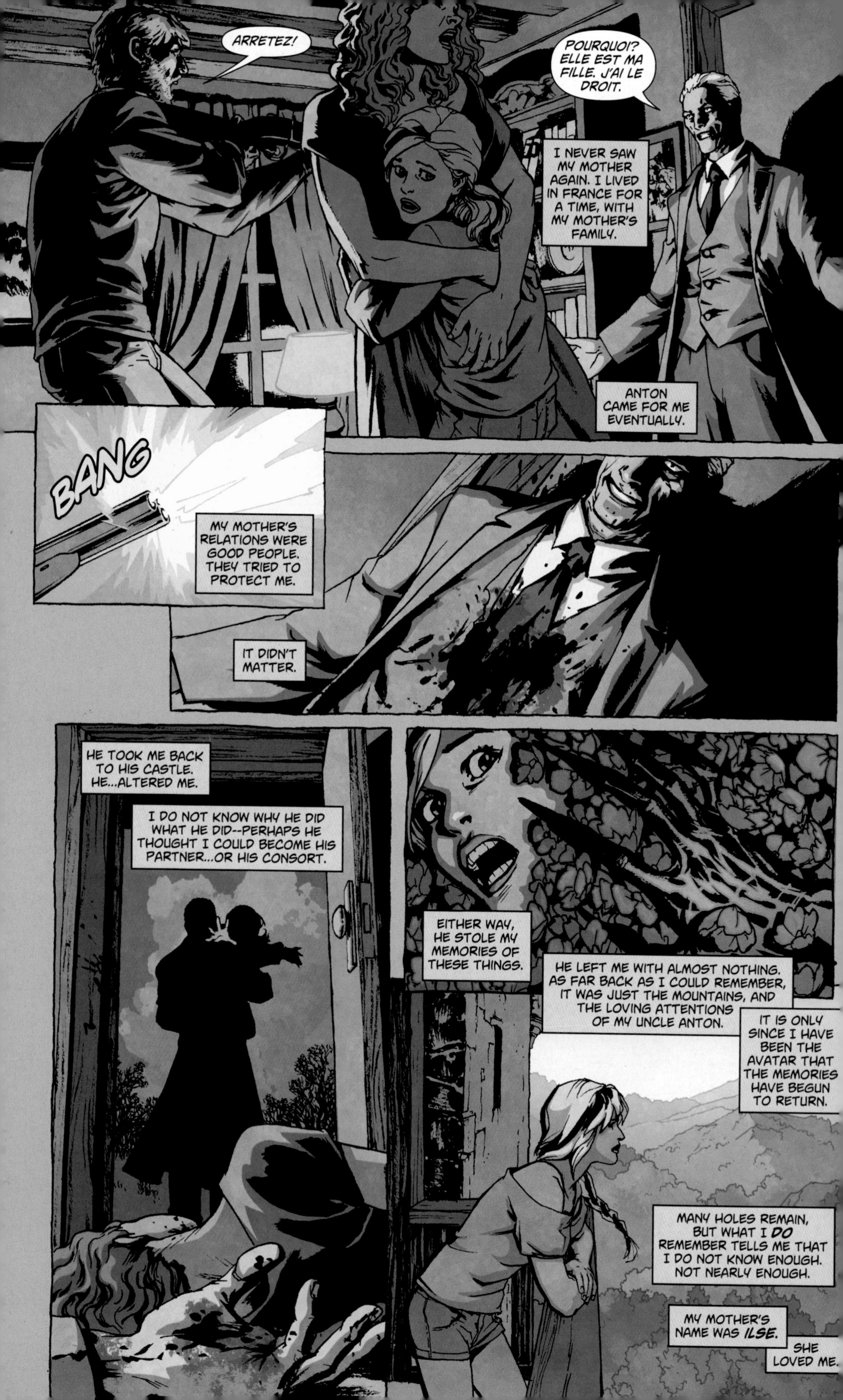
ARRETEZ!
POURQUOI? ELLE EST MA FILLE. J'AI LE DROIT.
I NEVER SAW MY MOTHER AGAIN. I LIVED IN FRANCE FOR A TIME, WITH MY MOTHER'S FAMILY.
ANTON CAME FOR ME EVENTUALLY.
BANG
MY MOTHER'S RELATIONS WERE GOOD PEOPLE. THEY TRIED TO PROTECT ME.
IT DIDN'T MATTER.
HE TOOK ME BACK TO HIS CASTLE. HE...ALTERED ME.
I DO NOT KNOW WHY HE DID WHAT HE DID--PERHAPS HE THOUGHT I COULD BECOME HIS PARTNER...OR HIS CONSORT.
EITHER WAY, HE STOLE MY MEMORIES OF THESE THINGS.
HE LEFT ME WITH ALMOST NOTHING. AS FAR BACK AS I COULD REMEMBER, IT WAS JUST THE MOUNTAINS, AND THE LOVING ATTENTIONS OF MY UNCLE ANTON.
IT IS ONLY SINCE I HAVE BEEN THE AVATAR THAT THE MEMORIES HAVE BEGUN TO RETURN.
MANY HOLES REMAIN, BUT WHAT I *DO* REMEMBER TELLS ME THAT I DO NOT KNOW ENOUGH. NOT NEARLY ENOUGH.
MY MOTHER'S NAME WAS *ILSE*.
SHE LOVED ME.

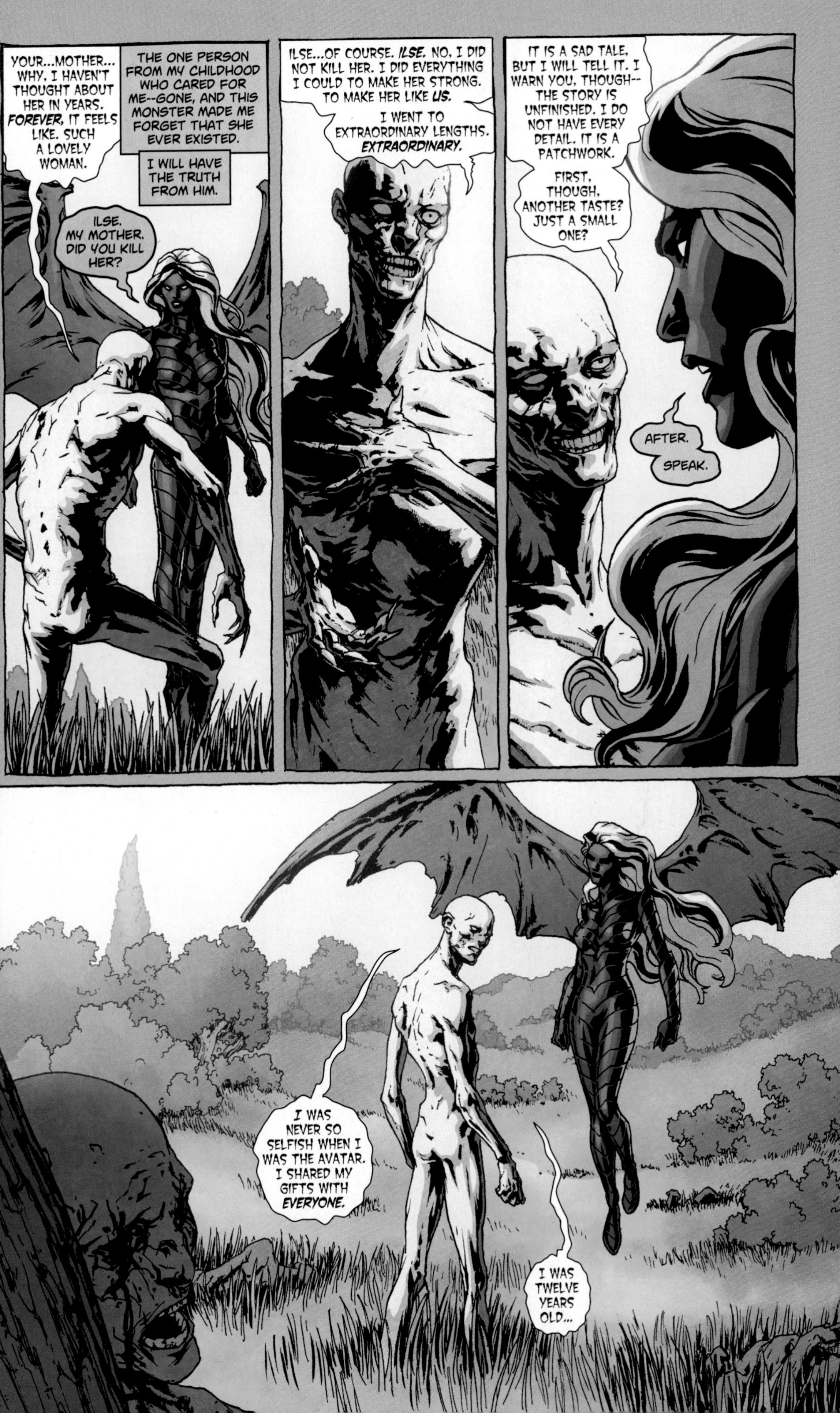
YOUR...MOTHER... WHY, I HAVEN'T THOUGHT ABOUT HER IN YEARS. FOREVER, IT FEELS LIKE. SUCH A LOVELY WOMAN.
THE ONE PERSON FROM MY CHILDHOOD WHO CARED FOR ME--GONE, AND THIS MONSTER MADE ME FORGET THAT SHE EVER EXISTED.
I WILL HAVE THE TRUTH FROM HIM.
ILSE. MY MOTHER. DID YOU KILL HER?
ILSE...OF COURSE. ILSE. NO, I DID NOT KILL HER. I DID EVERYTHING I COULD TO MAKE HER STRONG. TO MAKE HER LIKE US.
I WENT TO EXTRAORDINARY LENGTHS. EXTRAORDINARY.
IT IS A SAD TALE, BUT I WILL TELL IT. I WARN YOU, THOUGH-- THE STORY IS UNFINISHED. I DO NOT HAVE EVERY DETAIL. IT IS A PATCHWORK.
FIRST, THOUGH, ANOTHER TASTE? JUST A SMALL ONE?
AFTER.
SPEAK.
I WAS NEVER SO SELFISH WHEN I WAS THE AVATAR. I SHARED MY GIFTS WITH EVERYONE.
I WAS TWELVE YEARS OLD...

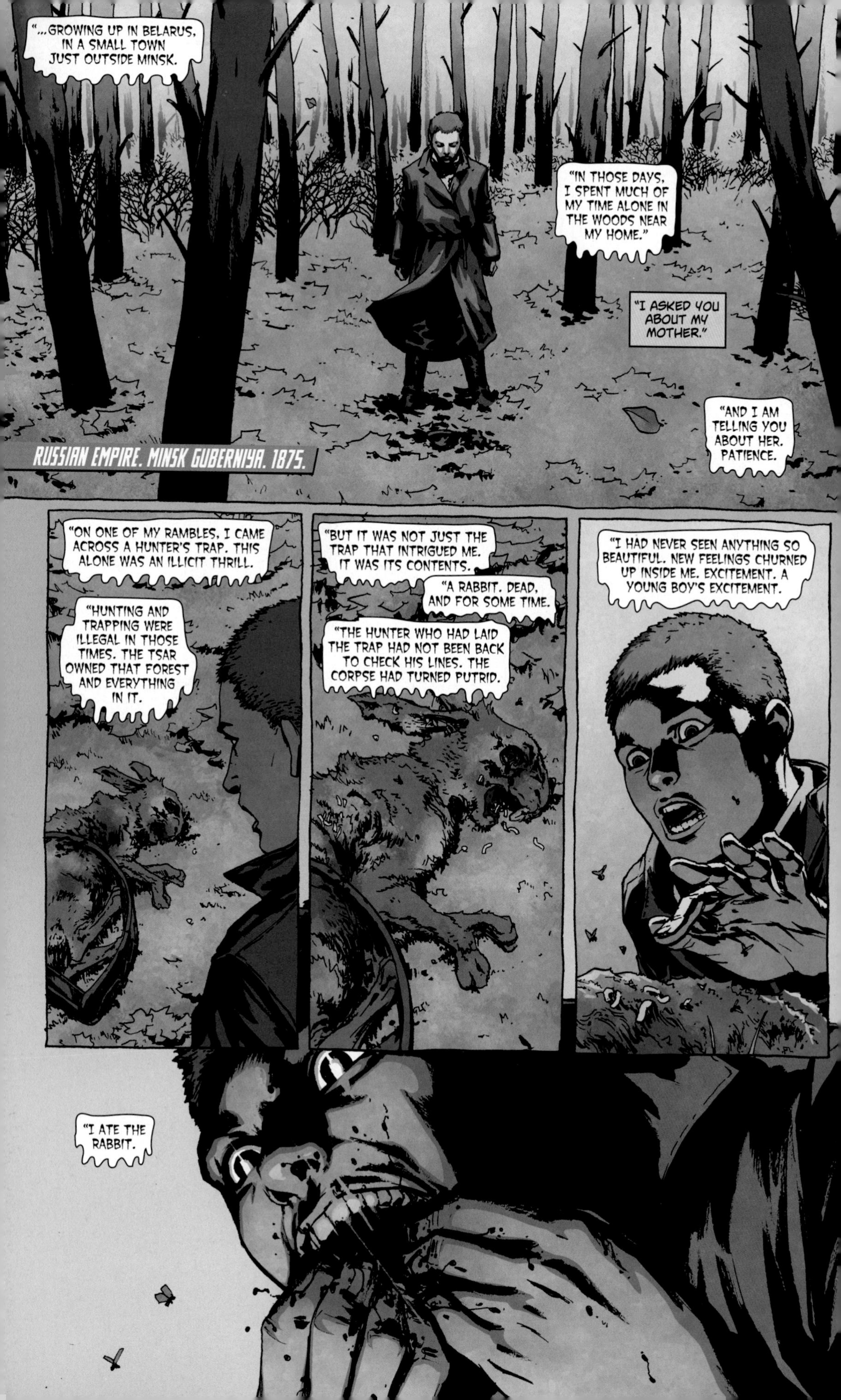

"...GROWING UP IN BELARUS, IN A SMALL TOWN JUST OUTSIDE MINSK.
RUSSIAN EMPIRE. MINSK GUBERNIYA. 1875.
"IN THOSE DAYS, I SPENT MUCH OF MY TIME ALONE IN THE WOODS NEAR MY HOME."
"I ASKED YOU ABOUT MY MOTHER."
"AND I AM TELLING YOU ABOUT HER. PATIENCE.
"ON ONE OF MY RAMBLES, I CAME ACROSS A HUNTER'S TRAP. THIS ALONE WAS AN ILLICIT THRILL.
"HUNTING AND TRAPPING WERE ILLEGAL IN THOSE TIMES. THE TSAR OWNED THAT FOREST AND EVERYTHING IN IT.
"BUT IT WAS NOT JUST THE TRAP THAT INTRIGUED ME. IT WAS ITS CONTENTS.
"A RABBIT. DEAD, AND FOR SOME TIME.
"THE HUNTER WHO HAD LAID THE TRAP HAD NOT BEEN BACK TO CHECK HIS LINES. THE CORPSE HAD TURNED PUTRID.
"I HAD NEVER SEEN ANYTHING SO BEAUTIFUL. NEW FEELINGS CHURNED UP INSIDE ME. EXCITEMENT. A YOUNG BOY'S EXCITEMENT.
"I ATE THE RABBIT.

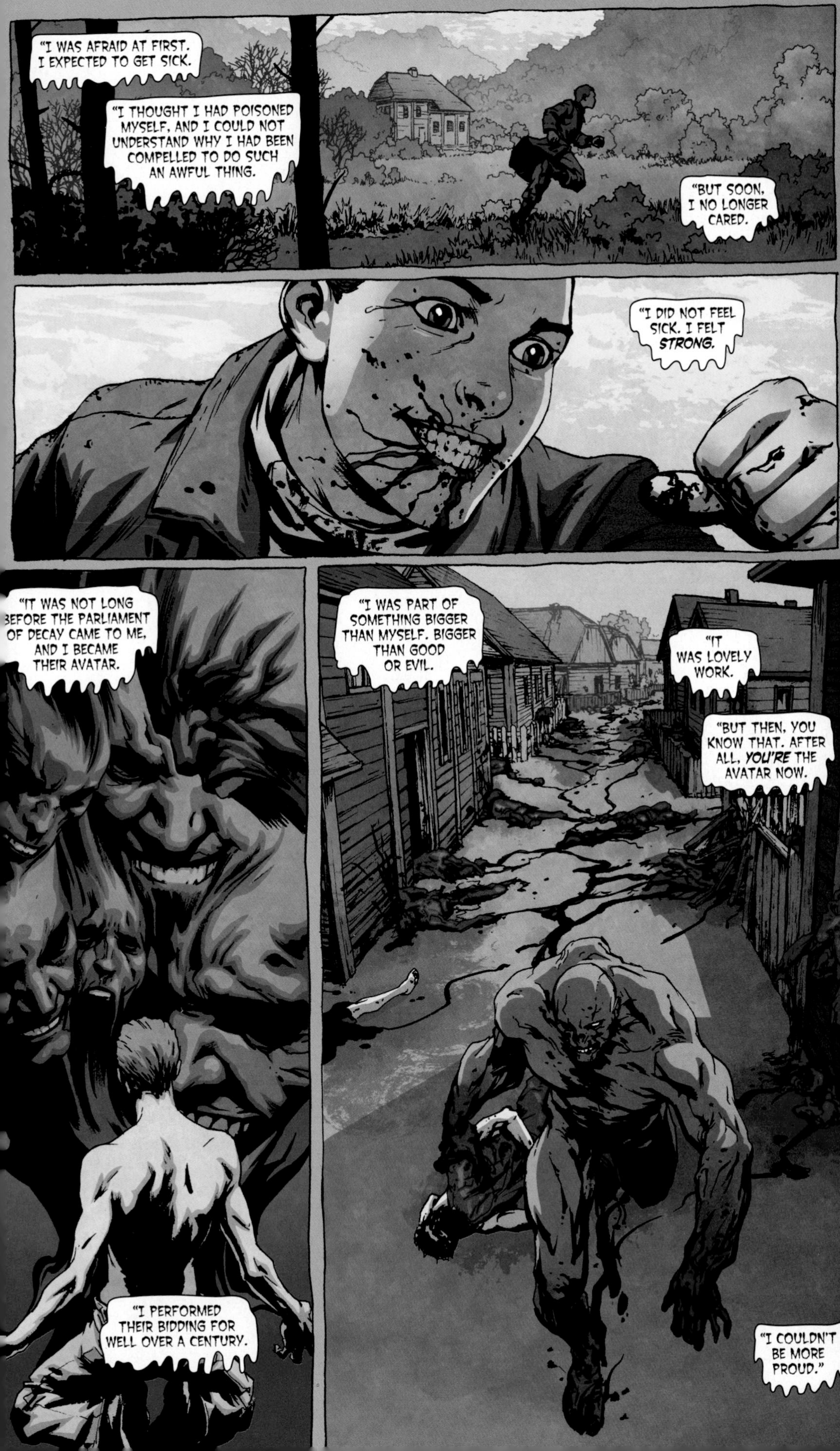
"I WAS AFRAID AT FIRST. I EXPECTED TO GET SICK.
"I THOUGHT I HAD POISONED MYSELF, AND I COULD NOT UNDERSTAND WHY I HAD BEEN COMPELLED TO DO SUCH AN AWFUL THING.
"BUT SOON, I NO LONGER CARED.
"I DID NOT FEEL SICK. I FELT STRONG.
"IT WAS NOT LONG BEFORE THE PARLIAMENT OF DECAY CAME TO ME, AND I BECAME THEIR AVATAR.
"I PERFORMED THEIR BIDDING FOR WELL OVER A CENTURY.
"I WAS PART OF SOMETHING BIGGER THAN MYSELF. BIGGER THAN GOOD OR EVIL.
"IT WAS LOVELY WORK.
"BUT THEN, YOU KNOW THAT. AFTER ALL, YOU'RE THE AVATAR NOW.
"I COULDN'T BE MORE PROUD."

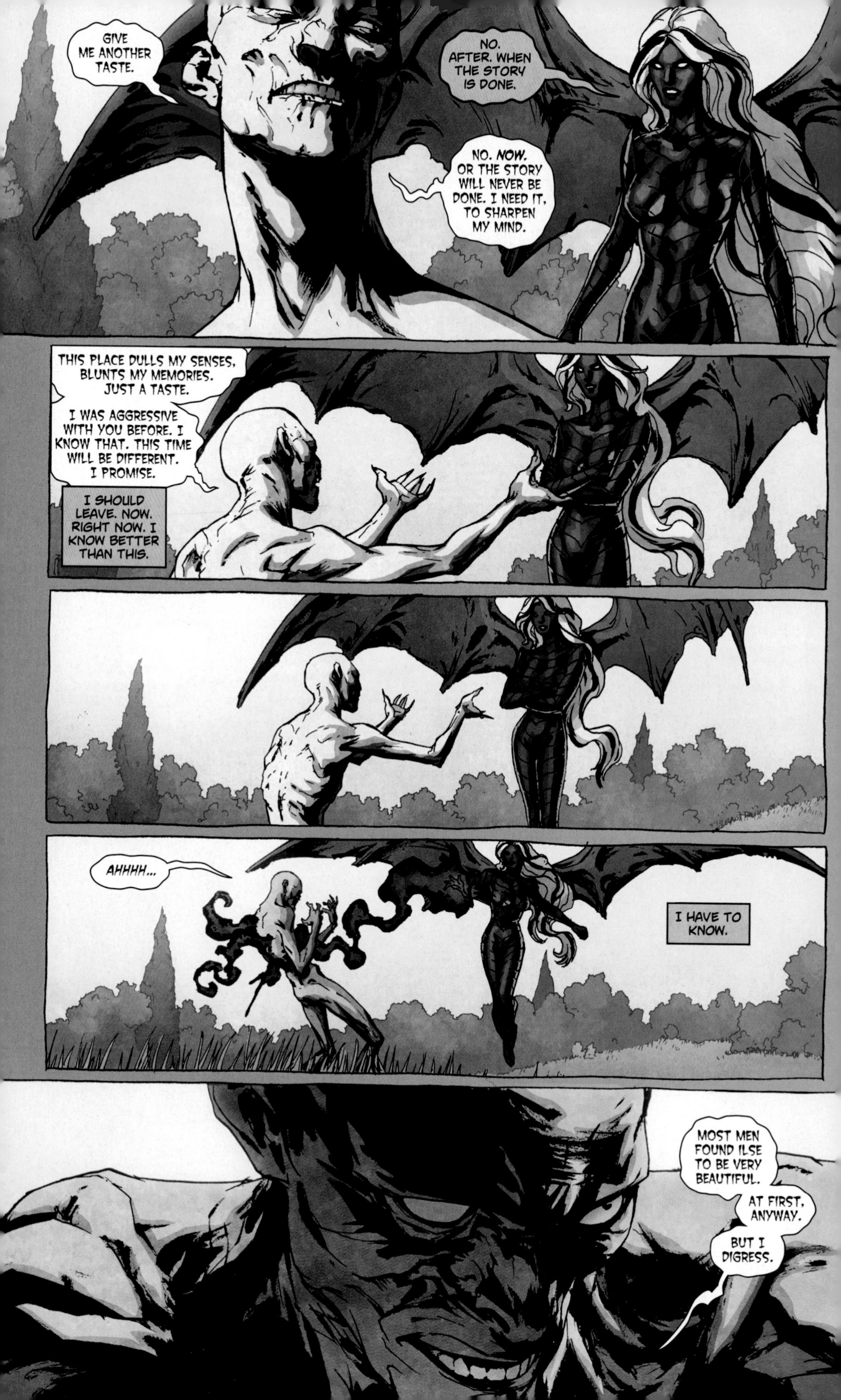
GIVE ME ANOTHER TASTE.
NO. AFTER. WHEN THE STORY IS DONE.
NO. *NOW.* OR THE STORY WILL NEVER BE DONE. I NEED IT, TO SHARPEN MY MIND.
THIS PLACE DULLS MY SENSES, BLUNTS MY MEMORIES. JUST A TASTE.
I WAS AGGRESSIVE WITH YOU BEFORE. I KNOW THAT. THIS TIME WILL BE DIFFERENT. I PROMISE.
I SHOULD LEAVE. NOW. RIGHT NOW. I KNOW BETTER THAN THIS.
AHHHH...
I HAVE TO KNOW.
MOST MEN FOUND ILSE TO BE VERY BEAUTIFUL.
AT FIRST, ANYWAY.
BUT I DIGRESS.

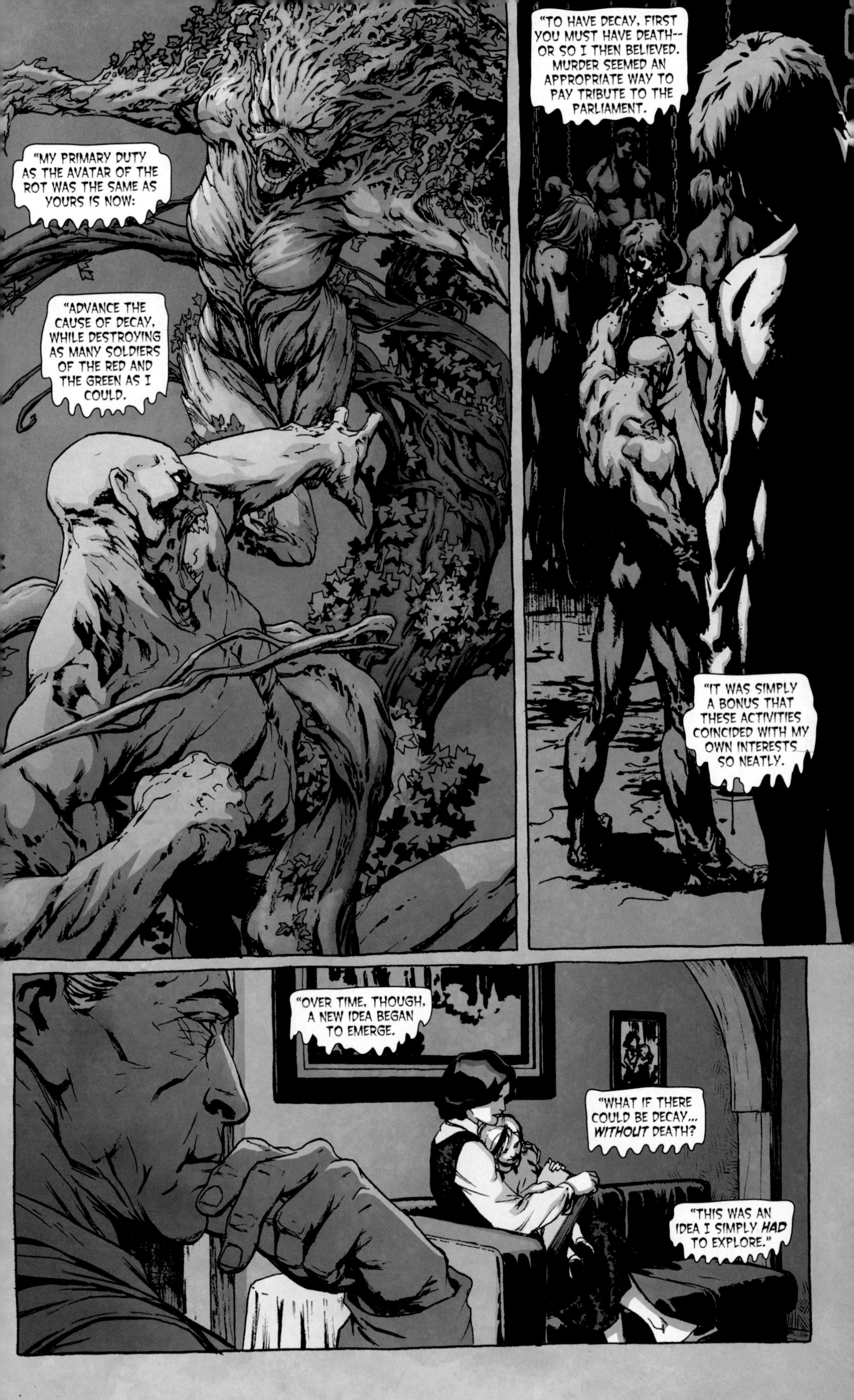
"MY PRIMARY DUTY AS THE AVATAR OF THE ROT WAS THE SAME AS YOURS IS NOW:
"ADVANCE THE CAUSE OF DECAY, WHILE DESTROYING AS MANY SOLDIERS OF THE RED AND THE GREEN AS I COULD.
"TO HAVE DECAY, FIRST YOU MUST HAVE DEATH-- OR SO I THEN BELIEVED. MURDER SEEMED AN APPROPRIATE WAY TO PAY TRIBUTE TO THE PARLIAMENT.
"IT WAS SIMPLY A BONUS THAT THESE ACTIVITIES COINCIDED WITH MY OWN INTERESTS SO NEATLY.
"OVER TIME, THOUGH, A NEW IDEA BEGAN TO EMERGE.
"WHAT IF THERE COULD BE DECAY... *WITHOUT* DEATH?
"THIS WAS AN IDEA I SIMPLY *HAD* TO EXPLORE."

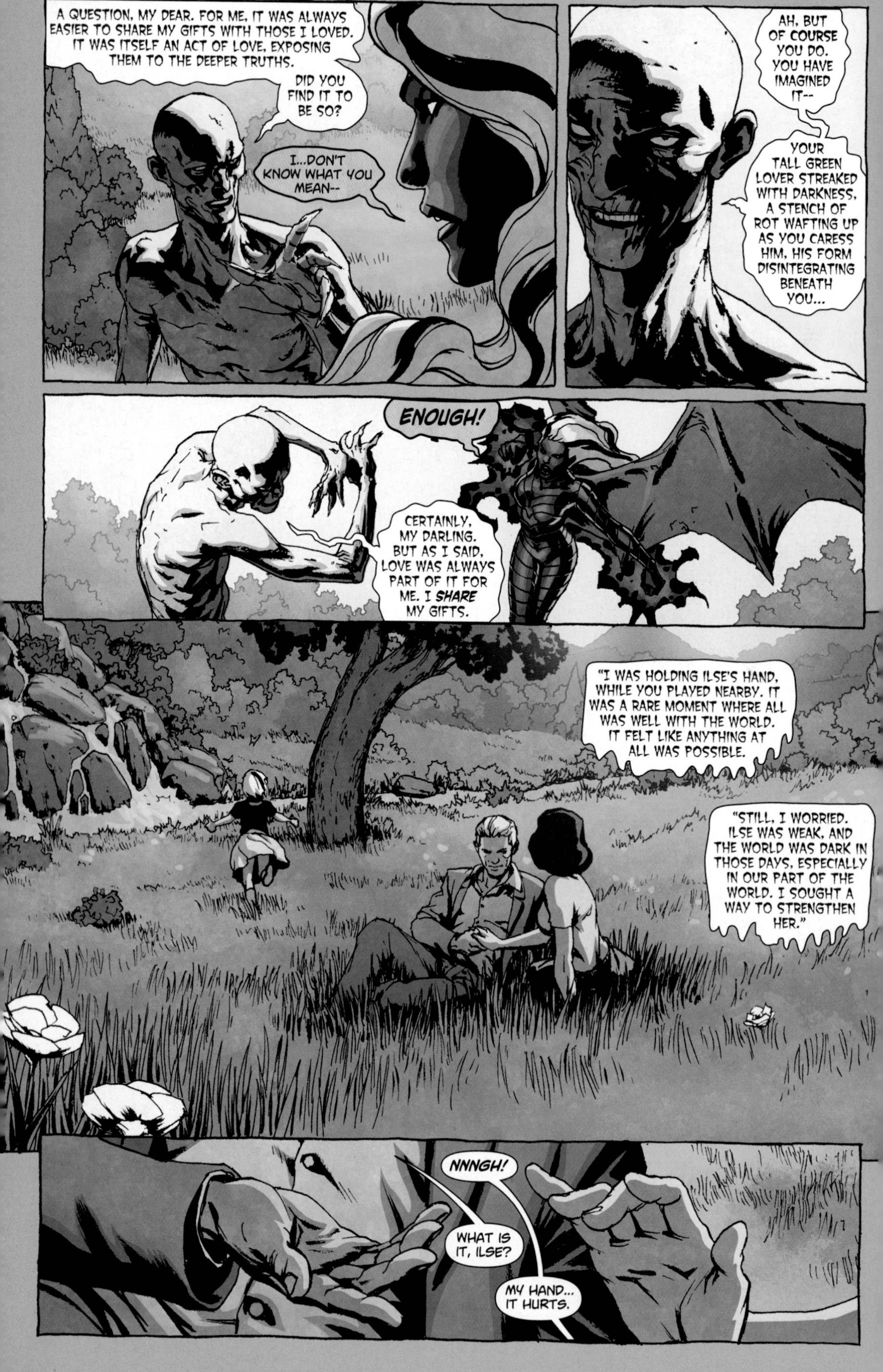
A QUESTION, MY DEAR. FOR ME, IT WAS ALWAYS EASIER TO SHARE MY GIFTS WITH THOSE I LOVED. IT WAS ITSELF AN ACT OF LOVE, EXPOSING THEM TO THE DEEPER TRUTHS.
DID YOU FIND IT TO BE SO?
I...DON'T KNOW WHAT YOU MEAN--
AH, BUT OF COURSE YOU DO. YOU HAVE IMAGINED IT--
YOUR TALL GREEN LOVER STREAKED WITH DARKNESS, A STENCH OF ROT WAFTING UP AS YOU CARESS HIM, HIS FORM DISINTEGRATING BENEATH YOU...
ENOUGH!
CERTAINLY, MY DARLING. BUT AS I SAID, LOVE WAS ALWAYS PART OF IT FOR ME. I SHARE MY GIFTS.
"I WAS HOLDING ILSE'S HAND, WHILE YOU PLAYED NEARBY. IT WAS A RARE MOMENT WHERE ALL WAS WELL WITH THE WORLD. IT FELT LIKE ANYTHING AT ALL WAS POSSIBLE.
"STILL, I WORRIED. ILSE WAS WEAK, AND THE WORLD WAS DARK IN THOSE DAYS, ESPECIALLY IN OUR PART OF THE WORLD. I SOUGHT A WAY TO STRENGTHEN HER."
NNNGH!
WHAT IS IT, ILSE?
MY HAND... IT HURTS.

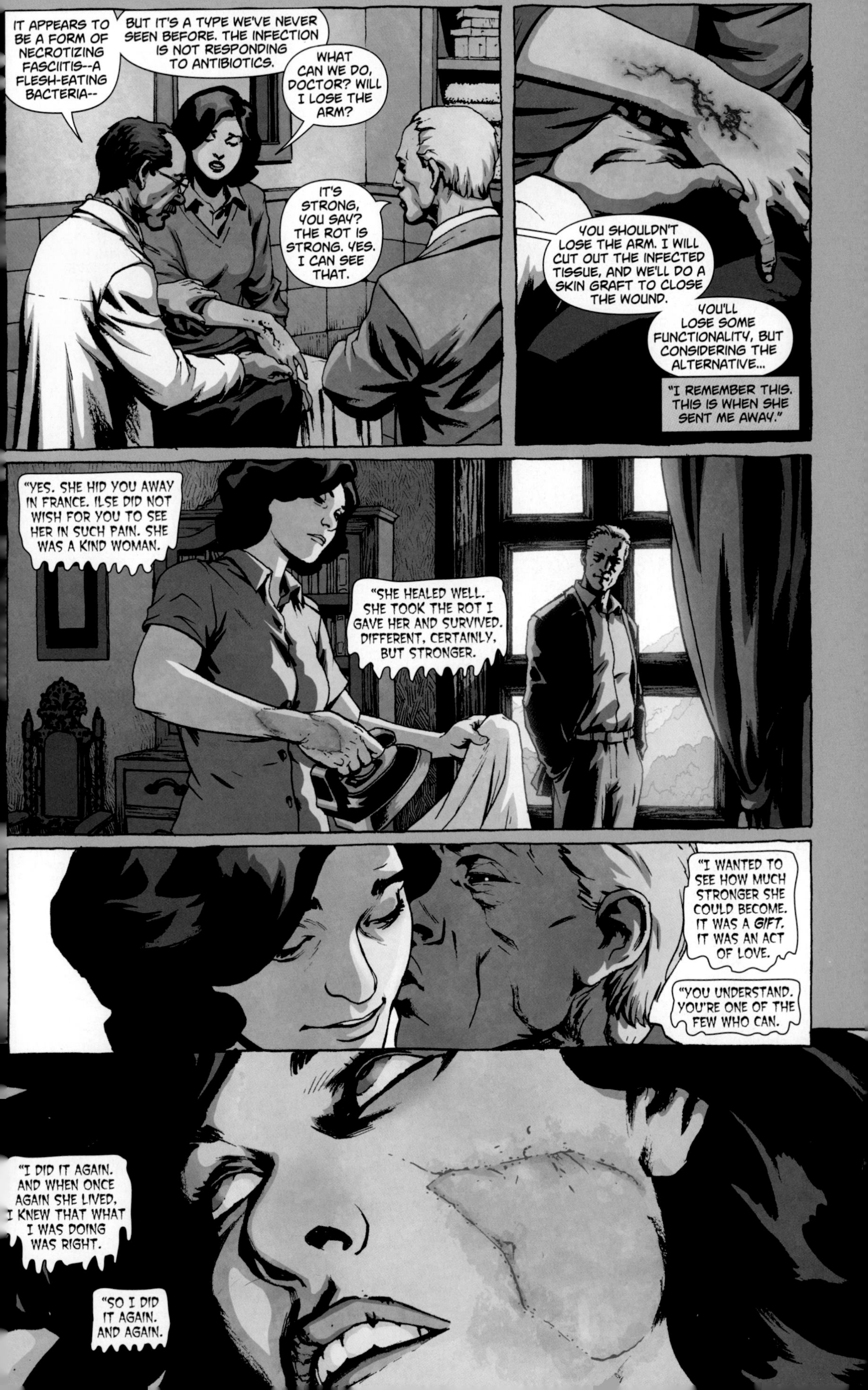
IT APPEARS TO BE A FORM OF NECROTIZING FASCIITIS--A FLESH-EATING BACTERIA--
BUT IT'S A TYPE WE'VE NEVER SEEN BEFORE. THE INFECTION IS NOT RESPONDING TO ANTIBIOTICS.
WHAT CAN WE DO, DOCTOR? WILL I LOSE THE ARM?
IT'S STRONG, YOU SAY? THE ROT IS STRONG. YES. I CAN SEE THAT.
YOU SHOULDN'T LOSE THE ARM. I WILL CUT OUT THE INFECTED TISSUE, AND WE'LL DO A SKIN GRAFT TO CLOSE THE WOUND.
YOU'LL LOSE SOME FUNCTIONALITY, BUT CONSIDERING THE ALTERNATIVE...
"I REMEMBER THIS. THIS IS WHEN SHE SENT ME AWAY."
"YES. SHE HID YOU AWAY IN FRANCE. ILSE DID NOT WISH FOR YOU TO SEE HER IN SUCH PAIN. SHE WAS A KIND WOMAN.
"SHE HEALED WELL. SHE TOOK THE ROT I GAVE HER AND SURVIVED. DIFFERENT, CERTAINLY, BUT STRONGER.
"I WANTED TO SEE HOW MUCH STRONGER SHE COULD BECOME. IT WAS A GIFT. IT WAS AN ACT OF LOVE.
"YOU UNDERSTAND. YOU'RE ONE OF THE FEW WHO CAN.
"I DID IT AGAIN. AND WHEN ONCE AGAIN SHE LIVED, I KNEW THAT WHAT I WAS DOING WAS RIGHT.
"SO I DID IT AGAIN. AND AGAIN.

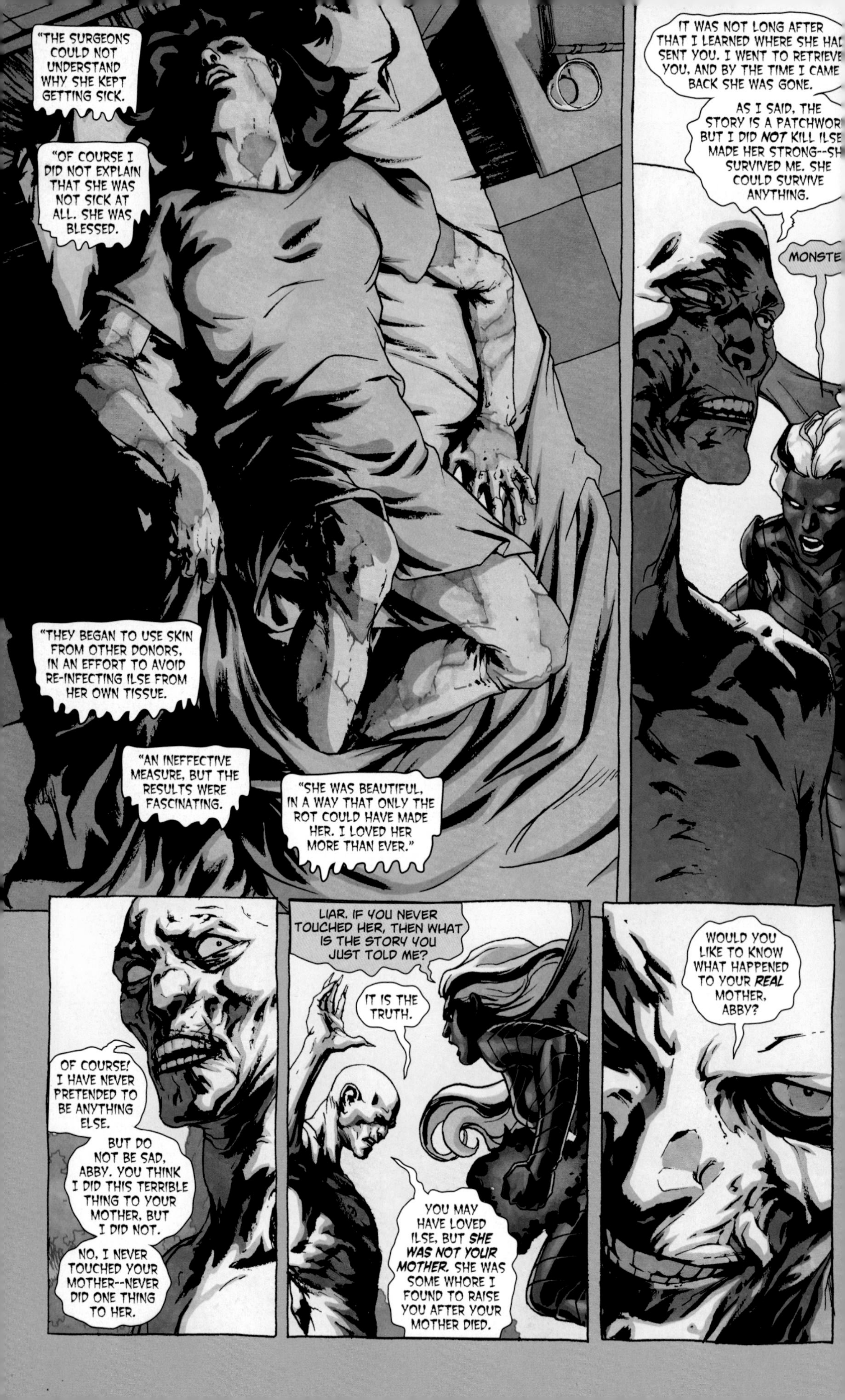
"THE SURGEONS COULD NOT UNDERSTAND WHY SHE KEPT GETTING SICK.
"OF COURSE I DID NOT EXPLAIN THAT SHE WAS NOT SICK AT ALL. SHE WAS BLESSED.
"THEY BEGAN TO USE SKIN FROM OTHER DONORS, IN AN EFFORT TO AVOID RE-INFECTING ILSE FROM HER OWN TISSUE.
"AN INEFFECTIVE MEASURE, BUT THE RESULTS WERE FASCINATING.
"SHE WAS BEAUTIFUL, IN A WAY THAT ONLY THE ROT COULD HAVE MADE HER. I LOVED HER MORE THAN EVER."
IT WAS NOT LONG AFTER THAT I LEARNED WHERE SHE HAD SENT YOU. I WENT TO RETRIEVE YOU, AND BY THE TIME I CAME BACK SHE WAS GONE.
AS I SAID, THE STORY IS A PATCHWORK BUT I DID NOT KILL ILSE. MADE HER STRONG--SHE SURVIVED ME. SHE COULD SURVIVE ANYTHING.
MONSTE
OF COURSE! I HAVE NEVER PRETENDED TO BE ANYTHING ELSE.
BUT DO NOT BE SAD, ABBY. YOU THINK I DID THIS TERRIBLE THING TO YOUR MOTHER, BUT I DID NOT.
NO, I NEVER TOUCHED YOUR MOTHER--NEVER DID ONE THING TO HER.
LIAR. IF YOU NEVER TOUCHED HER, THEN WHAT IS THE STORY YOU JUST TOLD ME?
IT IS THE TRUTH.
YOU MAY HAVE LOVED ILSE, BUT SHE WAS NOT YOUR MOTHER. SHE WAS SOME WHORE I FOUND TO RAISE YOU AFTER YOUR MOTHER DIED.
WOULD YOU LIKE TO KNOW WHAT HAPPENED TO YOUR REAL MOTHER, ABBY?

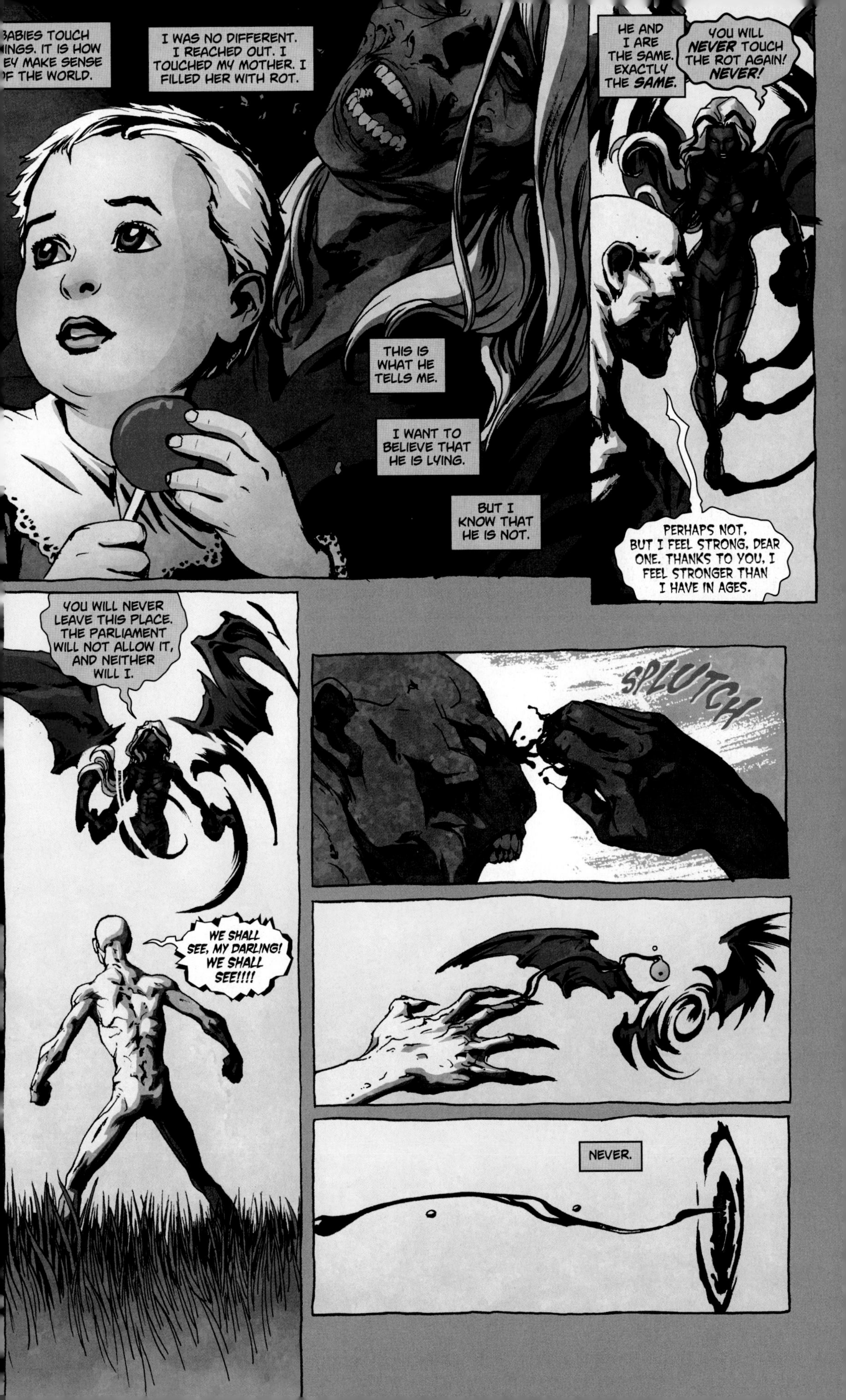

BABIES TOUCH THINGS. IT IS HOW THEY MAKE SENSE OF THE WORLD.
I WAS NO DIFFERENT. I REACHED OUT. I TOUCHED MY MOTHER. I FILLED HER WITH ROT.
THIS IS WHAT HE TELLS ME.
I WANT TO BELIEVE THAT HE IS LYING.
BUT I KNOW THAT HE IS NOT.
HE AND I ARE THE SAME. EXACTLY THE SAME.
YOU WILL NEVER TOUCH THE ROT AGAIN! NEVER!
PERHAPS NOT, BUT I FEEL STRONG, DEAR ONE. THANKS TO YOU, I FEEL STRONGER THAN I HAVE IN AGES.
YOU WILL NEVER LEAVE THIS PLACE. THE PARLIAMENT WILL NOT ALLOW IT, AND NEITHER WILL I.
WE SHALL SEE, MY DARLING! WE SHALL SEE!!!!
SPLUTCH
NEVER.

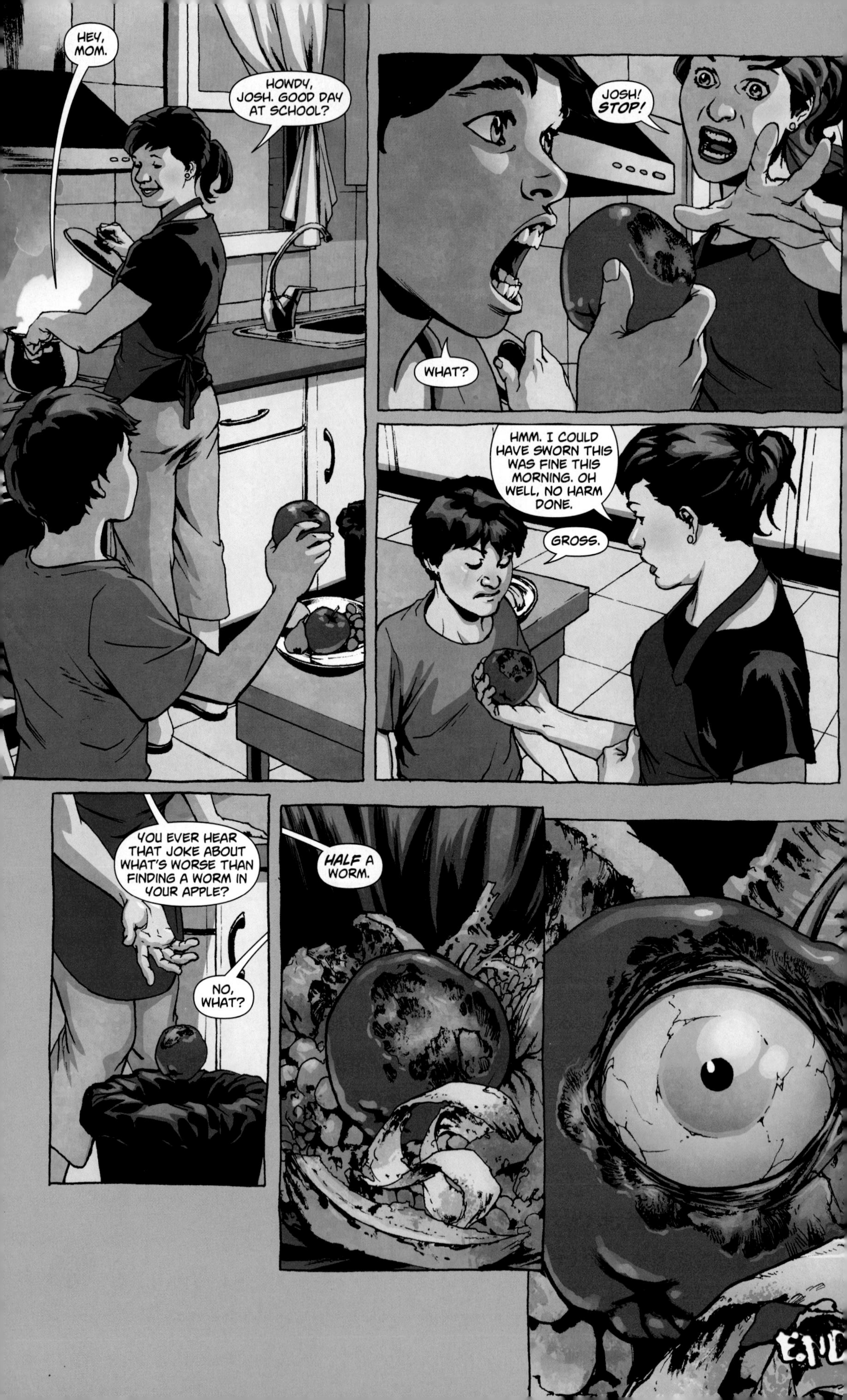
HEY, MOM.
HOWDY, JOSH. GOOD DAY AT SCHOOL?
JOSH! STOP!
WHAT?
HMM. I COULD HAVE SWORN THIS WAS FINE THIS MORNING. OH WELL, NO HARM DONE.
GROSS.
YOU EVER HEAR THAT JOKE ABOUT WHAT'S WORSE THAN FINDING A WORM IN YOUR APPLE?
NO, WHAT?
HALF A WORM.
END

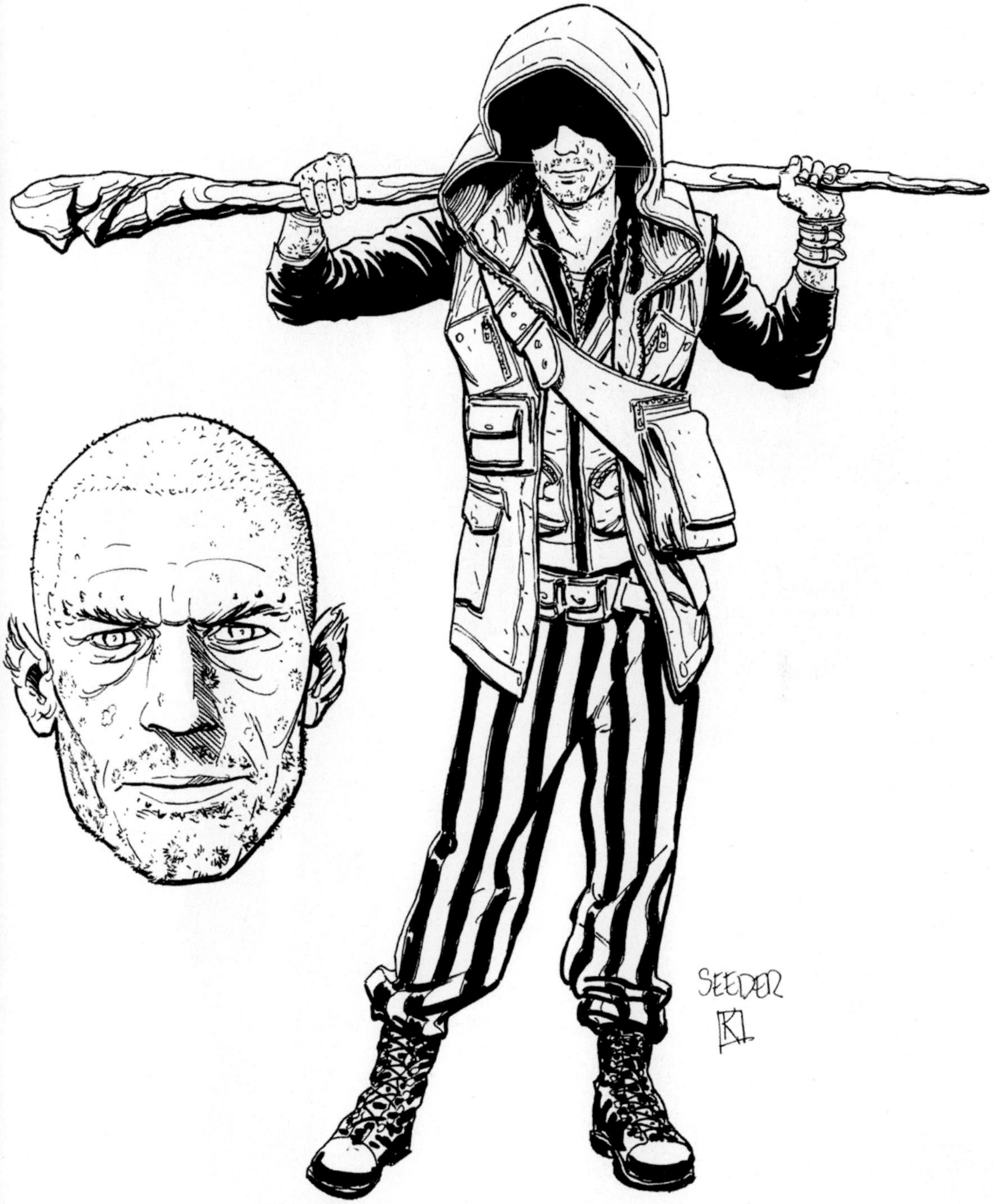
SEEDER

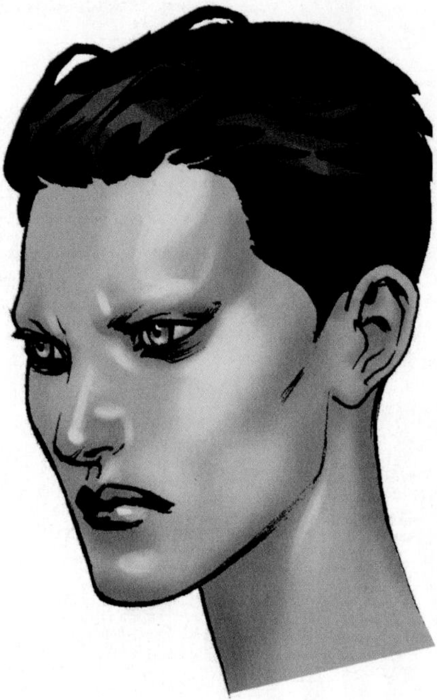
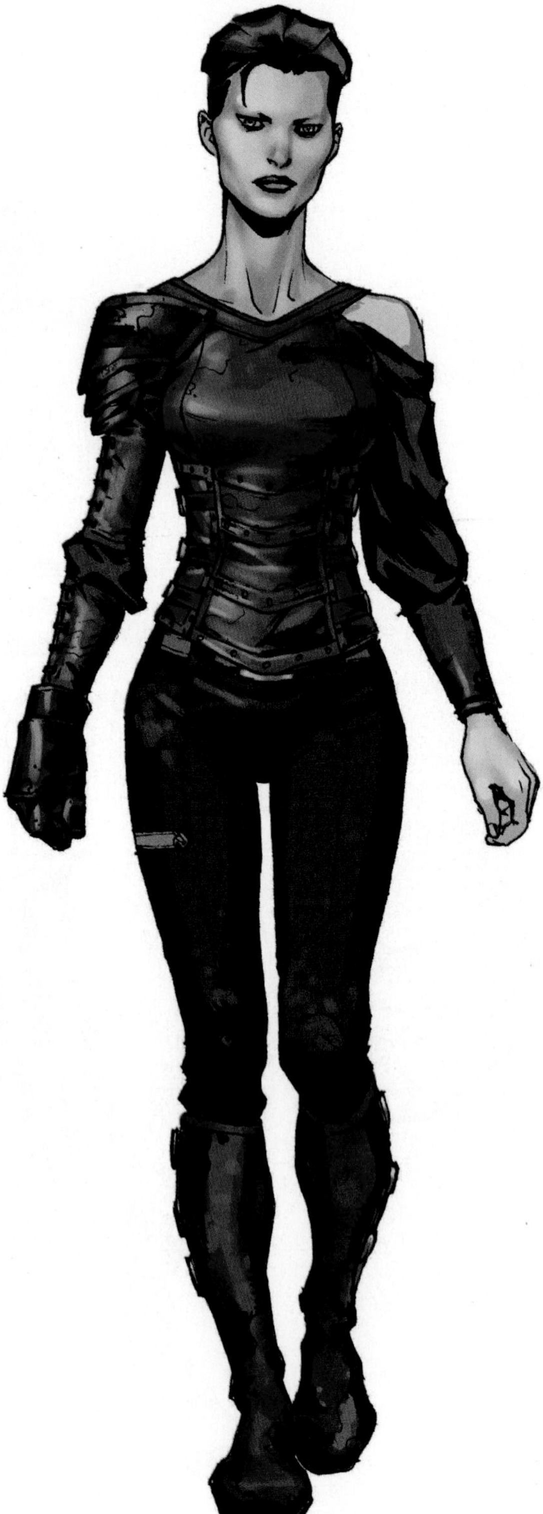

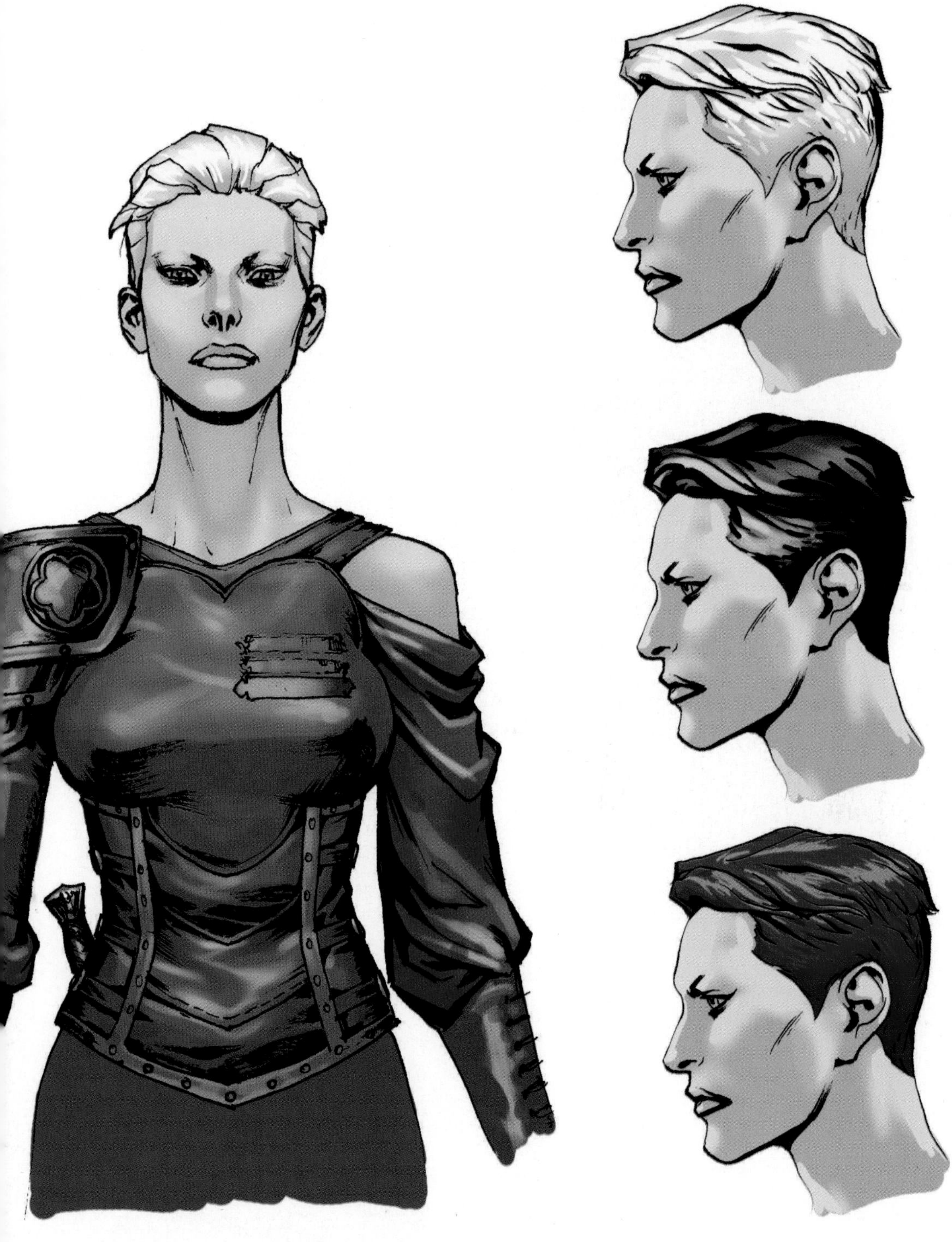

# SWAMP THING
## ISSUE #20 PENCILS BY KANO

MINIMUM BLEED 1/4" ALL AROUND
LIVE AREA
BLEED
CUT RIGHT-HAND PAGE AT THIS LINE
DOUBLE PAGE SPREAD: CUT AS SHOWN, ABUT PAGE EDGES, TAPE ON BACK, DO NOT OVERLAP
CUT LEFT HAND PAGE AT THIS LINE

MINIMUM BLEED 1/4" ALL AROUND
BLEED
CUT RIGHT-HAND PAGE AT THIS LINE
DOUBLE PAGE SPREAD: CUT AS SHOWN, ABUT PAGE EDGES, TAPE ON BACK, DO NOT OVERLAP
CUT LEFT HAND PAGE AT THIS LINE

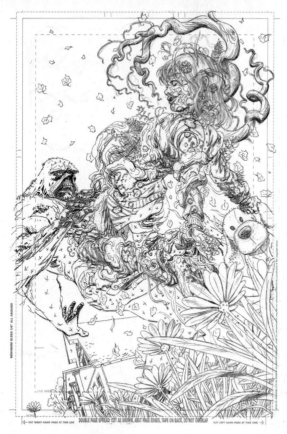

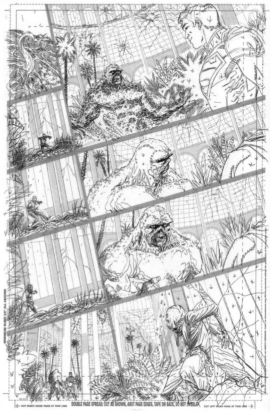

# SWAMP THING
## ISSUE #21 PENCILS BY JESUS SAIZ

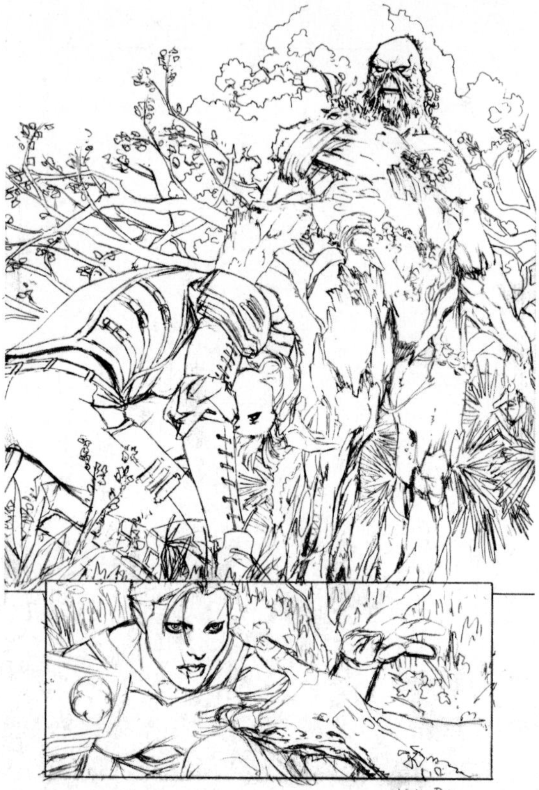

#21 P2

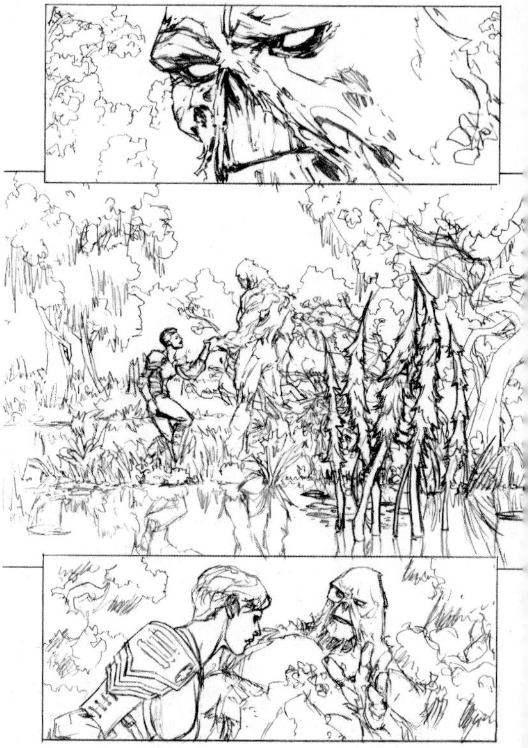

#21 P.3

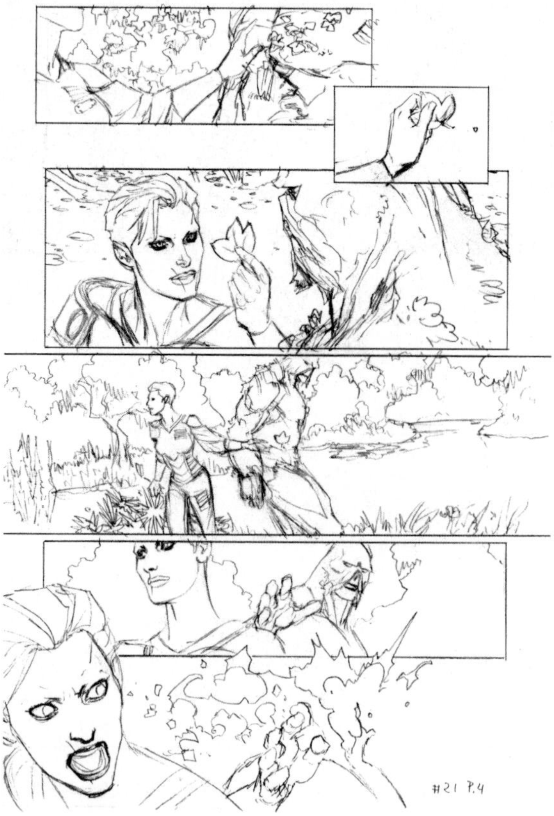

#21 P.4

Issue #22 cover sketches

Issue #23 cover sketches